GENTLE SHEPHERDING

For my nieces and nephews:
Gillian, Armin, Colin,
and Caitlin—who trusts her pastor.

GENTLE SHEPHERDING

Pastoral Ethics and Leadership

JOSEPH E. BUSH JR.

CHALICE
PRESS
ST. LOUIS, MISSOURI

Bible quotations, unless otherwise noted, are from the *New Revised Standard Version Bible,* copyright 1989, Division of Christian Education of the National Council of the Churches of Christ in the United States of America. Used by permission. All rights reserved.

Those quotations marked RSV are from the *Revised Standard Version* of the Bible, copyright 1952, [2nd edition, 1971] by the Division of Christian Education of the National Council of the Churches of Christ in the United States of America. Used by permission. All rights reserved.

Scripture quotations marked (TEV) are taken from the *Today's English Version*–Second Edition © 1992 by American Bible Society. Used by Permission.

Scripture quotations marked (TLB) are taken from *The Living Bible,* copyright © 1971. Used by permission of Tyndale House Publishers, Inc., Wheaton, Illinois 60189. All rights reserved.

Scripture quotations marked NKJV are taken from the *New King James Version.* Copyright © 1979, 1980, 1982 by Thomas Nelson, Inc. Used by permission. All rights reserved.

Material in chapter 3, "Permission for Mission," was originally published as "Informed Consent and Parish Clergy," in *The Journal of Pastoral Care & Counseling* 57, no. 4 (Winter 2003). Reprinted with permission.

Material in chapter 6, "Confidentiality in Care," was originally published as "Pastoral Confidentiality," in *Business & Professional Ethics Journal–Incorporating Professional Ethics: A Multidisciplinary Journal* 22, no. 4 (Winter 2004). Reprinted with permission.

Words on page 150 from "Bring Many Names" by Brian Wren. © 1989 Hope Publishing Co., Carol Stream, IL 60188. All rights reserved. Used by permission.

Cover and interior design: Elizabeth Wright

Visit Chalice Press on the World Wide Web at
www.chalicepress.com

10 9 8 7 6 5 4 3 2 1   06 07 08 09 10 11

Library of Congress Cataloging–in–Publication Data

Bush, Joseph Earl, 1956-
  Gentle shepherding : pastoral care in congregations / Joseph E. Bush, Jr.
    p. cm.
  Includes bibliographical references.
  ISBN-13: 978-0-8272-1250-3 (pbk. : alk. paper)
  ISBN-10: 0-8272-1250-X (pbk. : alk. paper)
  1. Clergy–Professional ethics. 2. Pastoral care. I. Title.
  BV4011.5.B87 2006
  241'.641–dc22

                                            2005025994
Printed in the United States of America

Contents

Acknowledgments

It is with joy that I give this book back to the ecumenical church that has nurtured me in the moral life and in the life of faith. I wish to thank my own teachers in ethics from both seminary and graduate school who have tried in good faith to instruct me: Edward LeRoy Long Jr., Donald G. Jones, Roger Lincoln Shinn, Thomas W. Ogletree, Larry L. Rasmussen, Bruce C. Birch, and J. Philip Wogaman. I wish to thank some of my current colleagues and friends at United Theological Seminary for reading parts or all of the manuscript for this book: Paul Capetz, Christie Cozad Neuger, and Marilyn Salmon. My good friends and colleagues Richard Knox and William Elkins have also read parts of this manuscript and encouraged me in its writing. Of course, I assume blame for any errors or misunderstandings apparent in these pages.

I especially want to thank members of my family who have supported me patiently and with love throughout this endeavor: my parents Joseph and Virginia, my wife Elizabeth, and her parents Don and Jane Ward. Finally, it is with deep gratitude that I thank the faculty, staff, and students in the School of Ministry for the Presbyterian Church of Aotearoa, New Zealand, located at Knox College in Dunedin. Much of the initial research for this book was conducted while on sabbatical from my teaching duties there, and some of the original composition was presented there in lectures. Your feedback was helpful, and your friendship is dear.

Finally, several libraries have given me access to their stacks and granted to me borrowing privileges. In New Zealand, I am grateful to the Hewitson Library at Knox College and the rest of the University of Otago Library system—especially the staff at the medical library (who welcomed me to their staff parties as well as to their stacks). In New Jersey, I wish to thank Drew University Library and the Gardner A. Sage Library at New Brunswick Theological Seminary. In Dubuque, Iowa, I was welcomed with privileges at the Wartburg Theological Seminary Library and the Charles C. Myers Library at the University of Dubuque. In the Twin Cities, I have enjoyed use of all the libraries within the Minnesota Consortium of Theological Schools, but I especially want to thank the staff of the Spencer Library at United Theological Seminary of the Twin Cities, who have been extremely helpful—Sue Ebbers, Dale C. Dobias, and Penny Truax.

Preface

This book concerns professional ethics for clergy. It is written for two audiences in particular: (1) seminarians studying pastoral ethics or social ethics, and (2) pastors or other leaders in the church who are interested in attending to their ethical responsibility in offering ministry.

The purpose of this book is to equip seminarians and pastors with some conceptual resources that will be useful for clarifying moral responsibility in the practice of ministry. This responsibility includes three levels: (1) the minister as a moral agent in offering care, (2) the minister as a moral enabler in encouraging virtue in others, and (3) the minister as a moral leader in facilitating congregational life and witness in society.

The book is written as an introduction or primer in pastoral ethics for those who may never have had a course in ethics previously. At the same time, I imagine that experienced pastors will be able to identify with the pastoral heart of this book, and find here resources for thinking anew about their responsibilities and moral quandaries in pastoral practice. Actually, very few books attempt to provide this kind of balance to this degree—to identify deeply with the pastoral vocation, *and* to bring it into conversation with a developed body of ethical theory.

This book begins "in the middle," with moral principles that are employed within society for thinking about the moral life. These principles are commonly used in discussions about applied ethics in general and in the particular area of healthcare ethics, e.g., fiduciary obligation, duties of nonmaleficence, etc. These principles are placed here within a Christian context and examined with regard to their applicability for Christian ministry. I have tried not to delve too deeply into extensive epistemological justification for this approach—either through philosophical argument or through biblical and theological interpretation. Many other resources are available to engage reflection at this "metaethical" level, and I hope that I have indicated some of those sources in the notes of this book as well as in the text itself.

I have tried instead to focus these pages as directly as possible on the nature of pastoral ministry and pastoral relationships. Moral principles and ethical methods are gradually introduced throughout the book to increasingly encourage ethical reasoning about the moral responsibilities of clergy acting within their profession. I have attempted to integrate ethical theory with ministerial practice from the very beginning. I have also provided case material for further reflection and to aid in class discussion. Each chapter has at least one case study or exercise for reflection. The case studies are based in truth but have been entirely disguised.

Chapter 1, "Moral Self in Community," begins with a general introduction to the subject of ethics as critical reflection on the moral life. It then proceeds to describe ways in which we might understand moral character to be shaped by culture and community, all the while affirming the role of the church in nurturing people of virtue.

Chapter 2, "Working Gently: Nonmaleficence in Ministry," argues simply, "First, do no harm." This is the popular understanding of the Hippocratic oath that applies in healthcare ethics. It is my contention that pastors would do well to recover this sense of respect for others and exercise a prudent caution about efforts to extend help. A method is suggested for determining when pastors are most obligated to prevent or remove harm, such as cases involving domestic violence or a risk of suicide.

Chapter 3, "Permission for Mission," emphasizes that pastoral ministry occurs within community. A pastor receives permission from others to extend care and to practice ministry. Respecting the nature of this permission is the subject of this chapter. Because many expectations for pastoral care are actually implicitly stated, ministers need to develop sensitivity to hear both requests for help and requests for privacy.

Chapters 4, 5, and 6 all speak about duties of fidelity. Chapter 4 emphasizes the importance of not lying, while chapter 5 looks more constructively at what it means to speak and act truly. Chapter 6 examines the importance and the limitations of pastoral confidentiality. Veracity and confidentiality are presented here in apparent tension—veracity seeming to require the sharing of information and confidentiality seeming to require the keeping of secrets.

Chapters 7 and 8 broaden the focus theologically. They are each about a theology of vocation, but each with different foci. Chapter 7 discusses the vocation of all creation to glorify God and the vocation of all of humanity to seek justice. Chapter 8 focuses on the evangelical vocation of the church and the particular vocation of the clergy. The thesis of these chapters is that the vocation of the pastor must be seen within the context of the vocation of the church, of humanity, of society, and of creation. The whole church is called to be steward of the mysteries of God, which involves a ministry of proclaiming a message of grace. Pastoral care to help individual persons and families flourish is also placed within the broader context of creation's vocation to glorify God. The minister is discussed as a moral leader and a moral guide, called to encourage the vocational faithfulness of the laity in the their homes, their careers, and their public lives—as well as in the church.

This book grows out of my experience as a pastor—primarily in the state of New Jersey, where I have served as a United Methodist minister. It also grows out of my experience teaching courses in ethics and in the practice of ministry at United Theological Seminary of the Twin Cities (a seminary of the United Church of Christ), the School of Ministry at Knox College in Dunedin, New Zealand (a seminary of the Presbyterian Church of Aotearoa, New Zealand), the ecumenical Pacific Theological College in the Republic of Fiji, and New Brunswick Theological Seminary (a seminary of the Reformed Church in America located in New Jersey). I am grateful for the many conversations I have had with students and with colleagues, with fellow clergy and with lay members of congregations, about the practice of ministry and about Christian ethics. I have learned from all of these conversations. It is my hope that this book will pass on to others some of the learning I have received from students and colleagues.

1

Moral Self in Community

Introduction to the Moral Life

Ethics can be defined simply as critical reflection on the moral life, or critical reflection on morality. Morality, however, is more difficult to define. Our understandings of the moral life vary considerably. Some think about morality in terms of duties. Some think in terms of rights. Some think in terms of law. Some think in terms of grace. Some think in terms of consequences to come. Some think in terms of promises made. Some think in terms of human nature. Some think in terms of nature itself. Some think about personal virtues and vices. Some think about interpersonal relations. Some think about public policy and social justice. Some think about moral reasoning and volition. Some think about the narratives that shape us as moral agents. All of this is about morality. Ethics tries to make sense of it all.

Ethics as the study of morality draws from many resources and bridges many disciplines. It draws from philosophical schools and from theological traditions. It draws from our contemporary experience in culture and from our analyses of that experience. Each of these areas of reflection can provide a beginning point for the study of ethics. Each provides a point of entry, but each also entails limitations.

First, it has been the way of many philosophers to argue deductively from the general to the specific—to look for first principles by which further lessons can be deduced and to articulate general theory from which particular conclusions can be drawn. Second, it has been the way of many theologians, similarly, to begin with theological affirmations and draw ethical conclusions, or to begin with questions of method (e.g., questions about the authority of scripture, the nature of revelation, etc.) and assume that ethical conclusions will then dependably follow.

These two beginning points, however, represent two temptations for ethical deliberation and moral reflection. In the first case, ethics tends to devolve into epistemology. In the second case, ethics tends to devolve into hermeneutics. Epistemology and hermeneutics are important, but ethics is not contained by either of these.

I prefer to begin in the middle. Ethics becomes important as people make decisions that affect other people and as they participate in lifestyles that have implications for future generations or for the earth as a whole. The perennial questions in ethics are huge in scope, e.g., "What is the nature of the good?" In actuality, though, people often begin with more immediate questions, such as "What should I do?" Everyone at some time or other asks this latter question. Many people, conversely, try to avoid the former. It may be, that such questions concerning the nature of the good are logically prior to, "What should I do?" Even more fundamental might be questions of identity, such as, "Who am I?" or, "Who are we?" But the importance of ethics, I would suggest, appears with salience in people's minds when we are wondering what to do, how to act, or how to respond in actual situations that have repercussions for ourselves or others. This is the middle—having to decide, to act, or to respond.

Pastoral ministers are fortunate in that we are able to encounter people in the middle. People come to us for advice or comfort in the middle of their quandaries or troubles. We frequently see people when they are in the middle of important decisions. We are not medical experts, but we visit people in hospitals as they are deciding about treatment for themselves or for their loved ones; these decisions can be matters of life or death. If death has occurred, we are with people in the midst of their grief and their struggle, with all the emotions, including guilt, that might be present.

We counsel people at pivotal points of commitment, based upon their previous experiences, and as they establish resolve for the future— moments of conversion, of baptism, of confirmation, and of renewal. Weddings also are significant beginnings that occur "in the middle" and that involve the moral resolve of persons together in family.

Even on a Sunday morning, if we preach a sermon to one hundred people, one hundred individual contexts for hearing the gospel are in the congregation that morning. Everyone will have his or her own struggles, own strengths, own relationships, own questions, own confusions, own regrets, and own hopes. As ministers, we are fortunate to be able to interact with people as they seek the grace to live their lives faithfully. For people and their pastors, ethics is not solely a matter of philosophical abstraction from life. Rather, ethics makes contact with life itself, but it does so utilizing the philosophical and theological resources that are accessible to us "in the middle."

■ CASE FOR DISCUSSION: Caught in the Middle

Pastor Anne has been serving for only three weeks in her first position as a minister. Her church is in an inner city neighborhood where poverty is prevalent, though most of the members of the congregation are in the economic middle class. Nevertheless, some do struggle to be able to afford even the basics of food, clothing, and rent. Many within the community are also affected by such problems as alcoholism and drug abuse.

Anne is excited to be in pastoral ministry. She is especially excited to be serving in a neighborhood where she thinks she might be able to make a difference in people's lives—where people's situations seem to call out to her for ministry. This early in her ministry, she is still attempting to establish a routine and to get to know the different members of the congregation. She has been putting a lot of energy into preparation for congregational worship on Sunday mornings. Worship is one of the aspects of church life that she enjoys highly.

On this third Sunday of Anne's pastorate, however, she is suddenly taken off guard. Just as Sunday worship is beginning, as she is seated behind the pulpit listening to the prelude and thinking about her sermon on the good Samaritan, a church usher approaches her and interrupts her meditation:

"Excuse me, Pastor, a woman here insists that she see you. She seems distraught. She says that her sister in Kansas has suffered an accident and that she needs to get to her right away. The bus leaves for Kansas in forty minutes, and she needs $70 for the fare. Do you want to see her? What should I say to her?"

Anne is not sure what to do. Should she delay the start of the service to see this person? If she chooses to see her, would she know how to respond to her request? If she chooses not to see her, is she hiding behind her robes and pulpit to avoid a neighbor in need? What ought she do?

■ ■ QUESTIONS

1. How would you imagine yourself responding if you were in Anne's position?
2. As you think about your response, what seems to carry weight in your own moral reasoning or moral inclinations? What seems to

"decide this" for you? Is it a moral intuition or hunch? Is it a rational principle? Is it a sense of duty? Is it a goal or a moral objective? Is it an identification with a biblical story? Is it a sense of one's role within the community of faith or within the neighborhood community? Is it a sense of loyalty or commitment? In other words, how do you find yourself thinking?

3. How satisfied are you with your response? Do you think you have taken into account the most morally important dimensions of this scenario? Are you relatively certain—or uncertain—that your response would be just? Do you experience a kind of moral conflict or dilemma in this situation—a kind of regret that a perfectly just solution would prove elusive? Even if you feel conflicted in this scenario, do you think you would be able, nonetheless, to justify your decision to others?

4. If you are answering these questions in the context of a class, share your responses to these questions with others. Is the reasoning of your neighbors similar or different than yours? Are you surprised by this similarity or difference? How would you describe the differences you are encountering with each other?

5. In analyzing this case, what aspects of the pastoral role become salient?

   a. Does this seem to be an issue of pastoral care—needing to respond in some way, primarily to the woman who is making the request for cash?

   b. Does this seem to be an issue of pastoral leadership—needing to respond in some way, primarily to the usher who is seeking guidance or direction to know how to proceed?

   c. Does this seem to be an issue of worship leadership—needing to be responsive to the community gathered for prayer and praise?

Anne is experiencing moral uncertainty or moral confusion. She is uncertain about how to proceed in response to the information she is receiving from the usher. Her confusion is heightened by the timing of the incident—just prior to Sunday worship. She feels under pressure to respond, but the right response is not immediately clear to her.

Anne must, nevertheless, do something, even if only to ignore both the usher and the woman and to proceed with the worship service as planned. Anne is a "moral agent" in this situation. Drawing on her understanding of the situation and on her moral resources as a person, she must make a decision. Her decision will reflect a number of factors:

- her own personal moral character
- her understanding of herself and of her roles in relationship to others
- the institutional parameters that might be defining her authority or limiting her power
- her moral reasoning about obligation or duty
- her perception of and sensitivity to the persons making requests of her

Her decision occurs within this complex matrix of perception, emotion, commitment, and reasoning. The same complexity is present whether the decision is made spontaneously or after long and thoughtful deliberation.

In their influential book, *Bible and Ethics in the Christian Life,* Bruce Birch and Larry Rasmussen distinguish between "an ethics of being" and an "ethics of doing."[1] This distinction provides one way of beginning to sort through the myriad moral factors at play in a situation such as Anne's. By an "ethics of being," Birch and Rasmussen are referring to matters of personal character—a person's moral habits, her virtues and vices. How is she disposed to respond in a given situation because of who she is? What are the strengths of character that enable her to respond in one way or another? While virtues of character may be thought of as a person's own particular moral dispositions, they develop within a person over time and through interaction with others in community.

An "ethics of doing" attends less to the person as a moral agent and more to action itself and to the options for responding that may be present in a given situation. While an ethics of being focuses more inwardly on a moral agent's personal character, an ethics of doing focuses more outwardly on the kind of action that might be called for and the kinds of moral principles that might function as guides for decision-making. In real life, of course, both "being" and "doing" are constantly related.[2] The distinction is a conceptual one that allows a person to explore the moral life, first from one angle and then from another.

Most of this book will center on the "ethics of doing" for persons engaged in congregational leadership and ministry. In the body of the book, each chapter will highlight a particular principle for moral action as it might apply in pastoral practice, e.g., nonmaleficence (not causing harm), veracity (truth-telling), and confidentiality. At the same time, though, an "ethics of being" will never be far away. To act in a way consistent with any of the principles suggested in this book would require the strength of character to discern one's duty in a particular situation and to respond with virtues such as compassion and courage. Nevertheless, the primary focus in the chapters to follow will be on the "ethics of doing" for pastors and congregational leaders.

This chapter, however, will continue with a discussion about an "ethics of being" and, in particular, how personal virtue might be seen to be related to one's culture and community. Culture and community, it will be seen, give shape to personal virtue. This is both empowering and delimiting. On one hand, culture provides us with the moral resources for virtue; on the other, it also limits and constrains virtue.

Character in Context

Character refers to our personal capacity to will good and to do good (or to will and do evil, as the case may be). In classical moral theory, a strength of character is referred to as a virtue (from the Latin *virtus*), and a weakness of character is referred to as a vice. In the above case, Pastor Anne seems to be presented as a person of good moral character. She is a person of good will in that she wants to do the right thing. She seems to display the virtues of compassion for people in need, diligence in the exercise of ministry, sociability in wanting to get to know others, and reverence in the practice of worship.

At the same time, Anne is aware of other, perhaps less virtuous inclinations. She is guarding against the vice of cowardice (concerned that she might be hiding behind her robes and pulpit) and the vice of indecisiveness (concerned that even if she meets with the woman she still might not know what to do). On balance, though, Anne appears to have sufficient strength of character to help her respond to the moral quandary she is facing. These are her personal moral resources, her capacities for moral action.

However, the same personal quality that appears as a strength or virtue can, in an extreme form, appear instead as a weakness or vice. For instance, Anne's virtue of compassion, in extreme form, might become codependency–her own need to be needed. Her diligence, in an extreme form, could appear to be a vice of overworking if she does not rest or take care of herself. Likewise, her sociability might appear to be a vice if she were uncomfortable being alone and so was always looking for a party. Even her reverence might be thought of as a vice if Anne appeared overly pious or self-righteous in her piety.

On the other hand, those qualities mentioned in the above paragraph as vices might, in more moderate form, provide the strength Anne needs to face her current challenge. Rather than being cowardly or indecisive, Anne might be demonstrating a necessary and prudent caution—especially if she is responding to a person who might represent a danger or threat to herself or to her congregation. Thomas Aquinas, following Aristotle, has suggested that for the most part virtue follows the mean rather than the extreme.[3] It is a matter of developing the right balance of personal disposition that enables one to respond appropriately in a given situation.

This discussion about virtue following the mean points to the potential for virtue theory to take cultural variability into account. To find a mean or to strike a balance between virtue and vice would seem to depend on cues from one's cultural context. Given the rich diversity of virtues encouraged by different cultures and the various kinds of strengths required of people in different circumstances, one would expect cultural influence to enter into our thinking about human virtue. One would think, furthermore, that moral character would be shaped by one's social location and the ways in which one experiences oppression or privilege in society. In other words, one might inquire about the kinds of social conditions that have challenged a person to develop particular moral strengths, and one might inquire as well about the cultural meaning that attaches to those strengths.

Katie Cannon provides an example of such culturally informed thinking about virtue. Cannon takes seriously the particular experiences of oppression that have formed the context for virtue among African American women. Cannon appeals to the primacy of experience. Her *Black Womanist Ethics* begins with an appeal to the experience of African American women rather than to ethical theory, and she draws out the ethical implications of this experience. "I believe," states Cannon, "that basic experiential themes and ethical implications can lead to norms lived out in the realities of day-to-day experience."[4] Analyzing the life and literature of Zora Neale Hurston as a source reflecting African American women's experience, Cannon highlights the importance of survival itself as a central virtue in Hurston's "unctuous moral agency":

> Zora Neale Hurston came to appreciate that surviving the continual struggle and the interplay of contradictory opposites was genuine virtue. Hurston knew that there could be no "perfectionism" in the face of the structures of oppression she experienced as a Black-woman-artist. For her, the moral quality of life was expressed not as an ideal but was to be fulfilled as a balance of complexities in such a way that suffering did not overwhelm, and endurance with integrity was possible.[5]

Cannon continues by describing corollary virtues of "invisible dignity," "never practiced delicacy," and "quiet grace."[6]

Cannon's work demonstrates how one can attend to a particular person's experience to describe moral virtue both as the unique set of virtues of a particular person and also as suggestively representative of that person's cultural community. She also demonstrates how this list of virtues might be shaped by a people's historic need to exercise moral agency while contending with powerful social forces that attempt to constrain that agency. Katie Cannon is able to portray an understanding of character and virtue that is relatively free from previous Western theories about character.

We now turn to some of these Western theories about character and conceptions of the moral self.

Models of the Moral Self

Any discussion about personal moral qualities or capacities (virtues) must assume some understanding of the self or some psychological model. For such an understanding of the self, Western moral theory has tended to rely on psychological categories from classical Greek philosophy–Plato and Aristotle–as these categories were further developed and shaped in Christian tradition–particularly by Saint Thomas Aquinas. The language of virtue in this tradition distinguishes between reason, will, and the appetites. The classical model of the self has produced a high degree of system in Western theory concerning the intricacies of virtue, vice, and character.

Traditional Model of the Self

Classical categories of virtue can still be seen as influential today. In the last twenty-five years, many writers have shown a renewed interest in the relevance of virtue and moral character for thinking about ethics. Some are explicitly critical of modernity and find in classical virtue theory an ancient alternative to categories of the Enlightenment.[7] Others voice a preference for biblical teaching over Greek philosophy, but can still be seen to assume categories characteristic of this philosophical tradition.[8] Some have applied virtue theory specifically to the practice of ministry.[9] Still others have emphasized the role of the church as a community that nurtures people of virtue.[10]

However, while the classical systems of virtue continue to be inspiring and instructive, it is probably not advisable to approach them in too literal a fashion. Alasdair MacIntyre is among those ethicists responsible for the renewed interest in virtue. Voicing appreciation for Thomas Aquinas's system, MacIntyre nevertheless notes that even the most "exhaustive and consistent classificatory scheme ought always to arouse our suspicions." The reason for MacIntyre's caution is that our knowledge of the virtues is primarily learned empirically rather than deduced neatly from theory, and that there is therefore a necessary "empirical untidiness" in our experience and knowledge of our own and others' virtue.[11]

Resonating with MacIntyre's insight, we noticed the empirical untidiness of beginning in the middle. Decisions that confront us suddenly, such as the decision that confronted Pastor Anne, evoke from us those moral resources–those virtues or strengths of character–that have been developing within us over time and in concert with others. Our personal virtue is nurtured within community, and it takes on meaning within culture.

Classical psychology and virtue theory assume the existence of a personal soul able to willfully participate with one's environment in shaping one's own personality. The classical model presents the individual as developing morally in dynamic interaction with his or her social environment. Nevertheless, because of the high degree of system achieved in this line of thought, the importance of cultural influence can sometimes become obscured in favor of a detailed taxonomy of individual virtues.

New psychological perspectives in both modernity and postmodernity have stretched our self-understanding of what it means to be human. At the same time, we need to reconsider our understanding of human moral capacity. Contemporary theories of psychology, as often as not, avoid the question–thus making difficult any articulation of a correlative theory of virtue. A major theoretical challenge for theological ethics early in the third millennium is to develop such contemporary understandings of moral virtue.

Contemporary Models of the Self

The Behaviorist Model

In the middle of the last century, the behavioral psychologist, B. F. Skinner, championed the idea that environment is determinative of the behaviors of individuals. Skinner presented this challenge with such hyperbole, though, that many moralists rather easily dismissed him. In *Beyond Freedom and Dignity,* Skinner pronounced the death of "autonomous man."[12] By this he meant that a person's behavior could be explained by reference to a person's environment alone–thus negating the relevance of questions of virtue entirely. Skinner was unapologetically reductionistic in this regard, but his theory about environmental conditioning continues to be very influential in behavioral science. Many in our congregations have studied his or similar theories.

The Cognitive Developmental Model

A psychological model more directly influential on congregations' own educational programs is cognitive structuralism, or cognitive development theory, inspired by the work of French philosopher Jean Piaget. This model presents learning as a dynamic process in the relation between "organism" and "environment." As children mature in interaction with their environment, they develop mental structures for understanding their world in increasingly complex and abstract ways. Learning occurs on different levels; as the child's earlier cognitive structures become inadequate over time for assimilating new information and experiences, the child "accommodates" by developing more adequate structures to take account of the newer complexity of mental perceptions.[13]

Psychologist Lawrence Kohlberg further developed Piaget's model and applied it to the cognitive development of moral reasoning. Kohlberg examined moral reasoning as a matter of the development of cognitive structures. He identified a pattern of development that progresses through stages. "Preconventional morality" in young children emphasizes avoiding punishment, while "conventional morality" in older children and many adults stresses conformity to rules and the approval of others. Finally, "postconventional morality" emphasizes abstract principles and the development of a more autonomous conscience.[14]

Sunday schools are often organized according to age levels to facilitate instruction of children at particular stages of cognitive development. Mainline Protestant Sunday school curricula have been written with these cognitive levels in mind, so as to communicate lessons in a way that is appropriate for a particular age level and that offers children a fitting degree of cognitive challenge. The intent is to present matters of morality and religion in a manner most appropriate for maturing minds. In this way, congregations are attempting to provide educational environments conducive to developing people of good moral character and Christian faith.

In testing Kohlberg's moral development theory cross-culturally, however, cultural differences have been found. One study examined the use of Kohlberg's stages in twenty-seven different countries and found cultural variation, especially with regard to Kohlberg's higher stages. It would seem that Kohlberg's stages are far from universal, and that cultural relativity characterizes the so-called higher levels of moral reasoning.[15]

Carol Gilligan, Lawrence Kohlberg's former colleague, has criticized Kohlberg's theory of moral development with regard to differences in gender. Gilligan has argued that Kohlberg's understanding of the higher stages of moral reasoning is biased toward the experience of men. Whereas men tend to reason formally and abstractly with regard to justice, she points out, women tend to focus more on relationships and to the actual obligations and responsibilities entailed in those relationships.[16]

Cultural Constructivist Model

More recent investigations in cultural psychology have become increasingly expansive in portraying the very structure of the "self" as cultural construction. This new line of psychological enquiry also poses new challenges for conceptualizing moral character. Cross-cultural studies have shown that people in different cultures can have very different perceptions of the "self." Westerners tend to view themselves with a higher degree of independence than do many non-Westerners. In the typical Western perspective, a person's attributes become internalized; they are personal virtues and characteristics, the self-identifying marks of the individual. For many Asians and other non-Westerners, however, a greater degree of fluidity exists between the self and the self's relationships with others. For people in these non-Western cultures, the significant characteristics of the "self" remain attached to these relationships themselves–the roles, responsibilities, and feelings associated with particular relationships– rather than internalized more abstractly as personal character traits.[17]

In his book, *People: Psychology from a Cultural Perspective,* David Matsumoto reviews some of this cross-cultural research. His examples help illustrate these cultural differences. He notes that if people are asked to describe themselves by listing abstract traits of their personalities (e.g., "I am sociable"), Americans will list more of these traits than will Asians. Conversely, people from China, Japan, or Korea are much more likely to describe themselves in terms of social categories or relationships. However, if the context is explicitly described so that an individual is able to imagine the specific social occasion and the particular relationships that are most salient in this hypothetical occasion, Japanese people are able to list a greater number of personal feelings and attributes than their American counterparts. The Japanese individuals would seem to be able to identify their own personal attributes best within the complex nexus of particular relationships rather than as isolated or abstracted from these relationships.[18]

The significance of this cultural difference became clear to me through interaction with theological students in the Pacific Islands. I was lecturing in a course on psychology at the Pacific Theological College in Fiji. The students in this class came from throughout Oceania: Fiji, Samoa, Tonga, Tuvalu, and the Solomon Islands. Almost all of the students in the class identified with the more interdependent understanding of the self. When asked, they would each describe their "self" within complex sets of relationships—including chiefs, elders, ancestors, and church, as well as family and friends.

After class, one student came to me with a further question. This middle-aged Fijian man was a very well-respected minister in the community. He was intelligent and articulate in English, but seemed less Westernized than some of the other students. He presented me with a sack of yams from the firstfruits harvest in his parish and asked his question: "Excuse me, I am confused. Would you please explain to me the difference between the 'self' and the 'others?'" The very idea of a "self" was actually confusing to him.

Cultural psychology, like conventional psychology, focuses on the development of the "self," but it gives greater attention to cultural variability in the constitution of personality and self-understanding. In so doing, it suggests not only cultural differences in values, moral teaching, and personal virtues; it also questions the universality of the basic model of an individualized self as moral agent who possesses virtue apart from the actuality of social relationships in cultural context.

The cultural constructivist model of the self described by cultural psychology seems to offer a rich alternative to the earlier, more reductionist behaviorist model. The behaviorist model, by comparison, seems impoverished with its emphasis on environmental stimulus and behavioral response. In the behaviorist model, both the self and the environment are diminished: The self becomes a reactive "organism," and similarly the "environment" loses its own "personality" of cultural complexity and meaning. Both models, though, emphasize the importance of the wider world in shaping the individual person. Moreover, both models raise a challenge for conceptualizing moral character and moral agency when the individual's self is so greatly shaped by the social and cultural environment.[19]

Anthropologists have always studied and compared cultures. They have attended to various moral systems and the ways that moral values are taught, expressed, displayed, and internalized. Writing in 1934, the anthropologist Ruth Benedict articulated a case of cultural relativity. She referred in particular to different patterns of vengeance considered laudable among the Dobu people in Melanesia, and among the Kwakiutl of the North American Pacific Coast. She then challenged people's tendency to extrapolate from their own localized experience to generalize more universally about morality and human nature. "We do not any longer make the mistake of deriving the morality of our own locality and decade directly from the inevitable constitution of human nature," she writes.[20]

Culture not only contributes to moral diversity, however; culture also allows us to communicate with each other and to develop shared conceptions of the moral life. Because we live together in culture, together we construct a shared world of meaning as we interact with each other and as we converse together. Culture enables us to interpret and to reinterpret our moral traditions to address new circumstances as they arise. Our moral world is made possible by culture.

Culture is not monolithic. It is permeable. It is composed of many overlapping subcultures, and it overlaps with other cultures within the global community of communities. We are constantly recognizing both similarity and difference as we communicate with others. Culture allows us to affirm this similarity and to recognize and learn from this difference. When people approach one another or when they approach the minister with a moral quandary, for instance, it is an invitation to further explore together our shared world of moral meaning. Communication rather than uniformity is to be expected in these encounters between people about moral matters. Culture allows for this communication of both similarity and difference.

Pastoral Response

For the pastoral minister interested in virtue and the formation of moral character, the emphasis on cultural and environmental influence presents two challenges. The first is the rather academic problem of how to conceptualize moral agency if so much of a person's actions and habits are shaped by the cultural environment. In other words, how do we begin to understand a person's will and a person's capacity to choose good or ill? The second challenge, though, is more pastoral than academic: How do we individually as ministers, and corporately as church, exercise our responsibility in shaping people's habits and actions? In other words, if people are shaped by their environment, how can the church be a responsible environment in helping to shape people of virtue? These two challenges are related to each other as theory to pastoral practice. They shall each be addressed briefly below. H. Richard Niebuhr provides one example of conceptualizing moral agency to take into account cultural factors. Following the discussion of Niebuhr, we will address the second challenge concerning the church's role in nurturing virtue.

The Responsible Self

H. Richard Niebuhr provides one theological approach to conceptualizing moral agency in culture. A contemporary of Ruth Benedict, Niebuhr acknowledged the fact of cultural relativity in morality. Moral relativism is an unavoidable cultural phenomenon, according to Niebuhr, especially during times of social change. Nevertheless, Niebuhr noticed that every culture has some way of conceptualizing the moral life, even though these conceptions all vary. He then argued that individuals and societies have an obligation to pursue their best understandings of moral good even though these understandings vary among cultures.

Niebuhr even suggested this as an "absolute" obligation that people have relative to the moral insight of their respective cultures. In his own words, he affirmed an "absolute obligation of an individual or a society to follow its highest insights."[21] Niebuhr perhaps begged the question of the criteria for determining a culture's "highest" insights; he certainly did not consider all cultural values and virtues to be of equal worth. Nevertheless, the idea of cultural relativity, to interpret Niebuhr's thought, does not negate the task of ethics. Instead, cultural difference becomes a part of that very moral reality to which the subject of ethics must attend.

Niebuhr's model of moral agency emphasizes the important role that interpretation plays within a community of shared meaning. Niebuhr's understanding of "the responsible self" was informed by the social psychology of George Herbert Mead. Mead's understanding, much like some of the psychological theories discussed above, views the "self" as developing in interaction with one's particular social environment.[22] According to Niebuhr's understanding of moral agency, we respond to each other in accord with our interpretation of "what is going on," and we further anticipate that our actions will be interpreted meaningfully by others. This "meaning" includes an understanding of the moral import of our actions in response to one another.

The emphasis is on responsibility as responsiveness. H. Richard Niebuhr states that we respond to an event in accord with our interpretation of that event and expecting a response to our response.[23] By "expecting a response to [our] response," Niebuhr is acknowledging that as moral agents we internalize a pattern of interpretation that we expect to be held by others with whom we are interacting. Moral meaning is something we share with others within culture. This openness of moral agency to cultural meaning allows Niebuhr's model to remain relevant even as we become influenced today by contemporary models of the self as shaped by culture.

Various value systems can enter into this process of interpretation, according to H. Richard Niebuhr. As a monotheist, Niebuhr affirms that ultimately God is the center of value for all that exists in interrelationship.[24] The value theory of Niebuhr's monotheistic theology, however, allows for the construction of many relative value systems with different provisional centers as one considers "the interaction of beings on beings, now from the point of view of [humanity], now from the point of view of society, now from the point of view of life."[25] These value systems allow us to interpret our world and to weigh alternative courses of action. They also allow us to recognize that our actions will, in turn, be valued by others in accordance with their interpretation of our actions. Niebuhr's model of moral agency is able to combine two concerns that may at first seem to be in tension: (1) an attentiveness to society and to culture as a shaper of moral agency; and (2) faith in God as the ultimate source of morality.

Character in Congregation

The church has opportunity to participate in defining good character and in nurturing people of virtue. As a community, the church can provide a culture or subculture in which persons can be shaped and their character formed. In *Bible and Ethics in the Christian Life*, Birch and Rasmussen maintain this emphasis on character formation within the context of congregations. Describing the church as a "shaper of moral identity," Birch and Rasmussen notice that character is both formed and reformed as people read scripture, worship, and deliberate together in community. The church, according to Birch and Rasmussen, contributes to the formation of moral character not only as a direct influence on people's lives but also as a place of centering where people can faithfully integrate various experiences and influences.[26]

Similarly, Stanley Hauerwas's primer in Christian ethics, *The Peaceable Kingdom*, promotes the idea that the virtues of God's commonwealth are nurtured within people through their participation together as church. Hauerwas recognizes that many social forces influence us as moral agents. He suggests that character be thought of as a matter of selection within and between these influences, rather than as a claim of radical human freedom apart from them.[27] Moral character necessarily develops within a set of social relationships, social expectations, and cultural narratives. Freedom, according to Hauerwas, "is dependent on our being initiated into a truthful narrative."[28] In particular, Christians learn to identify themselves as "forgiven people" as they find themselves incorporated into God's story of salvation.[29]

As the title of his book implies, Hauerwas understands peaceableness to be a necessary virtue of Christian community. Such peaceableness reflects God's commonwealth and God's intentions for human society. It stands in contrast to the realities of the current fragmented and violent world. Personal virtues such as hope and patience are corollary to this central vision of peace in community, and are nurtured in us as individuals within the Christian community.

Another Christian writer, Tom Sine, has brought further urgency to the character-forming mission of the church as a kind of alternative culture in postmodernity. "If we try to follow Christ on automatic pilot," cautions Sine, "the values of modern culture will wind up defining the direction and the character of our lives."[30] Sine is especially concerned with helping to strengthen the church as an alternative community to counteract powerful forces of globalization.

The peaceable theme articulated by Hauerwas, I would emphasize, becomes urgent for the church during times of war or when the wider society is tempted toward violence. As the society as a whole turns to an increasingly martial culture, the church is in a position to provide the kind of alternative culture advocated by Sine, Hauerwas, and Birch and Rasmussen. This is perhaps one of the greatest opportunities for the mission of the church—to continue in times of war as well as in times of peace—nurturing people of faith rather than fear, people of peace rather than violence, people of moral virtue rather than moral weakness. The members of a congregation can do this for one another in every aspect of their lives together in fellowship. Even by simply encouraging such virtue among themselves, church members provide a witness and an influence to the larger society, which may be in need of that alternative vision.

Professional Ethics in Society

One of the complicating factors for Christians, however, is that we exist simultaneously in more than one community. We are members of churches with sacred scriptures and with traditions of interpretation pertaining to those sacred scriptures. We are also members of a national community with its own foundational texts and moral norms, such as a tradition that identifies and interprets human rights and civil liberties. We are also members of other communities—neighborhoods, extended families, places of work. Indeed, people can identify very strongly with the culture and ethos of their profession or of their workplace. Strong and important moral resources are available to us in these other areas of social life as well as in the church.

The church's relevance depends as much on its appreciative attentiveness to the rest of society as it does to any dogmatic or judgmental criticism of that society. It is not simply that the other institutions in society are intellectually vacuous, morally bankrupt, and spiritually inert. It would be incredible (*in-credible*: without faith!) for the church to think so. Society has moral traditions that inform our understandings of political justice and that guide our understanding of ethics for professional practice in such areas as medicine, law, and business. In fact, during the last several years, courses in ethics are blossoming in colleges and graduate schools.

The church needs to attend for its own sake, as well as for its social relevance, to the moral conversations that are occurring in the other arenas of society. To do so is to recognize that various spheres of life are, in fact, held within the care of the Creator and that the culture, the tradition, and the society all provide resources for thinking about the moral life. There needs to be a common language about moral expectations as well as a difference in perspective. Indeed we need a common language about the moral life to even be able to communicate our important differences as well as agreements with each other.

A degree of shared expectations is necessary for morality to be mutually meaningful. We need to know that our kindnesses to each other are at least appreciated as kindnesses, that our injustices to each other can be recognized as such in order to be corrected, that our trust in each other can be reciprocated. This all presupposes a common language of moral discourse—or at least a common basic vocabulary. One might want to transcend the vulgar ethics of the secular society to attain a more perfect state, but one is likely to be surprised that one's perfection is perceived as unwanted or even dangerous by one's neighbors whom one is called to serve and with whom one is called to live.

A wider, pluralist culture contains us as Christians along with peoples of other faiths and beliefs. A wider society of political, economic, and social institutions numbers church organizations among them. This wider society and culture contains traditions of moral interpretation that may seem to make only occasional contact with the particular theological beliefs held by Christians. The civilizational ethics of the wider society tends to affirm values and principles, however, that are often (but not necessarily) held in common with the Christian groups within society. Earlier Enlightenment thinkers (such as Immanuel Kant and others) shaped much of this moral tradition, but it continues to be interpreted as a lively tradition. The liveliness of this ethical tradition can be seen in the continuing development of courses and programs in professional ethics: medical ethics, research ethics, business ethics, legal ethics.

The following chapters are concerned with the professional ethics of clergy as leaders of congregations and as caregivers. Pastoral ethics will be brought into conversation with other areas of professional ethics in Western society. Pastoral ethics will be seen to share with other areas of applied professional ethics a common tradition of moral discourse. As pastors we must draw on the best of the moral insights we hold in common with other professions, so others with whom we reside in society and with whom we share cultural patterns of meaning can appreciate (or judge as the case may be) our own professional ethics.

The justification for appealing to this tradition of moral discourse is not the same as the arguments used in the past by Enlightenment thinkers, from whom we now inherit many of these categories. The presumption is not made for absolute certainty in rational argument. The presumption is not even made that all of the principles here discussed will necessarily be rationally consistent with one another. Rather the appeal is to four factors that suggest that society's moral discourse may be relevant as well for the church's ethics.

First is simply the prevalence of these moral categories within our shared moral world.

Second, the prevalence of these moral categories gives them a "track record"; there would seem to be a pragmatic dependability of these categories for achieving a modicum of responsibility among the professions.

Third, for our own practice to be recognized as just, the church's morality must be consistent with the best moral insights of culture.

Finally, we share H. Richard Niebuhr's confidence that there is one God whose grace prevenes our moral formation and whose providence informs culture as well as church.

We now move to the "ethics of doing" in pastoral practice. As a primary concern, we turn now to the matter of not hurting others.

2

Working Gently

Nonmaleficence in Ministry

"[B]e wise as serpents and harmless as doves."

MATTHEW 10:16B (NKJV)

The day before I was ordained as a United Methodist minister, the bishop called all of us who were to be ordained together (along with our spouses if they desired) to put certain questions to the ordinands that the church required. To be honest, we thought of it as a kind of *pro forma* test that we did not have to study for. After all, we had graduated from seminary, and we all felt ready to pursue God's call into ministry.

"Do you know the General Rules of our Church?" inquired the bishop.

We looked at him blankly. None of us seemed to know what he was asking about. Some attempted to mumble guesses as their minds plumbed the depths of their biblical knowledge, theological learning, and Methodist doctrine.

"There are three rules," said the bishop at last. "Do no harm; do good; and attend to the ordinances of God."[1]

"O brother!" my wife verbally exclaimed a little louder than she had intended and somewhat to my embarrassment. It sounded to her banal and trivial, as if we were children again in Sunday school. I thought so as well at the time.

In retrospect, though, I think the bishop's reminder to us was important and necessary–especially the rule about doing no harm.

While it might be stated simply and seem to be very obvious, I find that few pastors think about "not harming" as a first principle for pastoral practice. They tend to be much more interested in trying to "do good" than "avoid harming." People often enter Christian ministry to help others and to be of service. To speak of refraining from harm sounds tentative—even cowardly. Ministers prefer to ask themselves, "What would be the most loving thing to do?" rather than, "How should I take care not to hurt those who come to me for help?" But isn't the caution represented in this latter question also important?

The relative lack of attention ministers give to refraining from harm is in contrast to the fundamentals of ethics for other so-called helping professions. "As to diseases, make a habit of two things," the Hippocratic Oath suggests: "to help or at least to do no harm."[2] The principle of nonmaleficence (literally, "no-harm-doing") has been repeatedly established in codes of healthcare ethics. Textbooks on medical ethics typically begin with this principle or have an entire chapter devoted to it.[3] Until recently, though, books on pastoral ministry have tended to make little mention of nonmaleficence.

Karen Lebacqz, however, has consistently attended to the duty not to harm in writing about pastoral ethics. Her book coauthored with Joseph Driskill provides some of the philosophical context in the West for this duty.[4] Contrasting the duty "not to harm" (nonmaleficence) with the duty "to do good" (beneficence), Lebacqz and Driskill cite the philosophers Immanuel Kant and W. D. Ross in referring to the greater stringency of nonmaleficence over beneficence:

> Generally speaking, philosophers have considered the ethical mandate to do good to be less stringent than the mandate to avoid harm. Kant considered avoiding harm a "perfect" obligation—always mandatory—while doing good was an "imperfect" obligation that applied with less rigor. W. D. Ross also placed not-harming as among the most stringent of the "prima facie duties" that guide ethical behavior. Thus, for most people, avoiding harm is a more stringent duty than is doing good.[5]

While affirming the importance of the duty not to harm, Lebacqz and Driskill provide further nuance to their understanding of this duty so that it is not as strictly contrasted with beneficence as the above quotation implies. Before proceeding with an examination of their position later in this chapter, however, further attention needs to be given to this suggested distinction between nonmaleficence and beneficence in Western philosophy and Christian ethics. To do this we need to attend to an explanation of this rather technical language about "perfect obligations," "prima facie duties," and "stringency."

Perfect and Imperfect Obligations

The language about "perfect obligations," "prima facie duties," and "stringency" refers to the degree to which any moral rule or principle might be considered binding or morally mandatory. Of concern here is the question of moral relativity and moral absolutes. Few contemporary ethicists argue for absolute principles of moral action or argue on the basis of such absolute moral principles except of the most general nature. Philosophical Kantians, however, do affirm the absolute validity of certain moral principles, even though they, too, must determine the actual implications of their moral principles for the particulars of each situation. The language about "perfect obligations" comes from Kantian philosophy and refers to these putatively inviolable moral principles. Obligations that are considered to be perfect never admit of exception. Imperfect obligations, by contrast, are understood to have exceptions.

To determine whether an obligation is perfect or imperfect, Kantians test it logically by means of Kant's "categorical imperative." The categorical imperative is usually stated in one or two forms, which Immanuel Kant considered to be equivalent. First, always act by that maxim (or principle) that you could imagine to be a universal law. Second, always act so to treat humanity, whether in yourself or others, as an end and never as a means only. Kant considered these two statements equivalent because of his confidence in the rational nature of human beings and because of his grounding of ethics in this rational nature or "autonomy."[6]

Several duties, then, appear to be perfect obligations because they can be imagined as universal principles without logical contradiction. Kant argued that the duty not to inflict harm on another human being is one of these perfect obligations, along with other duties such as telling the truth and keeping promises. These duties, according to Kant, do not admit of exception. In contrast, the duty to "do good" cannot be perfectly realized, because there is always some good that one is not doing. The potential number of good deeds is endless, but the capacity to do any of them is finite. One cannot therefore be blamed for not doing any particular good. One is still obliged to do good, but imperfectly so, since the principle itself logically allows for exception.[7]

Imperfectly Good?

The logic behind the imperfect duty of beneficence (doing good) becomes apparent to anyone asked to serve as a trustee for a charitable fund. Typically, there is no lack of good causes that could benefit from such a fund, so that conceivably requests or applications for grants from the fund could be endless. Those who manage charitable funds, however, must decide to grant some requests and to deny others. The decisions are sometimes difficult, even painful.

Managers or trustees of a charitable fund are still generally obliged to do good, but this obligation is not extended perfectly to each and every request made of the fund over which they are stewards. Rather, we understand that they have faithfully discharged their duty to do good when the funds have been distributed to some but not to others according to their best judgment. In such a situation, to be able to do good at all necessarily involves choices and priorities that simultaneously deny good to some. Beneficence is obviously obligatory, but it can only be imperfectly realized or expected.

The logic behind the imperfect duty of beneficence also becomes apparent to pastors who are in ministry in situations in which human need is constant and unrelenting. This can be the case, especially, in some parishes that are in impoverished urban neighborhoods. When nearly everyone in the parish struggles to afford adequate food and housing, and when violence is distressingly common in the streets and even in the homes, one must concentrate one's efforts to be in ministry at all. To feel equally obliged to do good to all would render one relatively ineffective and certainly very tired. Individuals entering such situations of ministry unprepared for the kinds of tragic choices involved in helping others either develop a capacity to make discriminating choices in offering help, or they find themselves burning out. We find that we simply cannot do all the good that we would like to do. The duty is constant but imperfect.

Urban ministers can sometimes be ambivalently baffled and grateful (sometimes even angry) when suburban and rural colleagues offer to help out in the "inner city" because their own congregations need a mission—something to do to help others. It can be hard for the urban minister to imagine a situation where beneficence is not overwhelmed by human need. Even in such suburban and rural parishes, though, I would argue, the opportunities for beneficent action are still endless. The possibility of doing all possible good for all people in the suburb or countryside is still unrealistic. The needs for help may be less obvious, though, and the pace of requests for help less hectic. It is probably nonetheless empowering of ministry in suburban and rural contexts as well as in cities for pastors to be deliberate in choosing how to focus their own beneficence as well as that of their congregations.

Also, decisions regarding beneficent ministry should probably not be based solely on proximity. It is empowering for all congregations to be involved in mission both locally within their own communities as well as cooperatively in locations outside of their local communities. This is so for urban congregations as well as for suburban and rural ones. Again, though, choices will be made about the kinds of good that can best be accomplished, whether locally or farther away. Part of being in Christian mission is learning to trust the Holy Spirit to empower that ministry to which a congregation may feel called and, at the same time, to trust the Holy Spirit to empower those ministries that a congregation might need to leave for others. Even when making these choices, though, prayer can still unite into one body people and congregations involved in disparate ministries. Part of beneficence for Christians is to pray for one another in different ministries and in different locations.

Perfectly Harmless?

The duty of nonmaleficence, to "do no harm," can be more perfectly realized than the duty of beneficence because, at its most basic level, it requires simply that we leave one another alone. It requires that we not hurt each other. This is a different kind of obligation than beneficence. Beneficence would have us consider the good that we would actually do given the infinite possibilities of good that we might do. Nonmaleficence, more simply and more strictly, demands that we not hurt anyone. Two aspects are involved in the notion of a perfect obligation such as nonmaleficence. First, in Kantian fashion, it can be thought of as an exceptionless obligation without logical contradiction. This logical test of universalizability might hold regardless of how hard it might be to actually realize such a harmless lifestyle in practice. Second, nonmaleficence requires our forbearance, that is, our refraining from acting harmfully, rather than choosing from among myriad possibilities for positive action.

One might object at this point that in actuality these abstract distinctions can get very fuzzy and impractical. When we attempt to apply Kant's categorical imperative to the idea of nonmaleficence, that is, to imagine it as a universal duty without exception, it is actually rather easy for many people to imagine instances where doing some degree of harm may be required and morally justified. Many medical procedures, for instance, risk harm to the patient to provide benefit for the patient. Risk of harm exists, for instance, anytime someone undergoes general anesthesia during surgery. In this example of the medical patient the same individual who is exposed to risk of harm is also intended to be benefited.

In other instances, though, we might risk harm to one person to benefit others. Ministers sometimes experience this kind of moral trade-off in the context of church meetings and congregational planning. Decisions to relocate the church building from one neighborhood to another, for instance, or even to alter the time of worship on Sundays, can disenfranchise some parishioners for the sake of others. Yet, we make these kinds of decisions, justifying the trade-offs either in terms of the greater number who can benefit from the proposed change or in terms of our understanding of the wider mission of the church within the community. It is not easy to consistently avoid harm in the practice of ministry. Pastors who are especially sensitive to people's pain might even say it is impossible.

In actual practice it would seem to be difficult to maintain an absolute distinction between perfect and imperfect duties on the basis of their formal universalizability or their conceptually exceptionless character. Even the most perfect duties, such as nonmaleficence, seem sometimes to admit of exception. Also, even the supposedly imperfect duty of beneficence seems always to be obligatory to us in some manner—even if never perfectly realizable. The distinction between perfect and imperfect obligation can become blurred in real life. If this is so in practice, then ethical theory should also realistically reflect this blurring.

Moral Presumption

W. D. Ross and Prima Facie Moral Duties

The philosopher W. D. Ross proposed a more fluid way of thinking about the moral life. Rather than distinguishing between perfect and imperfect duties on the basis of whether or not they admit of exception, Ross considered all moral principles to be only "prima facie" binding. By this he meant that he considered it possible to justify exceptions to every moral principle; none was perfectly exceptionless. At the same time, though, a prima facie moral principle does tell us something about our obligations; it describes our moral obligation in part. A prima facie obligation is a beginning point; it tells us how to act unless we can justify acting otherwise on the basis of competing moral obligations. In effect, Ross recognizes that life is complicated and that we are typically obligated in more than one direction at once.

Ross distinguishes instead between our actual duty and our prima facie duty. Prima facie duties are those moral principles that might describe our moral obligations in general, that is, in principle. Our actual duty is more circumstantial and situational. Our actual duty, according to Ross, is the particular course of action that we understand to be obligatory to us given the actual situation and the many different moral principles that might be relevant in that situation.

Because the moral life occurs in human relationships, those relationships themselves help determine the very nature of our moral obligations. Obligation often has a history. If we have made promises, we have entailed obligations to keep those promises. If we have done somebody wrong, we have a prima facia obligation of "reparation"– to right that wrong. If someone has shown us a kindness, Ross suggests, we feel obliged to repay that kindness–a prima facie duty of "gratitude."

We also have prima facie duties of justice and prima facie duties to improve life's conditions–whether for oneself (a duty of self-improvement) or for others (a duty of beneficence). Ross seems to consider the duty of nonmaleficence to be distinct from and more "stringent" than beneficence:

> No doubt to injure others is incidentally to fail to do them good; but it seems to me clear that non-maleficence is apprehended as a duty distinct from that of beneficence, and as a duty of a more stringent character. It will be noticed that this alone among the types of duty has been stated in a negative way.[8]

Ross does not argue that the duty of nonmaleficence is absolute or exceptionless. He does, however, suggest that the duty not to harm might be considered to be "more stringent" than beneficence because it requires forbearance rather than positive action.

The Stringency of Moral Obligations

The language about stringency can be confusing. Stringency refers to the degree to which a principle should be considered morally obligatory rather than optional. By saying that a moral principle is "stringent," one is saying that it is morally obligatory to a high degree. Hearing this language for the first time, listeners sometimes confuse stringency with difficulty. However, as is explained above, it is more difficult to act consistently with beneficence than with nonmaleficence, because the good one might conceivably do is never exhausted. Nonmaleficence, in contrast, is considered to be the more stringent of the two moral principles because its requirement is actually more finite or "do-able." It is phrased negatively—requiring merely forbearance rather than positive action. The logic about stringency is similar to that about perfect duty; the chief difference is that—in contrast to the idea of perfect duty—we recognize that even the most stringent prima facie principle still allows for exception.

Developing Moral Principles

Though they may vary in stringency, all prima facie moral principles, according to Ross, describe right-making or wrong-making qualities of human action. Actual duty is found not in the principles themselves but in the actual situation. Situations determine which moral principles are relevant for understanding one's actual duty. Nevertheless, these principles are not purely subjective thoughts in the mind of the moral agent. They describe the right-making or wrong-making characteristics of human actions. Ross makes no claim that those particular principles he happens to mention constitute an exhaustive list, or even that they are the most sufficient way of describing moral obligation. Moreover, Ross does not attempt to develop a method or system for weighing and comparing those moral principles he does affirm. He leaves much to the determination of the moral agent in the particular situation.

Where does Ross find these prima facie moral principles? Even though these principles have a history of philosophical debate, Ross claims to find them more intuitively. He appeals to common sensitivity rather than to philosophical heritage:

> The main moral convictions of the plain man [*sic*] seem to me to be, not opinions which it is for philosophy to prove or disprove, but knowledge from the start...[9]

He asks people to reflect on their own moral convictions to apprehend the moral qualities that he calls prima facie principles. In a sense, Ross encourages us to begin in the middle—with the moral sensibilities we already intuit or the moral convictions we already hold. From this perspective, it makes little difference how the principles might be philosophically or theologically derived or defended. They are important for moral deliberation in that they are already a part of our moral consciousness. We cannot assume a uniformity to this consciousness, but we can assume a sufficient commonality that enables us to converse together.

Ross's understanding of prima facie moral principles has been influential for Christian ethics, as well as for philosophical ethics. It has been influential in particular for pastoral ethics as well as for health care ethics. Some of Ross's interpreters stay fairly close to his suggested list of moral principles. Others respond to Ross's invitation to reflect upon their own convictions and have articulated alternative lists. Some of these are more theologically informed than others.

J. Philip Wogaman and Moral Presumption

J. Philip Wogaman, a Christian theologian, has drawn on Ross's philosophy in developing his own ethical method. Wogaman uses the easier English phrase, "moral presumption," rather than the relatively obtuse Latin, "*prima facie.*" Their meanings are roughly the same, however, and Wogaman's description of moral presumption can be helpful in understanding Ross's more difficult discourse. According to Wogaman, not only moral reasoning but most types of thinking occur on the basis of "initial presumptions" that we hold.[10] With regard to the moral life, moral presumptions are our basic guides. To be adequate as moral guides, however, these presumptions must be compared with each other and scrutinized for their applicability in particular circumstances. Our moral presumptions must be held open to revision and to exception, lest we become guided uncritically and even immorally by presumptive prejudice rather than insight.

Wogaman examines the Christian tradition in particular, but with an intent to bridge conceptually to the ethics of the broader civilization. He specifies four "positive moral presumptions" and two "negative moral presumptions": The positive moral presumptions are the following:

1. the goodness of created existence
2. the value of individual life
3. the unity of the human family in God
4. the equality of persons in God

Here are the negative moral presumptions:

1. human finitude
2. human sinfulness

These six presumptions reflect theological affirmation as much as they do moral content.[11]

Wogaman does not provide a detailed chart for navigating with this list of presumptions. Rather he suggests that we recognize our presumptions, test them against each other, and discover the degrees to which they might inform a course of action in a given situation or, more broadly, inform our policies across situations. Wogaman believes that this method provides an alternative to extreme situationalism, on the one hand, and a reliance on absolutes, which he calls an "ethics of perfection," on the other hand. Wogaman's method utilizing moral presumption is very similar to Ross's, but Wogaman has developed a theological dimension that is in keeping with our moral character as Christians. He has tried to do this, however, in such a way that the Christian moral life is seen as integrated with the larger moral world in society.

Healthcare Ethics

Other ethicists have stayed closer to Ross's formulation, and even to Ross's specific list of prima facie obligations. This is noticeable especially in the area of healthcare ethics. With regard to the principle of nonmaleficence in particular, writers in this field have reached general agreement that the basic duty not to harm does take general precedence over other obligations that might be understood as beneficence. They disagree, however, regarding the relationship between nonmaleficence and beneficence and whether or not they should be so strictly distinguished.

Dyck and Frankena: Preventing or Removing Harm

Arthur J. Dyck is a Christian ethicist who follows Ross's method closely.[12] He discusses such topics as euthanasia with reference to Ross's own list of prima facie principles: beneficence, gratitude, justice, nonmaleficence, promise-keeping, reparation, and truth-telling. Dyck interprets nonmaleficence, though, as a subset of beneficence rather than as a distinct principle itself. In linking nonmaleficence and beneficence in this way, Dyck follows the lead of philosopher William K. Frankena. Nevertheless, Dyck and Frankena both consider nonmaleficence to be the most stringent category of beneficence.

Frankena posits four categories of beneficence, with the duty not to harm being the most stringent of the four:

1. One ought not to inflict evil or harm (what is bad).
2. One ought to prevent evil or harm.
3. One ought to remove evil [or harm].
4. One ought to do or promote good.[13]

Frankena considers all of these to be prima facie duties, but they are listed in order of stringency. The duty not to cause harm has priority over preventing harm, which has priority over removing harm, which has priority over doing good.

The added middle dimensions of preventing and removing harm are helpful categories for conceptualizing some of the complexity of pastoral responsibility. The two extreme positions (do no harm and do good) have already been discussed above, including the idea that the duty not to harm others should take a kind of precedence over the general obligation to do good. A pastor is responsible first of all for his or her own actions and the direct results that follow from these actions. It makes sense that a first duty would be not to inflict harm on others oneself. Pastors, though, are frequently involved in questions pertaining to the actions of other people.

Pastors are consulted when individuals are making their own decisions and are seeking practical advice, emotional support, or moral counsel in their relations with others. Pastors also frequently interact with groups of people—e.g., exhorting an entire congregation during a service of worship, or facilitating decision-making in an administrative meeting. We help people to contend with suffering we did not cause. We help strengthen people in their own moral agency apart from our own actions. Between the poles of not hurting and promoting the good lies much pastoral territory—interacting with others to minimize harm or to help relieve a particular distress. John Snow, for instance, has suggested that this is a major aspect of the vocation of ministry—for the minister together with the members of a congregation to help one another make sense out of suffering in light of God's grace.[14] It would seem to be realistic to recognize a significant middle ground of "preventing and removing harm" that lies between the pole of not causing harm and the pole of doing good.

The lexical ordering of Frankena's four dimensions of beneficence/nonmaleficence also seems suggestive. The four dimensions seem to correlate with an increasing capacity to act. It is assumed that nonmaleficence is within a person's power because it requires simply forbearance. Doing good also lies within one's power, but much more proximately, in that some good yet to be realized always lies beyond one's immediate capability. In the middle territory, a duty to prevent harm assumes one has the power to actually prevent or minimize the risk of such harm caused by another or by chance. To remove harm assumes similarly that the removal of harm is in one's power. It also assumes that a source other than oneself has caused the harm. In other words, a middle ground of power, of agency, of moral responsibility exists that corresponds with the different degrees of stringency involved in the continuum between nonmaleficence and beneficence.

However, perhaps this linear ordering of stringency also entails some assumptions that could be stated more explicitly. In particular, two sets of concerns seem to be confounded in this linear order and could be more clearly differentiated. On the one hand are concerns about the nature of the harm (or conversely, benefit) itself—its relative severity or triviality. On the other hand are concerns about respective degrees of power and responsibility both for the parishioner as moral agent and for the pastor as moral counselor. The stringency of one's duty to prevent or remove harm would seem to be contingent on both these factors: the relative severity of the harm in question and the degree to which one has the power to act or an ability to make a difference.

Beauchamp and Childress: Rescuing from Harm

Tom L. Beauchamp and James F. Childress have suggested an alternative way of determining one's duty to remove harm. Beauchamp and Childress build on the insights of both Ross and Frankena. They affirm Frankena's four levels of beneficent/nonmaleficent action, but along with Ross they want to keep nonmaleficence as a distinct category in that it requires simply the duty not to act—to not harm. The other three levels, they say, require more positive action and more deliberation: to act to prevent harm, to act to remove harm, or to actively promote good. However, they insist that many acts of beneficence are morally obligatory and that some incidents of nonmaleficence are relatively trivial. They resist considering one to be necessarily more stringent than the other. They prefer instead to analyze situations of beneficence more carefully to determine the degree to which one is obliged in a particular instance to act beneficently.[15]

Using the parable of the good Samaritan as an example, they distinguish between "obligatory" and "ideal" beneficence. The good Samaritan's kindness toward the victim is purely an act of beneficence, in that the Samaritan was not responsible in any way for the victim's unfortunate condition in the first place. They even find in the good Samaritan's compassion for the victim an example of "ideal benefi-cence" rather than strictly "obligatory beneficence." Few individuals could be required to be "good Samaritans" in rendering such assis-tance, they suggest. Nevertheless, they argue that when the need is great and the ability to help is significant (such as a physician's professional skill), then one might be required to at least be a "*minimally decent* Samaritan" in rendering the necessary assistance.[16]

In particular, Beauchamp and Childress advocate five conditions that, when all five are met, greatly increase one's obligation to act beneficently.

- First, the risk of harm itself is great, such as the threat of death.
- Second, one's action is needed to prevent this harm.
- Third, one's action has a high probability of actually preventing the harm.
- Fourth, the risks, costs, or burdens to oneself would not be too great.
- Fifth, these risks, costs, or burdens are outweighed by the expected benefits to be gained.

If these five conditions are met, argue Beauchamp and Childress, one has a strong obligation to help—to act beneficently by preventing or removing harm. They refer to this as an obligation to rescue.[17]

Beauchamp and Childress's formulation has potential for informing the ethics of pastoral practice. Pastors often have a tendency to rescue. We refer to it in rather exaggerated fashion as a messianic tendency. Other Christians within our congregation have this same tendency. It can be especially difficult for clergy when members of the congregation project their own messianic tendencies onto the pastor so that the pastor's messianic tendency is reinforced by the congregation's expectations. Beauchamp and Childress's formulation provides a way of analyzing a situation to determine if "rescuing" is really called for, or if it is driven by other expectations or needs of the pastor or the congregation.

When are we obliged to help, and, conversely, when are we serving our own needs by helping? To answer this difficult question, a pastor must explore his or her own inclinations to become aware of his or her need to be needed. But in addition to this self-awareness, the pastor also should explore the situation and examine the objective possibilities within that situation for helpful action. Beauchamp and Childress's formulation provides a framework for this analysis of the situation itself—both in terms of the pastor's power to act and in terms of the risks or benefits to the pastor and to the parishioner alike.

I would argue, within the context of pastoral practice, when a contemplated situation meets Beauchamp and Childress's five criteria for "rescuing," it is morally obligatory to act to prevent or remove the harm in question. Moreover, I would consider such an act to be an example of nonmaleficence rather than beneficence. I say this for two reasons. First, in such a situation, a real and present danger or harm has been identified. It is about harm. Second, in such a pastoral situation, the pastor is constrained to respond in some manner by virtue of the pastoral office. Not to respond is not an option—though the course of action might be to refer or even to ignore. Not only has the distinction between beneficence and nonmaleficence been blurred, but so has the distinction between acting and not acting. Both action and inaction are responses within the pastoral portfolio. The distinction between action and inaction is less important than the question of how to respond safely to minimize harm.

If all five criteria are not met, however, the pastor still has the option to respond beneficently. Beneficence is not precluded if the five criteria are not met. In this sense, this checklist for "rescuing" is very different from, say, the just war theory, which also uses a checklist methodology. Just war theory includes an immensely strong moral presumption against war, so that war can be justified if and only if each one of the just war criteria are met. Rescuing has no such moral presumption against beneficence. Beneficence is always morally desirable; the question is how best to be beneficent and to whom? When the five criteria are met, it simply heightens pastoral responsibility to prevent or remove harm.

In Beauchamp and Childress's example using the good Samaritan, they argue that a physician's responsibility to remove harm increases by virtue of the physician's expertise or ability to act helpfully. Ministers can err like physicians in failing to provide remedial care when it is within their power to do so. However, one can err in the other direction as well. It is possible to err by attending to a problem beyond one's level of competence so that one causes or exacerbates harm rather than alleviates it. A minister must know not only when but how to act. The minister must also know how *not* to act at the same time. In situations of danger, a minister's abilities both to discern the danger and to refer become as critical as the minister's own ability to offer care.

■ CASE FOR DISCUSSION: Samson to the Rescue

Samson's ministry in an impoverished urban area was greatly appreciated by many of his parishioners. Many of the members of his church relied on government assistance for their income. They frequently found, however, that their income was insufficient for all of their needs—even basic needs such as food, clothing, and shelter. This was especially so if they were taking care of a number of children. Martha, one of Samson's parishioners, struggled with poverty. She was a woman head-of-household and the mother of three children ranging in ages from four to twelve.

Martha was very nervous—to the point of finding it difficult to accomplish basic chores such as cleaning the apartment. The middle child had been misbehaving significantly enough in school to come to the attention of the Child Protective Services as well as the school officials. The Child Protective Services determined that the child was not receiving adequate care at home and had recently acted to place this child in foster care. He nevertheless was able to see his mother occasionally. The placing of this child in a foster home, however, only increased Martha's anxiety.

The situation seemed to be reaching a critical point for her. The social worker was coming to visit that week, and the house was a mess. Martha was frightened that Child Protective Services would take away her other children. She had talked to Pastor Samson and had poured out to him all of her worry and concern.

Samson was concerned for Martha as well. He decided to help as best he could. He went over to Martha's home with cleaning supplies, and he cleaned the apartment for her. In this way, he helped her to prepare for the social worker's visit so that she could make a more favorable impression.

■ ■ QUESTIONS

Using Beauchamp and Childress's five criteria for intervention, analyze this case.

1. What is the risk of harm in this case?
   a. Who is at risk of harm?
   b. What is the source of this potential harm?
   c. Would you consider the potential for harm to be significant?
2. Is the minister's action needed to prevent this harm?
3. Is the minister's action likely to be successful in preventing the harm?
4. What are the risks, costs, or burdens to the minister?
5. What are the expected benefits to the parishioner(s)? Do these expected benefits outweigh the risks mentioned in the previous question?
6. Given the way you have answered questions 1–5 above, how then would you conclude? How strong is the moral requirement on Samson to help out in this instance?
7. Are there other options for pastoral action that Samson should consider as well? Would any of these be more appropriate, in your estimation, given your analysis above?

To Refer Out of Harm's Way

A friend of mine once said to me, "The trouble with the clergy is that they have only one tool; it is a hammer, so they like to make everything else a nail." He had not been impressed with the ability of clergy to discern diverse needs and to respond appropriately. Actually, my friend had been suffering from clinical depression. In his experience, even when the clergy do become aware that a person is depressed, they tend to want to address that need with prayer and verbal expressions of encouragement or sympathy. My friend had found this to be ineffective. His depression deepened. Fortunately, when he became afraid of his own suicidal tendencies, he sought psychiatric help. He was given medication and therapy. The medication evened his mood considerably, and he credits it with saving his life. No pastor had made this referral.

There are times when pastors face great urgency to make a referral. These are times when a crisis is clearly beyond the competence of the minister alone. When a person's safety is at stake, appropriate referral should be made to ensure a greater degree of security for that person. This is a matter of preventing harm. Two types of incidents in particular elicit this more urgent referral. The first are those types of incidents, such as the incident with my friend described above, in which a person may be suicidal. The second type of critical incident occurs when one person aggresses dangerously against another, especially in cases of domestic violence. Both of these types of critical situations will be discussed briefly below. In both situations, a pastor must act decisively to prevent the risk of harm or to prevent further harm.

Suicide

The pastor needs to attend to the signs and symptoms that indicate a risk of suicide and have at hand those places to which a person can be referred. In many communities, these might include a suicide prevention hotline, an emergency room in a hospital, or a psychologist or psychiatrist of the pastor's acquaintance. The police can also be called in an actual emergency. In making a referral, the pastor should respect the fact that many mood disorders characterized by suicidal ideation are effectively treated by a variety of different medications. When a pastor detects an indication that a person is at risk of committing suicide, the pastor should refer that person in such a way that he or she gains access to medical attention.

In his books on pastoral care in critical situations, David K. Switzer presents nine factors for evaluating the "lethality potential" when suicide is a possibility:

1. Age and sex. Older people and males kill themselves with a higher frequency than younger people and females, and whites more than blacks.

2. The suicidal plan. The more specific and detailed the plan, the more lethal the means, and the more available the means, the greater the danger. This criterion carries the most weight in the assessment of lethality. If the person hasn't given such details in the conversation, never fail to ask.

3. Contemporary external threatening events and situations: losses, failures, etc. How many, how severe, and how recent?

4. Symptoms. Persons who hear voices telling them to kill themselves, alcoholics and other chemically dependent persons, and especially those who are clinically depressed are more likely to kill themselves. Hopelessness is a major characteristic of depression, and that is what leads to suicide.

5. Resources. Available family members and friends, group membership, activities, a knowledge of agencies in the city, even money, versus the absence of these.

6. Lifestyle. Stability versus instability in work, marriage and other significant relationships, place of residence, etc. Prior suicide attempts are usually seen as indicating greater present lethality.

7. Degree of communication. Is the person still talking with and listening to others? A failure to communicate signals danger, as an important inner core of the person is increasingly isolated from others.

8. Reactions of significant others. Are they understanding and willing to be helpful? Do they withdraw? Do they criticize, condemn, or make light of the person?

9. Medical status. Is the person in reasonably good health; or is the person chronically, painfully, perhaps terminally ill, or *believes* himself or herself to be terminally ill?[18]

Of these nine criteria, Switzer suggests that primary importance should be given to the second criterion—the question of whether or not a person has a plan in mind for committing suicide. Of next importance, according to Switzer, are criteria 3 and 4, concerning stress and symptoms, respectively. Moreover, one should not minimize evidence of risk, but should make this evaluation of lethality erring on the side of caution. One's response then should err on the side of safety, referring the person as appropriate to minimize the possibility of self-inflicted harm.[19]

Obviously, to be able to respond safely in situations in which suicide is a possibility, a pastor should equip himself or herself with additional resources and training. The suggestions being made in this book are not intended to provide adequate tools for responding pastorally in such a situation. Rather, the intent in these pages is to argue that the duty of nonmaleficence requires ministers to equip themselves so that they can competently reduce the risk of suicide and self-inflicted harm among the people they are called to serve.

Domestic Violence

The second type of incident requiring urgent referral is the situation in which a person is being battered or abused and feels unsafe in her home.[20] She has to be referred properly, or her life could be further endangered by a violent response from her abuser. Again, this is a matter of preventing or stopping harm. Many communities now have established women's refuges and battered women's hotlines that allow for quick referral of women who are endangered at home. These refuges and hotlines are staffed by people trained to deal with exactly this problem. They are equipped to help a woman establish safety for herself and her children. The pastor should be able to provide a woman being battered with the phone number of the battered women's hotline and then let her make the phone call. With regard to the abuse of children, however, many states have laws about mandatory reporting to the authorities when one even suspects that child abuse is occurring. Ministers should have at hand the phone numbers and contact information for those agencies that can provide proper care in critical, abusive, or life-threatening situations.

There are two reasons why pastors should be prepared to make referrals for these two types of critical situations—suicide and domestic violence—in particular. The first reason is that the danger itself is real, and this danger needs to be recognized and responded to realistically. If a pastor is prepared from the outset to make a proper referral in these life-threatening situations, he or she will be less tempted to minimize the danger in his or her own mind and will be better equipped to respond appropriately. The second reason is that many people in the church and the community are facing these kinds of problems. It is almost inevitable that a pastor will have people approach him or her hoping to receive help for these problems—at least this would be true for pastors who convey sensitivity in these matters. On the other hand, pastors who do not notice or discuss the problem of violence in the home may send strong signals that discourage people from broaching the subject with them. I, myself, have never mentioned the problem of domestic abuse from the pulpit without someone approaching me afterward to confide in me about an abusive situation.

These critical situations highlight an enigma about pastoral professionalism. Sadly, life-threatening situations are unavoidable and will eventually come to the attention of any minister. To respond adequately to these situations, ministers will have to be honest with themselves about the limits of their expertise and ability. One should not try to deal with either domestic violence or potential suicide without referring the person to those professionals and networks that can provide the most adequate kinds of care and support. To refer is not just to defer.

To refer in these instances is to act both professionally and responsibly. Even to notice these problems so that referral can be made often requires training as well as sensitivity. It requires training and sensitivity to begin to discern suicidal potential when a person may initially complain only about feeling depressed or tired. It requires training and sensitivity to discover that a parishioner is being beaten when she indicates initially only that she and her husband are "not getting along so well these days." One cannot avoid encountering these problems by concentrating in areas other than pastoral counseling or by disavowing professionalism in general. The problems themselves paradoxically both demand attention and require discernment. It takes professional skill to be able to hear these cries for help and to refer responsibly for the sake of safety.

Ministering Safely in Violent Situations

This chapter has been examining the moral principles of nonmaleficence ("to do no harm") and beneficence ("to do good"). Nonmaleficence, which is often considered to be a first principle of healthcare ethics, has been examined concerning its relevance for pastoral ministry. In comparing and contrasting the two principles, we have attended to the argument that a greater degree of stringency should be attached to nonmaleficence because its requirement to refrain from causing harm seems to be more attainable and more immediate than beneficence. We have noticed, however, that pastoral ministry often occurs in between the two duties of "not causing harm" and "promoting the good." The pastor's duty to prevent or remove harm, I have suggested, increases with the risk of harm itself and with the pastor's capacity to act. Within the pastor's capacities should be included an ability to make a responsible referral.

Facilitating and Hindering Ministry

Ironically, the minister's role can both facilitate and hinder such gentle ministry. Because the minister is trusted as a helper, individuals–both members and nonmembers of the congregation–may approach the minister for sanctuary or for assistance when feeling threatened.

The minister, by virtue of the ministerial role, tends to be both accessible and trusted. Unfortunately, many of the duties of the minister can block pastoral perception of people's pain. First, the tasks of studying, preparing sermons, and preaching entail a considerable degree of private activity. A minister can be preoccupied with sermon preparation and not be fully present and perceptive when encountering a parishioner in pain.

Second, sermon delivery (a large part of the "job") tends to be one-directional communication. Without immediate feedback, a preacher can be unaware of the message actually conveyed to particular persons from the pulpit. An obvious example is provided in sermons touching on topics such as marital fidelity or patience. Although a preacher may not intend to convey the message that wives should patiently bear with violence from their husbands, this is exactly the way a sermon on fidelity or patience might be heard unless explicitly corrected by a perceptive preacher. I urge students for the ministry to always assume that members of their congregations have suffered or are suffering from abuse. The preacher should keep these people especially in mind in sermon preparation and delivery, so that the proclamation of God's grace on Sunday morning actually does allow God's grace to minister to their pain and to their need for empowerment.

Third, even when ministers are in counseling situations, they are not necessarily attentive to the victim's pain or to the potential for victimization in a situation. Marriage, while given to us as a blessing and even celebrated in some churches as a sacrament, tragically has the potential for victimization. Premarital counseling sessions should acknowledge this as at least a potential problem, and the sessions should clarify the nature and extent of a marriage covenant. Marriage simply *does not* include a vow to be abused. Battering violates the words of the marriage vows, the nature of the marriage covenant, and the person of the marriage partner.

Couples do expect the minister to help them interpret the nature of their wedding vows and the marriage relationship. A minister is acting within the ministerial role to caution bride and groom: "If he hits you, leave him." Unfortunately, ministers often miss this opportunity to offer practical advice and moral counsel either because (1) they are reticent to intrude on the romantic aura that sometimes surrounds premarital counseling sessions, or (2) they are primarily concerned with preventing divorce. Divorce is also a potential problem that should be addressed in premarital counseling, but not to the exclusion of a recognition of those kinds of real harm for which divorce itself would be a regretful remedy in the last resort.

In counseling sessions with people who are in established partnerships, and especially in counseling people about marital problems, one should not assume that violence is not already occurring until one has verified this with the counselee. If one begins with a moral presumption against harm, one needs to know whether or not violence is occurring early in the counseling relationship to determine how to proceed. Simply ask. Otherwise, a pastor may inadvertently encourage a parishioner to remain victimized in a situation that is dangerous for her or for her children.

Moreover, battering often occurs in a cycle of violence. The cycle can include a phase of remorse when the batterer seeks forgiveness from his victim and promises not to repeat the violence. Tragically, as time passes (sometimes a very short time) and stress builds up, the cycle comes full circle again; and the battering recurs. Minsters that counsel batterers during the phase of remorse should be wary in hearing a batterer's confession. The minister should not offer easy pardon to the batterer but should refer him to a program or a professional to encourage true repentance in breaking the cycle of violence. The minister, especially, should not encourage the victim to forgive her batterer during this phase.[21] Here is where the minister's intuitive role of mediating forgiveness and reconciliation can interfere with the role of pursuing peace and safety. The presumption against harm should guide the minister in discerning the proper role in such a situation.

Resources for Ministering in Domestic Violence

Some of the most helpful resources for guiding ministers and churches in situations of domestic violence are provided by Marie M. Fortune and her colleagues at The Center for the Prevention of Sexual and Domestic Violence. Fortune provides a list of nine warnings to clergy beginning with the negative caution "Do not":

✔ *Do not* use confidentiality as an excuse not to act to protect a child from further abuse.

✔ *Do not* interview a victim and an abuser as a couple. *Do not* attempt to counsel them together in order to stop the abuser's violence.

✔ *Do not* minimize the incidents that a victim shares with you. Assume that you are only being shown the tip of the iceberg.

✔ *Do not* refer couples who you suspect are dealing with abuse to marriage enrichment programs, mediation sessions, communications workshops, or the like.

✔ *Do not* try to deal with the problem alone. You probably don't have the time, energy, or expertise that you need. *Refer. Refer. Refer.*

✔ *Do not* become emotionally or sexually intimate with a victim…

✔ *Do not* be taken in by a batterer's claim to a religious conversion experience.

✔ *Do not* help the batterer avoid the legal consequences of the violent behavior. *Do not* provide a character witness or act as an advocate for this purpose.

✔ *Do not* forgive an abuser quickly and easily. Specifically, *do not* offer absolution without evidence of true repentance.[22]

Each caution indicates an area in which a minister's imprudent action could exacerbate harm in an abusive situation. These cautions urge the minister to first avoid exacerbating harm.

What should a minister do? Fortune advocates three basic goals: "(1) protect the victim from further violence; (2) stop the abuser's violence; (3) restore the relationship *if possible.*"[23] Fortune ranks these in importance in the order presented. It is instructing to note that the positive obligation of restoring relationship is presented as a priority only after attending to the other two goals that attempt to minimize harm: ensuring the victim's safety, and preventing the abuser's further violence. This order is in keeping with the emphasis of this chapter that ministers should "do no harm" as a first presumption before attempting other beneficial care. It is also consistent with the emphasis in this chapter on the need to refer properly in situations of danger.

The Ministerial Approach in Domestic Violence

However, when placing the first priority on minimizing harm in situations of domestic abuse, there may be more required of the pastor than mere forbearance. The particular style of pastoral counseling that is nondirective has been especially criticized for its use by ministers with parishioners in situations of domestic abuse. The nondirective listening approach was developed by Carl Rogers[24] and popularized for Christian ministers by such writers as Seward Hiltner.[25] In ministering to women suffering from domestic abuse, though, a much more directive—even interventionist approach—is sometimes called for, in which the woman is encouraged to seek her own safety. In counseling men who abuse, a more directive approach is needed to help hold them accountable for their actions and to enable true repentance. One simply cannot be value-free or nondirective when one's parishioners are suffering abuse in their own homes.

Carol J. Adams is one who has made this criticism and who has provided a valuable manual to help pastors respond in situations of woman battering. Adams has made the point that pastors tend to be too passive when counseling people in situations of domestic violence. She notices that it is a matter of personal comfort as well as the model of ministry or counseling that predispose many ministers to be inappropriately nondirective in responding to situations of domestic violence. She cites David K. Switzer with approval that ministers need to be: "questioning, searching, focusing, keeping the person on the present situation, interpreting, giving information, suggesting, mobilizing resources, and...calling for decision making."[26] She is especially critical of the use of "couple counseling" in situations when one partner in a relationship needs to find protection from the other. She advocates a "proactive" model of pastoral care.[27]

As pastors concerned about "harm," we must attend to two possible sources of harm: ourselves and others. Nonmaleficence proper would require that we ourselves refrain from harming. However, pastors are challenged frequently to know when and how to respond to others in order to prevent or remove harm that is being threatened by someone else. If harm *is* being threatened by someone else, a minister must act within the parameters of the minister's own power or be implicated in that harm. In doing so, though, the minister should be protective of his or her own safety as well as the safety of others. At any rate, the distinction between action and refraining from action becomes less important than responding gently and safely.

Neglect and Omission

Lebacqz and Driskill have also noticed that harmfulness is not avoided by forbearance in other types of pastoral situations besides those involving domestic violence. In exploring the question of "spiritual abuse," Lebacqz and Driskill examine various criteria for defining spiritual abuse, such as excessive judgmentalism or shame. They notice, though, that judging people and even shaming them, while potentially abusive, is sometimes legitimately done as part of the shepherding function of ministry. In and of themselves these activities do not determine abuse.[28] Moreover, they hesitate to encourage forbearance as a guard against harmful ministry. In fact, they caution against the kind of forbearance that results in harmful neglect. They particularly warn against neglecting social harm caused by political, racial, or gender injustice:

> True Spiritual care will refuse to ignore the Holocaust or our own painful history of slavery, broken treaties, and oppression of nonwhite peoples. True spiritual care will be social and political as well as personal.[29]

Clergy can also be neglectful, they remind us, in failing to provide for the spiritual growth and well-being of individuals and congregations.[30]

Lebacqz and Driskill here are putting pastoral responsibility for the congregation within the broader context of encouraging the church's responsibility within the world. The church has passively allowed much harm in society rather than actively confronting it with the gospel.

Matthew Fox, similarly, blames the ecological crisis on a sin of omission:

> The sinful consciousness that lies behind ecological sin is that of a dualistic mentality that treats other creatures in a subject/object fashion of manipulation and control. This dualism accounts for the sin of putting the egological ahead of the ecological. It is, when one thinks of it, a rather substantial sin of omission to omit the cosmos itself.[31]

Sin of omission, according to Fox, threatens the welfare of all future generations by threatening the earth that they will inherit.[32] It is not enough to do nothing.

Summary and Conclusion

This chapter has examined pastoral situations of violence as a paradigm for understanding nonmaleficence in ministry. It is not enough to talk about our forbearance or refraining from harm. This, indeed, is fundamental as a kind of moral minimum, and its importance should not be minimized. Along with healthcare ethics, pastoral ministry should seek first to do no harm. Gentle ministry, however, would seem to require a greater degree of discernment in deciding how to respond than can be satisfied simply by forbearance. In situations characterized by violence, nonmaleficence would seem to require referral to those better equipped to promote safety and accountability. At the same time, though, excessive passivity in pastoral counseling runs the risk of reinforcing the cycle of violence. The pastor seeking to prevent harm, it has been suggested, must at times be proactive rather than passive. A balance is pictured here between forbearance and intervention.

The question is not so much a matter of acting or not acting, of harming or promoting good. It is more a matter of gauging the degree of harm at stake and the degree of pastoral ability to help. Beauchamp and Childress's checklist method for "rescuing" is one promising way of comparing these two factors of degree. In addition to assessing the risk of harm, Beauchamp and Childress's method raises questions concerning the necessity and the likely effectiveness of any contemplated intervention.

We can distort our sense of power in either direction. We can minimize it so that we run the risk of not responding when it would be irresponsible not to respond, e.g., failing to make a referral in a dangerous situation. At the same time, we can overestimate our responsibility. In situations of domestic abuse, the victim must recover her own sense of responsibility for her own safety. Survivors have recovered this sense of their own agency despite the intimidation that they have experienced. The case above about Samson and Martha also illustrates a situation in which a minister may have assumed too much responsibility in a situation, so that (a) Martha herself is not encouraged to take responsibility for the safety of her children, and (b) the social worker is not able to realistically assess the degree of safety or danger that the children might be exposed to.

To act safely, then, requires both an assessment of the risk of harm and an assessment of the minister's responsibility and power to act in a situation. This chapter has highlighted primarily the first question concerning the risk of harm. Subsequent chapters will further address the other question concerning the minister's responsibility with regard to the subjects of vocation and authority. A person's call to ministry will be interpreted as a part of the whole church's call to authority and service. Moreover, the church's call includes a witness for justice on earth that enables all creatures to give glory to God. The next chapter returns to the question of pastoral authority and responsibility within the context of community.

3

Permission for Mission

Informed Consent in Pastoral Ministry[1]

*"Wherever you are welcomed, stay in the same house until you leave
that town; wherever people don't welcome you, leave that town and
shake the dust off your feet as a warning to them." The disciples left
and traveled through all the villages, preaching the Good News and
healing people everywhere.*

LUKE 9:4–6, TEV

When Jesus sent the disciples on a mission to preach the gospel
and to heal, he advised them to stay where they were welcomed but
to "shake the dust" from their feet if they were not welcomed. As
pastors offering ministry, it is important for us to be welcomed by
others if our message is to be heard or if our ministry is to be received.
It is respectful to respond to such welcome with pastoral care.
Conversely, a lack of welcome can be answered by respectful distance.

Consider this brief verbatim that is like many encounters all
ministers have:

> Rev. Rhodes saw his parishioner's father sitting on a sofa in
> front of the T.V. in the common lounge at the nursing home.
> He approached him.
> "Hello, Mr. Moody, I'm your daughter's minister. I've
> come to see you. Can I sit here while we chat a little?"
> "No. Bugger off!"
> "Okay, Mr. Moody. It was good to see you. I'll be going
> now."

Invitation and Permission

Fortunately, Mr. Moody was able to express his desires clearly, and Rev. Rhodes was able to respond lovingly by leaving. To have stayed would have been obviously intrusive and counter to the expressed wishes of Mr. Moody. A more complicated situation would have occurred if Mr. Moody were unable to express his wishes or if Rev. Rhodes were not able to understand Mr. Moody's attempt to communicate—if, for example, Mr. Moody's speech and motor skills had been affected by a stroke. In such circumstances, Rev. Rhodes would have had to exercise greater sensitivity and attend to more subtle or ambiguous forms of communication to discern Mr. Moody's desire for privacy.

Of course, Mr. Moody's desires are not the only determining factor in a scenario such as this. His desires and the expression of his desires, nevertheless, provide a basic beginning point for contemplating ministry to him. A minister has a strong prima facie obligation to respect his request. To impose care against his wishes would require justification. Ministry, normally, needs to be invited or welcomed. In addition to discerning Mr. Moody's desires, though, Rev. Rhodes would also want to be prayerfully attempting to discern God's grace in this instance—God's call to both Mr. Moody and to Rev. Rhodes. Moreover, others besides Mr. Moody may be in need of God's grace and Rev. Rhodes ministry at this time.

While a minister has a prima facie obligation to minister within the parameters of permission, this moral presumption is strongest when stated negatively—that is, that one should not impose care when it is contrary to a person's permission. It is a weaker presumption when it is stated positively—that is, that one should give care whenever others request it. Of course, a minister should always attend to requests for help, but not all such requests are equally obligatory on the pastor. Such competing requests for help typify pastoral visits in nursing homes. Most frequently when they make these visits, ministers find it difficult to disengage from the many, often lonely, appeals for their attention.

While we are called to "love our neighbor," there is a selectivity—even an "opportunity cost"—to the practice of ministry and to all acts of kindness. To offer one type of ministry to this one individual is simultaneously not to be offering ministry in many ways to many others. To a significant degree, one chooses where, when, how, and to whom to give care. So, not only as a matter of respect for Mr. Moody, but also as a matter of greater effectiveness in ministry, one ought to concentrate one's pastoral energies where they might seem to bring the greatest benefit. Mr. Moody's degree of receptivity in this instance is a factor in gauging the potential efficiency of Rev. Rhode's ministry in general, as well as his effectiveness toward Mr. Moody in particular.[2] Ministry and mission occur within community. Others give a pastor permission to extend care and to practice ministry. Respecting the nature of this permission in pastoral ministry is the subject of this chapter. The permission may be given in denominational policy, congregational expectations, or individual requests for pastoral care. At the individual level, permission for pastoral care can be understood as analogous to the notion of "informed consent" in healthcare ethics. Some of these areas of permission-granting may be explicitly clarified in the form of a contract. Some may be more implicitly articulated. Because many expectations for pastoral care are actually implicitly stated, minsters need to develop sensitivity to hear both requests for help and requests for privacy.

Informed Consent: Definitions

Different aspects of Western society have their own mechanisms or traditions to assist in clarifying mutual expectations and obligations. Business transactions typically take the form of a contract between parties predicated (one would hope) on truthful description of one's product and on honest representation of one's position. In medical care, a tradition has developed of obtaining "informed consent" whenever possible from patients before providing medical treatment. The obtaining of informed consent is also standard practice for scientific research involving human subjects. The principle of informed consent, in its most basic meaning, is that those who are placed at risk of harm should themselves be able to freely choose to accept or to reject the procedure that carries that risk.

The increased emphasis on informed consent in the last half of the twentieth century has developed largely in response to knowledge about atrocities committed in the name of medical science in Nazi Germany. In their book entitled *Ethics and Spiritual Care,* Karen Lebacqz and Joseph Driskill state that "...post-Holocaust Christian and Jewish spiritualities must attend to the significance of this event as an expression of extreme evil in the world."[3] Much of Nazi abuse in medical research became known at the conclusion of the war in the context of the Nuremberg trials. Prisoners in concentration camps had been deliberately infected with disease without their consent to test the effectiveness of drugs. Poisons had been tested on prisoners to determine their toxicity, and some prisoners had been intentionally killed to perform autopsies. Fifteen German physicians were convicted at Nuremberg in 1947 for such "war crimes and crimes against humanity."[4]

A result of the Nuremberg trials was the establishment of the Nuremberg Code of 1949 to provide ethical guidance both for medical practice and for research involving human subjects. Two principles have been particularly important for medical ethics since this time. Nonmaleficence is one. The other is informed consent. As discussed in the previous chapter, nonmaleficence is the affirmation that one should not inflict or cause harm on another. Risk of harm, however, is present to some degree in nearly every medical procedure.

People should be able to decide for themselves whether or not the risk of harm is acceptable given the intended benefits. In other words, a person—whether receiving treatment or participating in an experiment—should understand the potential risks as well as benefits from the procedure in question and should be able to freely agree or disagree to that procedure without coercion. This principle, implied in the compound phrase "informed consent," has two parts: (1) the need to be informed about different choices, including the potential for harm and benefit entailed in these choices, and (2) the need to be free or uncoerced in consenting or not consenting, that is, in making a decision.[5]

These two conditions have direct implications for the obligations of caregivers. Caregivers are obliged: (1) to disclose relevant information for the decision in question, and (2) to allow for voluntary choice without exercising coercion. In other words, caregivers or researchers have the duty, first, to ensure that patients or subjects are given the information necessary for making a rational choice and, second, to refrain from coercing that decision.[6] A third criterion is often distinguished: the person in question should be rationally unimpaired.[7]

Informed consent in healthcare ethics is a guard against harm and is related to nonmaleficence/beneficence in three ways.

First, it is assumed that when people are adequately informed and allowed to give their own permission for the care they receive, they will choose for themselves the least harmful and most beneficial course of action.

Second, even when the potential of harm is unavoidable (as it is in many types of treatment), the idea of informed consent ensures that the risk of harm for the sake of a greater benefit is considered as acceptable by the very person put at risk.

Third, not only does informed consent protect from nonmaleficence; it also functions as a guard against unwanted beneficence. It helps people, in other words, to avoid well-meaning but unwanted "paternalistic" interference in their lives.

Pastoral Ministry

How is informed consent relevant for the multifarious ministry that is more characteristic of most pastors? Fortunately, unlike other types of health care professionals, pastors do not normally have to get written permission from each person in his or her congregation to exercise pastoral ministry to these individuals.[8] Informed consent is nonetheless relevant for our ministry in at least four levels:

1. the relationship of the minister to those who come to her or him for pastoral care
2. the relationship of the minister to parishioners who are receiving care or treatment from providers other than the minister
3. the relationship of the minister to these other professional providers of care
4. the manner in which the congregation is engaged in mission in society

These will be discussed in reverse order.

Mission in Society

First, with regard to the church's mission within society, Margaret Battin analyses some of the practices of organized religion in the U.S. in her book *Ethics in the Sanctuary*.[9] She attends both to internal practices of pastoral care that affect mainly church members, and to missional practices of outreach that extend beyond church walls. Of particular concern to Battin is the idea of informed consent. She emphasizes the ethical importance of honest communication of religious purposes in offering ministry and the need to minimize coercion or manipulation in religious practices. She applies the idea of informed consent primarily to Christian ministries of "healing," as well as to other ministries that entail significant risk of harm. Even with relatively harmless practices, though, Battin advocates honest, noncoercive, and nonmanipulative practices.

Battin recounts her own encounter with a small group of Christian college students who were on an evangelistic mission in her neighborhood. They had come to her home ostensibly playfully in a game of "treasure hunt." In this game, people individually or in teams compete to find a list of objects. Battin realized that this was not simply a game but an evangelistic come-on only after one of the contestants asked for her help in finding "a person who has been thinking about the meaning of life."[10] By this time, she had already welcomed these missionaries into her home on a pretext and had revealed to them aspects of her private lifestyle by responding to requests for personal objects. Battin acknowledges that this "game" seems relatively innocuous. Nevertheless, she argues that these missionary tactics are ethically problematic in that they are intrusive and entail an element of deception.[11] She prefers a more straightforward approach to "invitational" evangelism that actually respects and empowers people's choice, rather than deceiving and manipulating.[12]

I agree with Battin in cautioning against dishonesty in Christian evangelism. I think it counterproductive if, for the sake of making Christian witness, one is perceived to be bearing false witness. I am especially suspicious of approaches to evangelism that include as an opening gambit, "Would you help me?" This is a moral appeal preying on people's kindness. In Battin's example, it is only playful help that is requested. Other approaches ask for "help" with a research project or survey, as if research itself is the desired end. In actuality, though, the "researcher" is not studying any particular subject, but is rather an evangelist seeking a point of entry. The evangelist does not actually desire to be helped, but is instead seeking to provide help—a relationship with Christ that can bring life and greater wholeness to the individual in question. This offer of help should be honestly stated as such and not couched as a plea for assistance.

A positive example can be seen in the Scripture Union Youth Camps in New Zealand. These camps tend to be very active in nature and attractive to nonchurched as well as churched youth, offering experiences in such recreations as skiing, biking, sailing, kayaking, and horseback riding. The organizers are intentional in all publicity to inform perspective campers about the Christian nature of the camp. The Scripture Union Web page explains:

> Scripture Union is a Christian organization and on camp you will have the opportunity to hear what Christianity is all about, and decide for yourself.[13]

Similarly, the brochure for the camps invites youth "to learn more about God."[14] This honest and straightforward approach seems to facilitate rather than hinder the camps' effectiveness for Christian witness.[15]

Deception—even the skewing of information—hinders responsible decision-making. For this reason, adequate informed consent includes a sharing of relevant information as well as a lack of coercion. Battin is especially critical of the absence of informed consent in the healing ministries of some religious organizations. She notices, for instance, that information provided by Christian Scientists about healing tends to be anecdotal in nature, does not include statistical data concerning success rates, nor does it include information about alternative treatments to Christian Science healing.[16] Such information about different courses of treatment and their likely benefits, side effects, and risks, according to Battin, is normally provided by other healthcare providers prior to obtaining consent for treatment. Otherwise, people are not adequately informed in order to be empowered to choose responsibly.

Battin is critical of some church practices not only with regard to the provision of adequate information but also with regard to the other two criteria of informed consent that she identifies: lack of coercion, and the need to be rationally unimpaired. She describes the coercive practices, for instance, of an organization called Faith Assembly located near Goshen, Indiana, which discouraged people from seeking medical attention by means of "fear of exposure, punishment, or excommunication for themselves or their children."[17] She recounts the story of one woman in particular whose husband refused her medical treatment while she bled to death asking for a doctor. Battin further indicates that one hundred such deaths within the Faith Assembly have been attributed to lack of medical attention.[18]

Even when there is no overt coercion, according to Battin, churches can develop a subculture that encourages an idiosyncratic assessment of risk. As a case in point, she describes the ways in which Christian snake-handlers in certain Holiness churches assess the risk involved in these religious practices. Even when people have adequate information and are uncoerced in, say, the choice to handle venomous snakes or to ritualistically drink poison, they may yet choose to accept such risk because of the way in which their assessment of these risks has been shaped by the particular religious culture. Whether or not this is a matter of impairment of rationality, it would seem to at least be a matter of ecclesial impression upon people's rationality. Battin cites Karen Lebacqz with approval that the church is engaged in the "social construction of reality" and that the clergy in particular are thus involved in "defining reality."[19] This is a persuasive power that is not always salient in ministers' minds when they plan congregational activities and the church's mission in society.

Ministry among Professionals

Knowledge about informed consent can also be helpful to clergy when they are interacting with other care providers in society. Clergy should not shy away from the task of being a moral resource for the congregation and for the wider community, including other professionals in the church and community. Part of our vocation as clergy is to encourage virtuous character in persons and to labor for just systems and procedures in institutions. Even those clergy who do not consider themselves to be healthcare professionals have within their congregations doctors, nurses, counselors, and other professionals who do provide healthcare. Beyond the congregation, the minister encounters healthcare providers in the hospitals and institutions that she or he visits. Scientists engaged in research are also members of our congregations and communities.

These researchers and healthcare professionals are often genuinely concerned for the people within their care. Nevertheless, even the most competent of them face moral quandaries in professional practice, and they work within institutional protocols that can both facilitate and frustrate good care. They can benefit from moral encouragement and ethical consultation that the clergy should be able to provide, assuming that the clergy are themselves critically conversant in the moral language that these other professions employ. Of course, overly strident or judgmental input from ministers would not be as appreciated as would sensitive conversation that respects the moral quandaries of the other. This is one of the areas in which an understanding of informed consent is helpful for pastoral ministry; a knowledge about informed consent helps a minister to serve as a moral counselor, consultant, and encourager to other professionals who are practicing in the community. The minister is able to help other professionals determine ways in which to respect the moral agency, the rights, and moral integrity of the people they treat as patients, clients, and subjects.

For example, in New Zealand an ecumenical InterChurch Commission on Genetic Engineering was established to facilitate Christian involvement in public debate about genetic engineering. Informed consent is one of the areas lifted up by this Commission for the attention of policymakers, scientists, and the general public. The InterChurch Commission states the following:

> As a commission, we re-iterate that in relation to the use or consumption of genetically modified foods, pharmaceuticals, organisms or other products the whole community (and the potential consumers in particular) must have the opportunity to give or withhold informed consent...There is also a requirement that all possible information be available,

including the extent to which possible risks are known and understood, or to which there is insufficient knowledge for risk assessment.[20]

Scientists and clergy alike were represented on this InterChurch Commission, and the subject of informed consent represents a node of intersection between their respective areas as well as a point of common concern between this ecumenical group and the larger secular society.

Ministry on Behalf of Patients

Another area in which knowledge about informed consent is helpful to the pastoral minister is in the minister's pastoral care for parishioners who are receiving treatment or therapy from others. The minister can facilitate communication between care providers and patients so that genuine informed consent occurs. Sometimes this might mean that the minister takes a role of advocate and speaks to care providers on behalf of a parishioner. More often, though, the minister can simply encourage a parishioner to ask the caregiver those questions that are important to the parishioner, but that he or she may be reticent to ask. People can be in awe of the medical professional and be reluctant consequently to challenge a perception of medical authority even if the medical professional is inviting an open conversation. The minister can be an encourager to parishioners in this regard—to help them communicate meaningfully with their caregivers so that they are properly informed.

The minister can also encourage parishioners on the "consent" part of informed consent. Many decisions about healthcare are difficult—not only because of a lack of information, but because of the import of the decisions themselves. Decisions that affect other people can carry a burden of guilt or at least the potential for guilt. Parents making decisions about healthcare for their children can agonize over these decisions and become distraught over their responsibility in this regard. Conversely, grown children deciding about the care of their elderly parents can be equally distraught. Eventually, almost all of us have to make healthcare decisions in matters of life and death for ourselves or for those we love. Modern medical technology sometimes allows for an imaginatively infinite maintenance of bodily function, so that death might follow only after decisions are made to remove life support. Few decisions are more difficult to make.

The minister can encourage people as they deliberate on these life and death questions. This might mean helping a person clarify for herself or himself that which is most important to her or him in making a decision. At other times, people are already aware of their own values but they may feel guilty for pursuing them and desire pastoral counsel in this regard. Sometimes, the minister may want to facilitate communication between family members so that they can give each other permission to pursue a difficult course of action. At other times, a minister may need to counsel with a person to help that person clarify his or her own thinking against a cacophony of family voices, demands, or expectations. Seldom would it be helpful for the minister to assert vigorously his or her own values to the decision-maker; this would likely be counterproductive to the pastoral task of encouraging the person's own moral agency as one who is freely able to give consent.

At the same time, though, a parishioner may genuinely want to hear the minister's own thoughts and ethical insight about a tough decision. When desired, such moral counsel should be given; to withhold such information when it is desired by someone would not be empowering of that person's moral agency. For a minister to withhold moral counsel when it is actually requested would be just as disabling to a person's informed consent as would a doctor's withholding of requested medical information. In sum, a pastor's knowledge of informed consent can prove helpful in several ways as pastors interact with parishioners who are making critical decisions. Pastors with that knowledge are better equipped to offer people moral counsel or encouragement or prayer or even absolution as they are making these decisions. Discernment is often required of the minister to determine how best to do this for particular individuals within particular circumstances.

Pastoral care at life's edge requires particular sensitivity to discern the desires that people have for care; this is especially so for those whose communication becomes impaired or whose competence becomes diminished. Our attention shifts to different foci during such times: a narrower focus on the "patient," a wider focus on the patient's family and community, a proximate focus on facing mortality, an ultimate focus on facing eternity. We should not lose sight of the ultimate focus. People are interested in our ministries at this particular time because we can voice prayer to God and assurance from God about a life and a love that are eternal.

While such soteriological conversations may not seem normal for most people most of the time, they are a part of our particular vocation as clergy—our call to be offering ministry in the first place. It may be awkward for some people to ask us for such a ministry, but it should not be awkward for us to hear such a request or even to discern such a need and to respond faithfully. Roman Catholic priests whose ministries include the sacraments of unction and extreme unction may be at an advantage over most Protestant clergy in this regard, because they are then prepared and equipped to listen for this request and to respond to it. Protestants, though, can likewise prepare themselves to offer prayer and ritual both for healing and for eternal salvation. No pastor should abandon this ministry of ultimate importance for attention to more proximate matters.[21]

The proximate, though, is also vastly important. People are concerned about their healthcare and their relative comfort as they face eternity. They are concerned about their loved ones and how to communicate with them during this time. The minister is frequently recognized as someone who may share a person's concern—whether of relationships or of medical treatment or of fear of death or of hope for death. One of the important proximate ministries that clergy might perform is to help parishioners and their families clarify their values and desires about life-sustaining medical treatment. This ministry can occur for us either during an emergency itself, when a family may be making critical decisions, or during a more distant or dispassionate conversation about so-called "living wills"—advance directives for healthcare.

■ CASE FOR DISCUSSION: Karen Ann Quinlan

A landmark case in medical ethics can also be discussed with reference to pastoral care. This case involved a family's decision concerning the medical treatment of a comatose loved one.

At twenty-one years of age, Karen Ann Quinlan had suffered brain damage due to oxygen starvation. As a result, she had been placed on artificial respiration to assist her breathing and to sustain her life. Karen lay in a coma for three-and-a-half months before her family, realizing that the organic damage to her brain would be irreversible, asked that artificial respiration be removed. Her mother, father, sister, and brother were all agreed.

Before reaching a decision about her respirator, Karen's parents consulted frequently with the family's priest, Father Thomas Trapasso. The Quinlans were Roman Catholic, and Mrs. Quinlan (Julie) worked in the parish rectory as Father Tom's secretary. Father Tom was able to reassure them that the Catholic Church's moral teaching did not require the use of extraordinary means of sustaining life in a situation without hope of recovery.[22]

In a book authored by the Quinlans, Father Tom recalls his conversations with Mrs. Quinlan approximately one-and-a-half months after Karen had lost consciousness. Referring to Mrs. Quinlan, Father Tom says the following:

> She could foresee that Karen might survive indefinitely on machines like the respirator, and this was simply inconceivable to Julie. She was just very, very sensitive to Karen's wishes and Karen's fears, and she kept repeating, "Karen would never want this."…
>
> I encouraged her to tell me everything that was on her mind, and she told me how painful it was to visit the hospital with Joe [Mr. Quinlan], because he would stand and talk to Karen as though she could hear him, as though she would wake up at any time. The doctors had made it clear that this was no longer a reasonable possibility, because Karen had no thinking brain left. "It is irreversible, irreparable," she said…
>
> I told Julie that once I had accepted the hopelessness of Karen's condition, I began to see her tragedy in theological terms.
>
> In terms of what I had been taught in my training, from a moral, theological point of view, this was a classic case of a hopeless life being prolonged unnecessarily through the use of extraordinary means. I explained this to Julie, and she just quietly listened…
>
> Julie had not heard of this concept before…
>
> She kept asking if the respirator, which was assisting Karen to breathe, would be considered "extraordinary" in the context of this Catholic moral law.
>
> I said there was no doubt in my mind that the respirator is extraordinary in Karen's circumstance.[23]

After being legally challenged, the Quinlans' right to make this decision concerning Karen's care was affirmed by the New Jersey Supreme Court. The Court ruled in this case that the "right to privacy" for determining one's medical treatment is not necessarily lost to a person even in a comatose state, but rather this right might persist even with such a loss of competency and autonomy.[24] In reaching a decision concerning Karen Ann Quinlan, the Supreme Court of New Jersey wrote the following:

> Our affirmance of Karen's independent right of choice, however, would ordinarily be based upon her competency

to assert it. The sad truth, however, is that she is grossly incompetent and we cannot discern her supposed choice based on the testimony of her previous conversation with friends where such testimony is without sufficient probative weight. Nevertheless we have concluded that Karen's right of privacy may be asserted on her behalf by her guardian under the peculiar circumstances here present.[25]

After the family was allowed to have the respirator removed from Karen Ann Quinlan, she nevertheless survived in a coma for nearly ten years, breathing on her own without the aid of a respirator before eventually passing away.[26]

■ ■ QUESTIONS

Discuss this case with reference to permission-granting for care.

1. Whose permission would normally be required in order to provide medical treatment to Karen? Whose permission would normally be required, do you think, for the removal of such treatment?
2. Since Karen was comatose and unable to express her own desires to medical staff, whose permission was necessary for determining Karen's course of treatment? How do you interpret the reasoning of the New Jersey Supreme Court in this case? Are you inclined to agree?
3. As Father Tom describes some of his conversation with Mrs. Quinlan, how does he hear her concern for her daughter? Do you think he is demonstrating care in his listening or not? How so, or why not?
4. What concerns or thoughts does Father Tom have to share with Mrs. Quinlan? In offering these thoughts, is he acting in faith with Mrs. Quinlan and her family? If he withheld his thoughts, would this be acting in faith with Mrs. Quinlan and her family? Is the information he conveys helpful to Mrs. Quinlan in thinking about consent for Karen's care?
5. In what way is Father Tom exercising pastoral care, and in what way is he providing moral guidance? Do these roles seem consistent with each other, or do they seem to be in tension?
6. How is permission for Father Tom's ministry given in this situation? Does it seem more explicit or implicit? Does Father Tom seem to be acting faithfully within the parameters of his parishioner's (implicit or explicit) permission?

7. How would you handle a similar situation if your secretary or a parishioner were facing the kind of tragic loss and difficult decision being faced by Mrs. Quinlan? Would your provision of care be similar or dissimilar to Father Tom's?

Care and Counseling to Individuals

A final area in which informed consent is important for pastoral practice is in the pastor's own provision of care to persons. Although most parish clergy are not engaged in the kind of therapeutic practice in which one formally contracts with individuals to provide a professional service and receive a fee in return, there are exceptions. In addition, many professional pastoral counselors and Christian counselors do see individual clients for therapy, much like other professional counselors. Those who are engaged in this kind of specialized ministry should comply with the ethical standards of the counseling profession as a whole.[27] This includes the notion of obtaining informed consent. "One of the most important elements to assure adequate protection for a pastoral counselor," according to Aaron Liberman and Michael J. Woodruff in their book, *Risk Management,* "is the written consent form."[28]

The importance of informed consent for Christian counseling is a point emphasized by several of the contributors to a "handbook" on *Christian Counseling Ethics,* edited by Randolph K. Sanders. Alan C. Tjelveit, for instance, states, "Christian mental health professionals need to act in concord with professional ethics and provide therapy fully informed by Christian ethics only when clients give their free, full and informed consent."[29]

In the next chapter of the book, Horace C. Lukens Jr. further spells out the kinds of information that should be conveyed by professional counselors if at all possible:

1. information about the services provided
2. goals of therapy and procedures to be used
3. financial issues
4. understandings about confidentiality
5. the qualifications of the counselor
6. any other pertinent information

This handbook also includes in the Appendix sample "consent forms" that could used for this purpose.[30]

Other matters could be added to Lukens's list, notably: information about the risks of therapy, alternative courses of treatment, whether or not the treatment is of an experimental nature, and perhaps even any relevant philosophical or theological commitments of the counselor or counseling agency. Thomas E. Rodgerson, for instance, recommends such an exhaustive list of topics for consideration in establishing informed consent for pastoral counseling. At the same time, though, Rodgerson cautions against overly detailed consent forms that are designed more for the legal protection of the counselor than the intended benefit to the client. While the conversation between the counselor and client should cover the relevant details, the consent form itself can be simply and succinctly expressed.[31]

For parish clergy, though, most ministers do not provide pastoral care structured so thoroughly according to a therapeutic model in which the relationship between therapist and client is contractually defined. In fact, some pastors' personal distaste with this particular model provokes them to disavow the whole idea of professionalism as it relates to pastoral care. Professionalism, however, does not necessarily refer to a particular style of working with individuals; professionalism can simply mean that one makes the effort to be competent in those areas in which one professes ability.[32] While most pastors are involved in many ways of caring and relating to parishioners beside this therapeutic model of counseling, they nevertheless do occasionally counsel with individuals as well. Whether they consider themselves to be "professional" or not, pastors do offer counseling of one kind or another at one time or another.

In their book on *Ministerial Ethics,* Joe E. Trull and James E. Carter approvingly cite Wayne Oates in saying, "[M]inisters, whatever their training, do not enjoy the privilege of deciding whether to counsel with people or not."[33] I agree with this statement that minsters do not usually have the luxury of avoiding the task of pastoral counseling in some form and to some degree. I would add, though, that whatever their level or type of training, ministers are responsible for clarifying with people the nature of their own ministerial competence and the type of pastoral care that they are willing and able to offer. This mutual sharing of information and clarifying of expectations is required by the notion of pastoral informed consent. Moreover, pastors should be careful not to prolong or extend any kind of pastoral care beyond their areas of acknowledged competence.

So far, I have defined the idea of informed consent and suggested its relevance for four areas of pastoral ministry and the church's mission: mission in the wider society, ministry among professionals, ministry on behalf of patients, and therapeutic pastoral counseling. To summarize with regard to these four areas, we have noticed that

1. outreach to the larger society should involve practices characterized by honesty, mutual respect, and invitation
2. the clergy are in a position to serve as a moral resource for other
   caregivers in respecting the moral integrity of their patients
3. the clergy are able to offer moral encouragement to patients as
   they contemplate giving consent for medical treatment
4. the clergy need to mutually clarify with perspective counselees
   the nature of any counseling they themselves may be providing

Ministers provide counseling to individuals within a broader
context of parish and community. Our communication with one
another occurs within this context even when we converse privately
and confidentially. The criterion of informed consent as applied to
pastoral ministry presupposes the context of a particular congregation
or a community of common concern. Let us examine the idea of
pastoral informed consent further in light of this broader community
of concern.

Consensual Communication

Informed consent is really about respect. It means that we do
not act toward persons in ways that are uninvited. For professionals,
it means that we are empowered to act, not so much by virtue of
special knowledge, but because we have been given permission. I
think that this is extremely important for ministry. It may be even
more important for ministry than for other professions, because
ministers are publicly proclaimed as being called by God to provide
their services.

The reader may think that I have exaggerated or overspoken.
The pastor may not want to see himself or herself in such an exalted
position. But the church, in fact, does publicly proclaim this call of
God in services of ordination and installation, and at least some
laypeople actually do ascribe divine authority to the minister–whether
done consciously or not and whether doctrinally sound or otherwise.
Irrespective of motivation, the high regard sometimes afforded the
pastoral office morally requires that the holders of that office hold
themselves accountable to the people who are investing their trust.
*Faithfulness to God Who calls, I would suggest, involves accountability toward
those we serve.* This accountability needs to occur on two levels–
corporate as well as individual. They will be discussed in turn.

Community, Covenant, and Contract

A minister's call is affirmed, empowered, and delimited within
the context of a particular community, which is the church. Different

denominations have different structures for testing, affirming, and defining a minister's call. These typically include responsibilities for proclaiming Word, administering Sacrament, and participating in some way in church order.

At the denominational level, different churches have different degrees of specificity in establishing expectations for the minister's duties. United Methodist ministers, for instance, are instructed in the *Book of Discipline* to visit people in their homes. While this visitation should be done in a way that respects people's privacy, it is considered to be a legitimate function of the minister in a United Methodist parish. Many other professionals could not even attempt to visit people in their homes without appearing intrusive and uninvited. I would be really taken aback, for instance, if my dentist wanted to check on me at home. Even for ministers, however, the most routine and denominationally sanctioned duties can appear unwanted and intrusive to people if more localized processes of consultation are ignored.

Regardless of national and regional structures, at the congregational level it is helpful to clarify expectations concerning the pastoral role—both the minister's own self-assessment and the congregation's expectations. When congregational expectations are clarified and communicated, it is like giving general "consent" for this type of ministry to occur, though it is still not giving consent on behalf of any particular individual who might be a recipient of pastoral care. In communicating with congregation or committees concerning their pastoral work, however, ministers should be guarded in speaking about individual members of the congregation so as not to betray the confidence of the individual in question or even to cause undue embarrassment.

Congregational consent is, nonetheless, important for clarifying expectations between the minister and members of the congregation. These expectations might have to do with any dimension of pastoral ministry or congregational mission: pastoral visiting, pastoral counseling, leading worship, work in the community, evangelical outreach, etc. It is of practical importance to clarify these expectations so that the workload of the minister can be manageable. Unclarified expectations tend to escalate to unmanageable proportions, becoming a problem of self-care for the minister and the minister's family. But moral obligations as well as workload are also clarified in the process of articulating expectations for the ministry of the pastor and congregation. Many pastors have written contracts with their congregations that spell out in detail expectations for ministry. Such contracts are especially helpful for ministers serving within more congregationalist structures of governance.[34]

Corporate consent, however, is not simply a matter of contracting between two parties–the pastor and congregation. It is also a matter of covenanting between the many individuals within the congregational community. In forming a community, church members constitute a culture with shared expectations for one another. These expectations may not be expressed in written clauses, but they may indeed find expression through performance in life and ritual.

As an example of the church as a covenanting community, consider the obligation to respect people's privacy. Most professional caregivers with access to information about someone's health or medical treatment would consider such information to be privileged, and they would not be right in sharing it publicly. (Patients themselves, of course, can share their own personal information about health and treatment with whomever they please; it is their privilege.) Ministers, however, and other leaders of public worship often make public proclamation about people's health not only during corporate prayer but also in published newsletters! This is not necessarily a betrayal of confidence, though it can be.

In worshiping communities in which prayer for one another is typical, however, it is frequently the case that people want and expect their need for prayer to be conveyed to the rest of the community. They would feel hurt if excluded from prayer because of a lack of communication. The rightness or wrongness of communicating this information is a function both of the individual's expectation and the community's expectation of what constitutes normal practice for that community. This can vary from one location and culture to another.

In New Zealand, the nation's Privacy Act is interpreted rather strictly, so that hospitals typically refuse to provide information about hospital admissions to patients' ministers. Some churches have also been under the impression that it is illegal and unethical to name individuals publicly when praying for their healing. Coming from New Zealand to the United States recently, I was startled to go to church on Sunday and find in the bulletin that morning a full page listing every ailing member of that congregation and their specific medical conditions. There is, fortunately, substantial middle ground in both countries.

A specialist in international privacy law, Paul Roth has indicated that the nature and expectations of the community to which people voluntarily belong determines to a degree what kind of information is personal and private and what kind of information is shared within the community. If people have agreed to share medical information with each other for the sake of a ministry of prayer–that is, if this is a shared expectation within the community–then it is appropriate to share this kind of information.[35] To interpret Roth's comments in this matter, the members of the worshiping community in effect give consent or "authorization"[36] to each other in this regard. This is so even if the community's expectations remain implicit; but the more explicitly these expectations are conveyed, the more confident one would be that one is acting appropriately in bringing a prayer concern about someone before the group.

On the other hand, even when a congregation has an established and expected practice of offering prayer for one another, some individuals nevertheless want their personal identity or their particular need for prayer to be kept quiet. It is important, then, to maintain this confidentiality. To determine whether or not it is appropriate to bring someone's personal concern to the community for prayer, one must consult with the individual in question. This can be done naturally and informally by simply asking someone during a pastoral visit, "Would you like your concern to be placed on our prayer list?"

Even to remark politely and indicatively, "We will be praying for you," gives the other person a chance to object, to express gratitude, or to clarify the nature of the prayer request. One would need to be sensitive, though, to discern whether the person actually felt free to object to the statement or not. Not everyone feels comfortable saying no to the minister, so ministers should be sensitive to degrees of "coercion" that might be an unavoidable ingredient in their ministerial presence, even if wholly unintended. Nevertheless, this is how informed consent typically works in pastoral contexts–not by legal forms but more informally by conversing together, listening sensitively, clarifying, and discerning. But there is nothing wrong with making such informal mutual understanding more explicit. When in doubt, simply ask.

Communication and Care with Individuals

Informed consent for pastoral ministry with individuals tends to be choreographed like a dance rather than drawn up like a formal contract. In this dance, we often have to adjust to changing steps as we change tunes. We have to learn how to communicate with our different dance partners. Sometimes we lead; sometimes we follow. Communication involves both parties; it is important both to speak and to listen with care.

Care-ful Listening

Pastoral "informed consent" occurs largely through conversation as expectations become clarified. Such clarifying conversations are especially important for the clergy because of the many roles we have in relation to people in the parish. It is not just that we see people in different community contexts: Sunday worship, parish session, golf course, school board, etc. These types of role differences are fairly easy to distinguish because of contextual cues, though we sometimes make a misstep by taking someone's comment on the golf course as jocular when it was actually a request for care. The more difficult role confusion occurs within the context of pastoral ministry itself.

Pastors, as pastors, do many things–church administration, education, worship, grief counseling, marriage counseling, emotional support, and the list goes on–and do so with the same group of people. We do not typically take appointments in our offices to deliver the same general type of service to each person. Lawyers interpret the law. Physicians treat medical conditions. Optometrists diagnose eyesight. Counselors counsel. Ministers, on the other hand, need to constantly clarify to know whether a person is in need of prayer, is asking for personal advice, is wanting help in interpreting scripture, is seeking safety from a battering husband, is offering to help in an evangelistic program, desires to make a contribution to the building fund, is confessing sin from a guilty conscience. Otherwise, we find ourselves offering assistance that has not been requested, or, conversely, ignoring pleas that require our attention.

This distinction between the clergy and other professions with regard to uniformity/diversity of care, obviously, is one of degree rather than a strict division. Actually, for the process of obtaining informed consent to work well for all healthcare providers, clarifying conversation needs to occur between the professional and the patient. In fact, communication is fundamental to the very idea of informed consent. To make an informed choice, medical patients must be told of their different options for treatment and the different risks involved. Conversely, healthcare professionals must listen to discover the patient's understanding of the choices, listening for the following:

1. what questions the patent may have about his or her condition or about the optional treatments
2. what concerns or reservations he or she may hold
3. the degree to which she or he may be feeling coerced

4. the extent to which the patient is understanding his or her own consent in this matter

If a medical patient has only been given a blank form to sign upon admittance to the hospital, then this respectful process of communicating has probably not been followed. This is especially so in cases when people may be inclined to interpret signing a blank informed consent form as a condition of admittance. If the medical procedure has not been described on the form, than the patient is actually consenting to nothing. Furthermore, if admittance is understood as conditional upon signing such a blank permission slip, then an element of coercion has also been introduced. Ministers can help both patients and professionals to understand the importance of communication in this process, and ministers are frequently in a position to facilitate such communication as well.

In our own pastoral interaction with individuals, however, such clarifying conversation is especially necessary for discerning the nature of the pastoral relationship in the moment. While many ministers may formally contract corporately with congregations, they rarely do so with individuals who approach them for pastoral help. The exception would be those ministers who are engaged in a specialized ministry of rendering individual care in a manner like other healthcare professionals. For congregational ministers, though, the very lack of a written contract with individuals for pastoral care heightens the importance of clarifying expectations conversationally. Such conversation is the primary means of communicating information and of conferring consent. We have to listen *care-fully*.

Care-ful Speaking

We also have to speak *care-fully*. Communication is a two-way process. With regard to informed consent, we have so far placed importance on the pastor being able to listen sensitively to people to hear their expectations, and being able to clarify with them the nature of those expectations. But the minister needs to speak as well as to hear. The minister needs to clarify his or her own abilities to minister as well as the other's expectations for ministry. An expectation is not an obligation unless it is agreed upon. Silence from the minister, though, can be interpreted as tacit agreement to provide the expected ministry.[37] The minister does not want to be blunt or offensive if at all avoidable, but he or she is obliged to communicate the extent to which he or she is reasonably able to meet these expectations. In other words, the minister should indicate what kind of ministry he or she is able to provide. This obligation for informing, I suggest, extends then to letting people know of other kinds of care that might be available from other types of providers.

Bill Blackburn has noticed that his parishioners seem genuinely appreciative when he communicates the limits of his competence:

> Many laypeople do not understand what pastors have been trained to do and what their training did not include. I have found, however, that when this is discussed, most persons appreciate the pastor being honest in confessing a lack of training, background or time to deal with the particular issue.[38]

Blackburn indicates, moreover, that in referring parishioners to other professions, he is careful to reassure them about the continuance of his pastoral relationship with them.[39]

Every semester, my students who are preparing for pastoral ministry ask me when one should make a referral. My response is that I refer constantly. Whenever parishioners begin to talk with me about difficulties they are having for which they are seeking help or advice, I respond by honestly reflecting back on what I or others in the church or others in the wider community are able to do. This is simply a matter of providing information. In giving counsel or in providing care, the notion of informed consent suggests that a person's free consent follows upon the caregiver having communicated relevant information concerning the full range of options available to the person. I let these conversations flow easily and naturally; they are seldom very awkward. I try not to be in a hurry to send someone in another direction; I listen as the person tells me of the problem or concern, and when I am asked to respond I do so with my assessment at the moment of the kind of care that might help. My suggestion is then received or rejected, and the conversation continues. Diagnosis, counsel, guidance, and referral all occur together in the context of mutual conversation. If a person is interested in my referral, I try to have the relevant information at hand so that I can facilitate contact.

Conversation, I am suggesting, is required in every step of the dance between pastor and parishioner in establishing informed consent for pastoral care. The conversation defines the particular expectations of the pastoral relationship in the moment and for the particular situation. This conversation requires both sensitive listening on the part of the pastor, and honest communication from the pastor about the kinds of ministry that he or she can offer. The pastor also needs to be able to communicate other possibilities for care within the church or community. The pastor is listening to the parishioner to know how to respond appropriately with the right kind of information or pastoral care.

There are limits, however, to the value of conversation. Conversation can help focus the nature of the pastoral relationship in a moment; it can also distract pastor and parishioner alike from the problem at hand, and it can detract from the pastoral relationship. Sometimes ministers are overly interested in the problems that parishioners bring to them. They ask questions beyond their own need to know. When a parishioner approaches the minister with a personal problem, it should be assumed that the parishioner is requesting advice, help, or even simply companionship concerning that problem.[40] This in itself constitutes the parishioner's consent to the minister to explore further together the nature of the problem and the possibilities for pastoral response. It is an invitation.

It is an invitation, however, for the specific purpose of receiving pastoral care. To respond faithfully to the invitation, the pastor should keep in mind the kinds of pastoral responses that he or she could offer that would be consistent with the nature of the pastoral relationship and that would be within the capabilities of the minister. Questions the minister asks should help to further clarify the situation for either the minister or the parishioner so that they will be able to discern together the way to proceed. Sometimes it happens, however, that the minister asks questions just to learn more without any real idea concerning an appropriate pastoral response. It is as if the minister is waiting for inspiration while absorbing the gritty details of who is sleeping with whom. When this happens, the pastoral relationship has devolved into voyeurism and gossip.

A parishioner who has asked a minister for help, who has invited the minister to listen, who has given consent for pastoral care is trusting the minister to ask questions that will help the minister to respond care-fully and helpfully. The minister has not been given permission or consent to intrude for any other reason. To do so is actually an invasion of privacy and a betrayal of trust for which the parishioner has not given consent. The parishioner, though, is very likely to continue to answer the pastor's questions because of the person's trust in the pastor. It is up to the pastor to notice his or her own motivations and to interact with the parishioner appropriately. This is a vulnerability of the parishioner who asks the minister for help, and it is a responsibility of the minister to keep faith with care for the parishioner.

This is not to say that ministers should not encourage people to "talk out their problems" and to "tell their stories" as a vehicle for helping people to discover their own resources for health or to discern their own spiritual journeys. Letting people talk as a way of empowering them is standard practice in both pastoral counseling and in spiritual direction. In giving pastoral care, pastoral theologian John Snow has noticed that only when people begin to tell their story and are allowed to go through the length of their narrative do they begin to find the resources for healing. Part of pastoral caring, according to Snow, is to take the time to listen to people tell their stories so that they, in the process, open themselves to receiving grace.[41]

Similarly, with regard to spiritual direction, Karen Lebacqz and Joseph Driskill describe the spiritual director's role as allowing people to describe their own journeys and listening together with them to discern the presence of God.[42] If a minister is offering pastoral care or spiritual direction in such a listening mode, however, the minister should be self-aware that this is what he or she is doing in interaction with the parishioner as the parishioner is speaking. Not only should the minister be intentional about his or her own involvement in this process, he or she should also let the parishioner know (when it is appropriate to do so) that this is what the minister is doing.

One thing is available to the minister to help discern whether it is the parishioner's need to talk, or the minister's need to hear, that is driving the conversation. The minister can notice whether she or he is listening as the story unfolds or whether he or she is more assertively provoking the telling with a series of questions. This is just a rule of thumb, of course; sometimes a lot of questions are entirely needed to know how to proceed, and sometimes the parishioner expects a line of insightful questioning from the minister. The point is simply for the minister to take care not to intrude unnecessarily, but to respect the nature of the pastoral relationship when responding to a person's request or consent for pastoral caring.

In her work on *Counseling Women,* Christie Neuger has developed a narrative approach to pastoral care that relies on "deconstructive listening" to women's stories. This is an intentionally empowering process that allows people to externalize and name a problem and to look for the unique deconstructive possibilities within their stories. A powerful quotation from her book is appropriate here:

> The narrative-oriented counselor has a strong conviction about the authority and agency of the other. The primary

stance of the counselor in narrative therapy is a compassionate, curious, and respectful listener who pays very careful attention to the story in order to find subplots that assist the counselee in resisting problem-saturated narratives and oppressive discourses. The counselor believes in empowering agency in the counselee and thus creates a counseling environment in which the counselee has primary agency in the therapeutic relationship.[43]

To respect people's agency, I am suggesting, to hear their consent for care, is seldom carte blanche permission to do whatever is in the minister's mind. It is usually a more specific if yet unarticulated request for help or discernment or companionship or guidance or prayer from the minister. The pastor's task is to clarify this person's consent and in so doing to clarify the minister's own call to extend care to this person with this request in this context.

Conclusion

I have been discussing communication as a constitutive requirement of informed consent in ministry. The pastor's ministry and the church's mission, I have argued, should proceed within the parameters of permission as provided through a process of communication. This permission-granting within the context of community is analogous to the requirement of informed consent in healthcare ethics. Pastors need to respect the dignity of parishioners as people created in the image of God.

As a moral presumption, a minister should respect virtually everyone's ability to make moral decisions concerning themselves and their loved ones. I would add, moreover, that a part of this respect is to accept degrees of apparent irrationality in others' decisions and actions. In other words, a minister should respect a person's rational choice even when it seems marked by irrationality, and a minister should respect a person" moral agency even when it seems marked by immorality. There are exceptions to this rule, I am sure, but they should require justification.

Priestly and prophetic pastoral care should seek to affirm and proclaim God's grace in every dimension of life. It would be self-defeating for the pastor as a moral enabler to constantly second-guess parishioners and paternalistically question their capacity for rational and faithful decision-making whenever they happen to disagree with the pastor's own reasoning. On the contrary, pastoral care requires faith on the part of the pastor to trust God's Spirit working in the midst of a person's struggle—even when a person seems to be in error, to discover (to *dis-cover*) their own moral resources and moral agency. By demonstrating such trust, the pastor is also encouraging others to respond with greater faith to God's grace. Pastoral care as moral enablement seeks to affirm and strengthen the moral character of people facing difficult decisions.

Finally, to respect people as created in the image of God includes not only a respect for people's "autonomy" as moral agents in the present moment; it also includes a respect for who they may yet become "in Christ." There is a teleological as well as a deontological dimension to pastoral care for persons. We seek to help people discern God's love for them, God's presence in their lives, and God's call to them to be perfected in love. Respecting the parameters of their permission in the present, their invitation, their welcome to us, is the beginning of our pastoral sojourn with them in this process of discernment and discovery.

4

Keeping Faith I

Veracity as Not Lying

"In the beginning was the Word," the gospel of John proclaims in its initial verse, and as the gospel continues we find the incarnate Word questioned in the context of power. "What is truth?" the interrogator asks in John 18. Questions of truthfulness are at the heart of the gospel and at the heart of a ministry that is called to proclaim that gospel.

Fidelity

The terms "fidelity" and "fiduciary obligation" are both related to the Latin word for "faith" (*fides*) and the Latin verb *fidere* ("to trust"). Duties of fidelity are a matter of keeping faith.[1] Typically, one hears the phrase with reference to such duties as keeping promises, telling truth, and honoring confidences. These duties all have to do in general with keeping faith, but they challenge us to determine what such faithfulness requires in particular relationships and under specific circumstances. Promises, for instance, can be explicitly written or spoken, or they may be more implicitly or tacitly inferred. Keeping faith in the context of a written contract entails fulfilling the written terms of the contract as promised, but often faithfulness requires discernment of duty beyond those contractual obligations. The ideas of faith and faithfulness are larger for most of us than the mere matter of a written contract.

In professional ethics, fiduciary obligation is understood to apply to relationships between professionals and their clients. This is especially important when there is a power differential between them so that the client is dependent on the professional's good faith. A professional's fiduciary responsibility toward a client is to keep the client's interest foremost and to act in a manner consistent with those interests. This is a legal duty as well as a moral duty and can be enforced in court when a professional is sued for breach of fiduciary duty. This legal duty can sometimes be applied to clergy as well. In this and the next chapter, however, duties of fidelity will be considered more broadly as a general moral category. They are present in every aspect of faithfulness, including but not limited to explicitly contracted responsibilities or to professional duties. Fidelity is as central to moral responsibility, I would suggest, as faith is central to life itself.

We find faithfulness called for in every relationship. It is fundamental in our very relationship to God Whose faithfulness endures to all generations (Ps. 119:90) and Who offers to each of us salvation by faith. Covenant with God asks for our response of faith—whether the covenant through Noah to respect life, the covenant through Abraham to bless all nations, the covenant through Moses to keep the law, or the covenant in Christ to renew creation. Covenantal relationship requires faithfulness—faithfulness on God's part to embrace us, and faithfulness on our part to respond to God's grace.

We keep faith (or we hope to keep faith) with one another as well as with God. We make promises to each other. We form relationships and we establish expectations. Every relationship we have entails some degree of faithfulness. Sometimes we expect merely a minimal degree of honesty, as, for instance, when we purchase a newspaper and cup of coffee in the morning from the "guy on the corner" and expect simply not to be overcharged. At other times we expect a great deal from one another, as, for example, when we enter into a covenant of marriage or when we give birth to children. These primary relationships involve a depth of intimacy and a breadth of legitimate expectations. Our responsibilities to each other are a function of the nature of each relationship and what it means to keep faith with each other in that relationship.

Sometimes we define as specifically as we can the exact nature of our mutual expectations; this is the case when we establish a formal, written contract. At other times, we let the relation grow more "naturally" as we develop and deepen friendship. Friendships rarely have written rules, but friendships always incur some kind of faithful care for one another. One of the areas of moral quandary members of the clergy often face pertains to the rather fluid boundary we can experience between viewing people as friends and as parishioners, between the role of friend and the role of pastor. There are likely to be similar but different sets of expectations entailed between the two types of relationships. To keep faith with our friends and to keep faith with our parishioners, we must be clear in our own minds concerning the nature of our obligations to each. When these roles overlap, as they sometimes do, it requires even greater clarity in our own minds to respond appropriately and faithfully.

It is apparent to us that our relationships actually occur not in pure pair bonds between one individual and another, but within webs of relatedness. Even in the privacy of romantic love, if two individuals decide to marry, they also become simultaneously "in-laws," and they each find themselves related to a new extended family. Friendships also occur in overlapping circles of friendship. Professional relationships are established within institutional contexts. When a minister enters a parish, he or she is already related to all the strangers in the congregation, not only spiritually by virtue of their common confession of faith, but also because of their mutual relatedness within the institutional church. The church itself, with its own institutional requirements, provides a context for defining the duties of fidelity between pastor and parishioners. Not only the church, but every place of employment regulates human interaction at a formal level. Every institution also includes a corporate culture that more implicitly contributes to our sense of obligation to one another. Such social and cultural complexity to human relatedness both helps to define our duties of fidelity at any given time and also introduces confusion as different sets of obligations or loyalties compete for our fidelity.

While it may be that God's faithfulness is primary for the sustaining of the universe (Ps. 136), and while our own ethics might always be dependent on God's faithfulness (1 Jn. 4:19), our duties of fidelity require faithfulness and loyalty on our part. God is always faithful to us; this is not the problem. The question that arises is, rather, "How can we keep faith with each other?" To identify my duties of fidelity to my neighbor, I ask myself how my neighbor is legitimately placing faith, trust, or confidence in me. The confidence, faith, or trust that we place legitimately in each other is the source of our duties of fidelity to one another. To begin to answer the question, "How am I obligated?" I might inquire, "How am I being trusted?"

This is not to say, however, that every social expectation placed on us is a responsibility in faith. We are not totally at the mercy of other people's trust. Sometimes trust is misplaced not because someone is untrustworthy as a person or as a professional but because the expectation itself may be inappropriate or unrealistic. For instance,

I was approached on my very first day as a minister by a woman who told me that my predecessor had been her regular means of transportation to her physician. She asked if I would be willing as well to take her to the doctor when she needed to go. It would have been a kindness for me to have said yes, but I was not yet aware of the other needs that might require my attention in this parish. I felt that I was being responsible in turning down her request while still indicating my willingness to help her find alternative means of transport. Fortunately she asked me, making explicit her expectation. By asking, she allowed me to clarify our mutual expectations of each other. Duties of fidelity have their source partly in the expectations that are placed on us in trust. They are also partly sourced in our acceptance and clarification of that trust.

Confusion enters at this point, though, when our role as pastors entails obligations that are already a part of that role. Official denominational policy also defines duties of fidelity. In The United Methodist Church, for instance, congregations are not allowed by denominational policy to prevent ministers from holding worship services in the church building. Ministers are expected to do this; they are also expected to be the administrative officer of the local church.[2] These expectations are already structured into the pastoral relationship in a United Methodist context, so they are already included among the obligations that exist between United Methodist pastors and parishioners.

By accepting the pastoral relationship within the particular context of a United Methodist parish, congregation and minister alike have accepted in trust certain obligations toward each other. If there is an exception to be made to these expectations, then it is this exception that needs to be clarified or negotiated between the parties (providing it is even permissible by denominational polity). Otherwise, the normal obligations of a United Methodist pastor can be assumed to be relevant and applicable. Other denominations have similar obligations structured into the relationship between a minister and a congregation. These obligations are assumed to be accepted when the pastoral relationship itself is accepted.

It may also be that there are certain basic obligations in the nature of fidelity across denominations. In fact, there may be basic fiduciary obligations that apply within society across the various professions. Christian ethicist Karen Lebacqz, in her book *Professional Ethics: Power and Paradox*, advocates fidelity or trustworthiness as a "key virtue" not only for the clergy but for other professionals as well. Lebacqz argues for the centrality of trustworthiness, not only theologically by appealing to our response to God's steadfast love and faithfulness, but also sociologically. She cites sociologist Talcott Parsons's insight that professionals are distinguished by the "independent trusteeship… of a major part of the cultural tradition of the society." Because society as a whole places such trust in members of the professions, those professions should be significantly guided by moral norms of promise-keeping, confidentiality, and honesty in the relations between the professions and society. She understands the virtue of trustworthiness to encompass these several norms of fidelity, and she commends it for clergy.[3]

There are different ways of being trustworthy or faithful to one another, though, and we sometimes experience these to be in tension. Two moral principles in particular seem to entail different expectations: confidentiality and veracity. Confidentiality requires that we keep quiet about information shared with us in trust. The word *confidence* literally means "to keep faith with" or "to keep faith together." The principle of veracity (from *verax*, the Latin word for "truthful"), on the other hand, refers to honesty and our need to communicate truthfully. Both of these principles are relevant to pastoral relationships. Part of pastoral practice is learning when to hold information privately and when (or with whom) to share information. Neither principle can be said to be absolutely binding without exception, but both principles can be seen to be constantly applicable. Pastoral practice occurs within the ebb and flow, it seems, of respecting secrets and communicating truth.

Both veracity and confidentiality can be seen as related to a third principle: "promise-keeping." Promise-keeping is a matter of speaking truly about one's own intents and purposes. To keep a promise is to keep true to one's word; it concerns veracity. Confidentiality, conversely, can be seen as staying true to one's promise to remain quiet about a matter or to keep communication confined within a limited circle. One is not always bound never to repeat information that one hears; rather, confidentiality is strictly applicable only in those situations where there has been an explicit or implicit promise made that communication should remain confidential. For clergy, though, implicit promises of confidentiality constitute part of the difficulty in knowing when and how to communicate. Because pastors are generally expected to maintain confidence, there is often an implicit but unspoken promise that a conversation will not be repeated. If this expectation of confidentiality is unspoken, however, an implicit promise may be assumed by only one party in the conversation. When ministers clarify with parishioners the extent to which confidentiality applies in a particular situation, they are in effect clarifying the promise they are making and the obligation they are therefore assuming. Pastoral confidentiality will be discussed further in the next chapter. In the present context, it is enough to notice the apparent tension between confidentiality and veracity, as well as their mutual relationship to the third principle of promise-keeping.

The moral principles of veracity and confidentiality nevertheless receive different emphases by ethicists writing about professional ethics in general or about pastoral ethics in particular. Richard Gula[4] and William Rankin[5] give central emphasis to the principle of confidentiality for pastoral ministry. Walter E. Wiest and Elwyn A. Smith, on the other hand, give central emphasis to veracity.[6] These are not exclusive emphases; all of these ethicists affirm the importance of both veracity and confidentiality. Their writing has simply provided a sharper focus on one or the other. In the following discussion, the principle of veracity will be explored in greater detail before turning more explicitly to questions of confidentiality in the next chapter. Both veracity and confidentiality can be understood as prima facie duties of fidelity that are important for pastors to hold in balance as they seek to be faithful and trustworthy in ministry.

Veracity

"What is truth?" (Jn. 18:38a), Pilate asks Jesus in John's gospel. Pilate's question is frequently interpreted as a cynical response to Jesus' claim of global scope: "For this I was born, and for this I came into the world, to testify to the truth" (v. 37b). Without addressing the question of truth in such global terms, however, Pilate immediately renders a particular verdict in the trial and tells those accusing Jesus: "I find no case against him." (v. 38c). The word *verdict* literally means, in its Latin etymology, "to state the truth." In the particulars of this trial, Pilate answers his own question.

There are many ways to discuss the ethics of truth-telling. Already, though, a distinction can be made in our discussion regarding the universality or the particularity of truth as a moral principle. Can the idea of truth and its moral requirements be defined as global in scope, or, conversely, should the idea of truth and its requirements be more narrowly defined within particular contexts?

This ambiguity concerning truth-telling—the question of its universality or its particularity—can also be illustrated with reference to the Ten Commandments. *The Living Bible* paraphrases the commandment in Exodus 20:16 to simply and universally read: "You must not lie." This translation would seem to apply to truth-telling (or at least to not-lie-telling) as a general rule without reference to particular contexts or circumstances. *The Living Bible* adds a footnote, however, that provides an alternative, more specific translation: "You must not give false testimony in court." In court or during a legal trial is suggested as the context in which truth is of particular importance. Most other translations offer a reading consistent with this more particular, contextual interpretation. The *New Revised Standard Version,* for instance, reads: "You shall not bear false witness against your neighbor." The context provides particular import to the principle of truth-telling. Since people's welfare, livelihood, reputations, and freedom are at stake in the courts of power, one ought not to wrongly accuse or testify falsely against another.

Arthur Dyck

Because of the potential for causing harm from lying in court, Arthur Dyck, in his introduction to ethics, discusses the prohibition against bearing false witness as a matter of nonmaleficence. He discusses not bearing false witness as a matter of "not-harming," even though he also separately affirms a more general principle of truth-telling. His argument is that legal structures of authority depend on being able to ascertain the truth as a basic prerequisite if they are to render justice, promote community, or restrain evil. Conversely, deception in legal proceedings can not only inflict particular harm on accused individuals, but this deception also tends to undermine the court's very ability to promote the good ends that the legal system should serve, Dyck says:

> The court is an institution that, when dedicated to truth-telling, prevents the escalation of injurious actions within the community that would surely result from failures to test the veracity of accusations against one's neighbor.
>
> At this point we can begin to see that the evils cited and prohibited by the Mosaic covenant involve obligations of the most stringent character. Lying in the courtroom is not tolerated at all.[7]

Dyck interprets the Ten Commandments as protecting the institutional and moral requisites of community for ancient Hebrews, and he finds a parallel importance in preserving the beneficent character of contemporary courts. The courtroom context magnifies the importance of veracity as a matter of preventing harm.

Nevertheless, other areas of social life in addition to the legal system depend on truthful communication for their proper functioning. Dyck acknowledges, for instance, that science by its very nature as a quest for truth depends on truth-telling.[8] This implies open and honest communication between researchers themselves, as well as between the scientific community and the general public. Similarly, pastoral ministry depends on service to the truth as essential to ministerial integrity. "Truth," insist Walter E. Wiest and Elwyn A. Smith, "...is the key both to ministry and the ethics of ministry."[9] The business community, too, as frighteningly illustrated by recent scandals on Wall Street, depends on honesty in reporting financial matters for its own integrity as well as for the economic health of the larger society. While dishonest practice in accounting might constitute criminal behavior in specific instances, such dishonesty on a wide scale threatens the stability of the entire economic system and has repercussions for the well-being of all members of society. Indeed, the first years of the third millennium in the United States seem to have been characterized by a crisis in honesty. Not only leaders in business, but both Democratic and Republican leaders in the United States have come under public scrutiny for failing to communicate with an expected degree of honesty.

In fact, a case can be made that we depend on veracity at nearly every level of society as a basic precondition for a coherent morality, or even for the establishment of community itself. Dyck makes this argument for veracity as a "constitutive"–rather than a "constituted" or derived–rule. In making this argument, Dyck appeals to distinctions drawn by Jean Piaget and by Bishop John Robinson. Piaget distinguished between "constitutive" rules upon which other rules depend, and "constituted" rules that are logically derived from or built upon the constitutive rules. Dyck explains, "Constitutive rules are requisite to the very processes of formulating or deciding upon rules."[10] Piaget's distinction was with regard to the moral reasoning of individuals. Bishop John Robinson, according to Dyck, made a similar argument with regard to the basic requirements for human relationships and societal moral norms:

> As a variant of Bishop Robinson's formulation, we might say that lying, breaking promises, and unfair procedures would be destructive of the human relationships that are endemic to the formulation and acceptance of any standards, laws, and procedures needed for cooperative behavior in community, and that all communities recognize, implicitly or explicitly, their general wrong-making character.[11]

According to this argument, veracity is a basic moral principle upon which other aspects of community and morality depend.

Sissela Bok

Philosopher Sissela Bok argues similarly that veracity is foundational for society. Bok's argument examines veracity with reference not only to the violence that can be done to individuals through deceit but also to the larger harm that can occur to society from a lack of trust. Society depends on at least some level of "trust in communication," she states. Regardless of other moral principles held within society, she reasons, a certain level of truthfulness is essential to avoid not only personal misunderstanding but even social collapse.[12] Thus, "trust in some degree of veracity," she writes, "functions as a *foundation* of relations among human beings; when this trust shatters or wears away, institutions collapse." "*Whatever* matters to human beings," she emphasizes, "trust is the atmosphere in which it thrives."[13] Bok affirms a basic moral presumption against telling lies, which she defines as messages that are "stated" and "intentionally deceptive." She also expresses this affirmation for the worth of truthfulness positively as a presumption in favor of the principle of veracity.[14]

By affirming veracity as a prima facie moral principle, Bok is recognizing that dishonesty might sometimes be morally justified because of conflicts between veracity and other moral duties. She is indicating, however, that such exceptions to the principle of veracity do indeed require justification. Such exceptions should be a last resort, and the circumstances surrounding them should always be clarified. She suggests several criteria that might be considered when determining the stringency of veracity in a particular situation.[15] Some of her more important considerations can be summarized and enumerated as follows:

1. Consider lying only as a *last resort*. If the same desired ends can be achieved through more truthful or honest means, then the option of lying should not even be considered.
2. Identify the rationales that seem to be employed in excusing this lie and compare them to the reasonable counter-arguments that can be made in response to these rationales. How convincing are these counter-arguments? How valid or empty do these rationales appear?
3. Describe the desired ends and the particular circumstances surrounding the question of lying in a given situation. Is the situation dire enough to justify dishonesty? Is there a harm at stake that is severe enough to warrant lying?
4. More widely, clarify the possible harms to oneself as a moral agent or to the level of trust in one's community.

5. Determine whether lying will expand to further levels and forms of dishonesty by oneself or others, or whether the lie itself and its consequent damage will be more of an isolated instance.
6. Ask how legitimate the claim of the intended hearers of the lie normally is to have honest answers and/or accurate information?
7. See if one's reasoning about this contemplated lie can survive the scrutiny of a "public of reasonable persons." Would such an imagined public agree or disagree with the lie's justification?[16]

Because Bok considers deception akin to violence, her reasoning tends to take into account the potential for various forms of harm. Bok's treatment of veracity can be seen in this regard to be related to the subject of nonmaleficence.

By describing veracity as a prima facie principle in such a way that it allows for justified exception, Bok is distinguishing her approach from two more extreme positions. On the one hand, she is distinguishing her position from more absolutist interpretations of veracity, such as that exemplified by Immanuel Kant, that do not allow for exception. On the other hand, she is also distinguishing her position from entirely utilitarian positions that give little or no prima facie weight to truth-telling. Each shall be considered briefly below.

Immanuel Kant

Immanuel Kant, as mentioned briefly in chapter 2, considers the duty not to lie to be a perfect duty. In Kant's view, one is always obliged to tell the truth—even if it means risking great harm. Kant argues that one would not even be justified in lying to a would-be murderer about the location of the intended victim in an attempt to prevent that murder. Part of his argument has to do with distinguishing between the respective responsibility of each moral agent—that the murderer is responsible for his/her own actions while the other individual is responsible for speaking the truth or telling a lie. The core of his argument, though, is that speaking falsely denies the very principles of autonomy and rationality that are central in his thinking about ethics. Indeed, Kant argues that to lie is to dehumanize oneself and all of humanity, and he categorizes the duty not to lie primarily as a duty that one has toward oneself as a moral being.[17]

Utilitarianism

For utilitarians, however, the morality of lying in any given instance is determined by appeal to the harm that can be avoided or the good that might be produced by lying or by telling the truth. Utilitarians advocate a single moral principle: utility. Jeremy Bentham, as an influential example, defines that principle with reference to promoting happiness as follows:

> By the principle of utility is meant that principle which approves or disapproves of every action whatsoever, according to the tendency which it appears to have to augment or diminish the happiness of the party whose interest is in question: or, what is the same thing in other words, to promote or to oppose that happiness.[18]

Utility is a broad understanding of happiness—encompassing "benefit, advantage, pleasure, good," and, conversely, preventing "mischief, pain, evil or unhappiness."[19] From this perspective, one is justified—indeed, one is morally required—to do whatever will maximize utility in a given situation for all involved. Utilitarianism is consequentialist: an action is justified by looking at its consequences—the harm or benefit that might result. Moreover, when considering a course of action, a utilitarian is concerned with maximizing utility for everyone—the greatest good for the greatest number. Some Christian interpretations have been very favorable to utilitarianism—notably that of theologian Joseph Fletcher, whose influential book *Situation Ethics* identifies the principle of utility with love.[20] Several observations can be made here about utilitarianism as moral theory.

First, even though popular language sometimes refers to "utilitarian" pejoratively, utilitarianism is actually an intellectually rigorous approach to ethics that sincerely attempts to promote the good and to minimize harm.

Second, it *only* seeks to promote the good and to minimize harm; this is the single principle of utility.

Third, benefit and harm tend to weigh against each other equally when one is determining the balance of utility; there is not the same priority given to nonmaleficence over beneficence as was advocated above in chapter two of this book.

Fourth, it is *consequentialist*: anticipated consequences are the only factor used in determining the morality of actions. In this perspective, not only do the ends justify the means, only the ends are ever able to justify the means.

Fifth, utilitarianism tends to be *situational*; that is, it tends to focus on particular actions being considered within specific contexts and with reference to the possible consequences from those actions. There are, however, exceptions to this last point about situationalism. Many utilitarians do argue that the consequences are best for society—that utility is maximized—when prima facie rules or policies can be established that do act as guides for moral action across similar situations.

It can be seen that utilitarianism and Kantian philosophy represent counterposing approaches to ethics on most of these points. For Kant, the ends can never justify the means. Far from being situational, according to Kant, ethics should always strive toward that which can be imagined as a universal maxim. Nevertheless, Sissela Bok incorporates both Kantian and utilitarian concerns in her treatment of veracity. With the utilitarians, she would interpret the ethics of lying with reference to the possible harm that might result as the consequences of lying. With Kant, though, she also wants to include a broader concern for the kinds of harm that occur to oneself as a moral being, or to the wider human society as a result of lying. Hence, like W. D. Ross, she argues for a moral presumption of veracity. She suggests as well that utilitarians might even agree with this presumptive principle of veracity since, as she argues, utility is normally served by telling the truth. Against Kant, though, she argues that lies can sometimes be justified. Her manner of reasoning, as outlined above, enumerates the ways in which the requirements and stringency of veracity might be weighed under particular circumstances.

■ CASE FOR DISCUSSION: The Cheese

Pastor Alfred was rector of a parish located in a depressed, post-industrial city. The average income in this city was actually less than the "fair cost of housing" there. He pastored there during a time of governmental budget cuts, curtailment of some governmental services, and the reduction of governmental assistance for people of low income. During his tenure, the church's food pantry had expanded to become a major charitable mission in the city, since it was becoming unfortunately common for many families to need supplemental food provided to them regularly.

One source of charitable food was government-subsidized USDA cheese. The mission was given a considerable amount of this cheese, but the mission was also responsible for keeping account of the cheese and reporting its distribution. Whenever a block of cheese was given to a family, the family was asked the reason for that family's "emergency" requiring food assistance. These reasons were then recorded on a form provided with each block of cheese for this purpose and returned to the government agency that was responsible for the program. The mission had been told that "ran out of food" or "chronic poverty" were not valid reasons to write on these forms. There had to be a specific emergency articulated. However, the mission's clients (some of whom spoke languages other than the English and Spanish used by the volunteer staff of the mission) often seemed baffled by the question that was being put to them. They wondered, out loud, what kind of "emergency" other than being hungry was required of them.

Pastor Alfred wandered into the mission one afternoon and discovered the staff's solution to this problem. They had made a pot of tea and were sitting pleasantly around the table together. The government forms for that month's cheese were in the center of the table, and each staff member had a small stack of them. They were each filling in the forms with random "emergencies" if that part of the form had been left incomplete at the time that the block of cheese had been distributed. The rest of the information on the forms seemed accurate, but many of the "emergencies" were being expanded upon or even fabricated as they sat together around the table.

Everyone was glad to see Pastor Alfred. "Have a cup of tea, Alf. Join us. Would you like a stack of forms?"

■ ■ QUESTIONS

  A. As a utilitarian, how do you analyze this case?
    1. What are the likely consequences from this activity?
    2. What harms and benefits do you see resulting from this activity?
    3. Harm to whom? Benefit to whom?
    4. How is utility maximized here? Do the harms outweigh the benefits, or do the benefits outweigh the harms?
    5. On the basis of utility, is deception justified here? Is it morally required? condemned?
    6. Are there differences between the moral agents in this case with regard to the realistic options before them? If so, is utility reckoned differently for their respective choices?
    7. How situationally are you reasoning?
      a. Is there a difference in consequences between lying on a single form and lying on a stack of forms?
      b. Is there a difference in consequences between deception for a single month and deception as the institution's regular *de facto* policy?
      c. Is there a difference in consequences between this particular mission's practice and the cumulative practice of all such missions?
  B. Given what you have read about Immanuel Kant both in this chapter and in chapter 2, how might a Kantian respond to your utilitarian analysis?
  C. Deepen your analysis using some of Sissela Bok's questions:

1. Is deception in this instance a last resort? Or are there truthful ways of achieving the same worthwhile ends? If so, what are they? (According to Bok, if a truthful alternative exists then it should be used.)

2. What are the rationales that might be employed in excusing this deception? What reasonable counter-arguments can you employ in response to these rationales? How convincing are these counter-arguments? How valid or empty do these rationales now appear?

3. What are the desired ends and the particular circumstances surrounding this practice of deception? Is the situation dire enough to justify dishonesty? Is there a harm at stake that is severe enough to warrant lying?

4. What are the possible harms from this deception that might result to the staff and rector? What are the possible harms that might result to the level of trust in the community–the church, the neighborhood, the country, humanity?

5. Will such deception expand to further levels and forms of dishonesty, or do you see this deception and its consequent damage as more of an isolated instance?

6. How legitimate is the claim of the government agency to normally have accurate information on these forms and an honest response to this particular question about the "emergency"?

7. Could your reasons for this deception survive the scrutiny of a "public of reasonable persons"? Would such an imagined public agree or disagree with your reasoning?

D. After thinking about this case from each of these three perspectives suggested above (utilitarian, Kantian, and Bok's presumptive method), which seems to have the easiest fit with your own manner of moral reasoning–the way you tend to think? Which of these methodological approaches seems to challenge your thinking the most? Which seems to offer the most realistic way of dealing with the ethics of veracity and deception–at least in this case? Do these ethical methods seem to contradict, compliment, or supplement each other?

Right to Truth?

Perhaps, in reflecting on the above case, some readers may have encountered a degree of complexity or confusion in addressing Sissela Bok's question about the rightful claim of someone (in this case, the government agency) to have the truth. It may feel like a disrespectful intrusion–even an invasion of privacy–to press someone about their "family emergency" when they are already humbling themselves by requesting charity for something as basic as the family's food. Nevertheless, the government would seem to be exercising some legitimate responsibility in ensuring that the cheese is actually given to those in need of it because of their hunger. If the cheese belongs to the government, then such possession might seem to entail a right to the information that is necessary for determining proper distribution.

At the same time, however, the staff members understand themselves to be prevented from telling the truth on these forms as they see it–the problem of chronic poverty exacerbated by the government's own policy. From this perspective on the question of the right to a truthful answer, honesty is actually being prohibited rather than requested. By requiring a particular type of explanation for hunger–that is, an "emergency"–hunger is presented as a series of unfortunate anomalies rather than a chronic condition shaped by public policy. Governmental assistance is thus presented in this manner as a beneficent act of kindness rather than a more stringent need for nonmaleficent removing of harm.

This may seem like a deception on the government's part, but would this putative deception justify the staff's additional deception? Perhaps so; perhaps not. On one hand, one might argue that the government has forfeited its claim to truth by requesting a *de facto* misrepresentation of the problem; on the other hand, to humor this request by falsifying information on the forms tends to reinforce that very misperception of poverty and to compound the deception.

Dietrich Bonhoeffer, a theologian in Nazi Germany, faced directly the challenge of being truthful at a time when absolute truthfulness posed a danger. The Nazi government was requiring conformity in every area of German life–including the church's life. Bonhoeffer and others established the Confessing Church, which declared against Nazi totalitarianism that "Jesus Christ…is the one Word of God which we have to hear and which we have to trust and obey in life and in death."[21] Bonhoeffer became increasingly involved politically in the German resistance. He became forbidden to lecture or to write, and eventually he was imprisoned and executed after his involvement with an unsuccessful plot to kill Hitler was discovered.[22]

Such resistance to totalitarianism required secrecy and even deception as well as boldness and proclamation. For Bonhoeffer, truth was to be sought in the actual relationships in which people live, and it was to be shaped by the circumstances surrounding those relationships. This is a broader concern than that of whether or not one's words are true. Bonhoeffer writes, "When the various orders of life no longer respect one another, words become untrue."[23] In a dangerous situation, Bonhoeffer recognized that not all requests for information carried the same kind of requirement for veracity. "Account must be taken of one's relationships at each particular time," Bonhoeffer wrote. "The question must be asked whether or in what way a man is entitled to demand truthful speech of others."[24]

It is this kind of situation that Sissela Bok has in mind when she asks about the rightful claim of people to hear the truth. She recognizes that Kant had denied the very idea of another's "right to truth"; for Kant, this phrase held no meaning since he understood veracity to be a duty primarily to oneself and to one's humanity.[25] Nevertheless, she cites Bonhoeffer on this matter, acknowledging that different individuals and groups make different kinds of claims on us for truthful speech. Bok writes about unjust or unwarranted requests for information as follows:

> In this category fall...all the illegitimate inquiries regarding political beliefs, sexual practices, or religious faith. In times of persecution, honest answers to such inquiries rob people of their freedom, their employment, respect in their communities. Refusing to give information that could blacklist a friend is then justified; and in cases where refusal is difficult or dangerous, lying may fall into the category of response to a crisis. One has a right to protect oneself and others from illegitimate inquiries, whether they come from intruders, from an oppressive government, or from an inquisitorial religious institution.[26]

Claims for information need to be realistically weighed if privacy and safety are to be protected. Nevertheless, according to Bok, a truthful alternative is preferable to a dishonest one if the same necessary ends can be achieved.

In conclusion, we have been discussing the principle of veracity primarily in its more stringent, negative form as a moral presumption against telling falsehood, that is, against lying or intentional deception. With Sissela Bok, we have affirmed this principle of veracity, and we have begun to examine those special conditions under which we might consider ourselves justified in overriding this principle. It has been recognized that veracity may not require total candor to all listeners at all times, but we have pondered when we might be justified to actually tell a lie rather than simply to remain silent.

We have not, however, entertained to the same degree the principle of veracity as entailing a positive obligation–that is, to speak the truth, to proclaim the truth, to name reality.[27] We now turn to questions pertaining to truthfulness as positive obligation.

5

Keeping Faith II

Veracity as Truth-telling

When are we obliged to speak or even shout the truth whether it is asked for or not—or indeed whether it is even welcome or not? The discussion previously about Dietrich Bonhoeffer points in this direction. It is not simply that the realities of social relationships occasionally justify the telling of falsehood; rather, it is these same realities that can determine the very meaning of veracity in context and which require us to live in a way that is true within these social relationships.

Truth-telling involves us in naming and renaming reality. This understanding of veracity becomes particularly important in situations of social oppression or abuse. In such situations, a difference in power results in a division between perspectives. The more powerful, whose voice is dominant, presume the privileged position of determining reality and of defining "truth" for both themselves and for the rest. To reclaim truth, the more marginalized or oppressed in society must find their own voice, name their reality, and give expression to alternative "truths." This liberationist understanding of truth-telling will be considered briefly here before returning to a consideration of the specific vocation of pastoral ministry and the task of clergy to proclaim a gospel of truth. Liberationist understandings of truth will be discussed here with reference to Latin American, African American, and feminist perspectives.

Truth as Naming

Latin American Liberation

Latin American theologian Rubem Alves used a parable to illustrate perspectival differences on truth due to economic class. At an ecumenical study conference on the subject of "Faith, Science and the Future," Alves noted that tigers and wolves, which are predators, have eyes in the front of their faces, whereas deer, which are preyed upon by tigers and wolves, have eyes on the sides of their heads. Tigers and other predators have binocular vision to see prey. Deer have eyes on the sides of their heads to be vigilant against predation. Alves explains:

> [O]ur sense of the future is determined by our social, econ-
> omic, and political situation. The powerful want to preserve
> their power. For them the future has to be the development
> and perpetuation of their domination. Tigers cannot imagine
> a world dominated by deer.
>
> The situation of the poor and oppressed is exactly the
> opposite. Their future must not be an improved form of the
> present.[1]

The powerful are interested in "truly" describing a world in which their power is secure. The poor are able to see the rich differently than the rich see themselves, and they are able to describe the world and their own oppression with a different truth as well. If you want to know about tigers and wolves, Alves suggested, ask the deer.[2]

This perspectival advantage of the oppressed to see the truth of their own oppression and their need for justice is often referred to as the epistemological privilege of the poor. It is not an automatic in-sight, however, since the perspectives of poor and rich alike are strongly influenced by the dominant perspectives of the rich. That dominant perspective works to define reality for all of society. The poor, though, by virtue of their different social location, have an alternative point of reference from which to begin to critique the dominant perspective.[3]

The well-known work of Paulo Freire on teaching adult literacy in Latin America was predicated on this insight from the sociology of knowledge. Freire chose images from the social world of the poor and then used these images in pedagogical exercises of naming, spelling, and reading. His students were able to see and name the contradictions represented in these images—to see and name the different perspectives of the dominant ideology, on one hand, and their own experience, on the other. This process of conscientization developed concurrently with the development of literacy, each pedagogical process reinforcing the other. This pedagogy was simul-taneously empowering the student as agent of her or his own learning and agent of her or his own history.[4]

African American Theology

Building on African American experience, James Cone applied a similar sociological critique of knowledge in his development of a Black theology of liberation. The first chapter of his book *God of the Oppressed* is titled "Speaking the Truth." The first section of that chapter highlights the importance of Black experience as a source of theology. Cone concludes that section by stating clearly, "to *speak* the truth we black theologians must set forth the authentic experience of blackness."[5] The following quote is instructive of Cone's own summary of his liberative understanding of truth:

> [T]ruth is not an intellectual datum that is entrusted to academic guilds. Truth cannot be separated from the people's struggle. Truth is that transcendent reality, disclosed in the people's historical struggle for liberation, which enables them to know that their fight for freedom is not futile. The affirmation of truth means that the freedom hoped for will be realized. Indeed, the freedom hoped for is already partly realized in our present history, because the realization of hope is the very ground of our present struggle. We do not struggle in despair but in hope, not with doubt but from faith, not out of hatred but out of love for ourselves and for humanity. And as black theologians, who have been grasped by the truth, we are accountable to black people.[6]

Truth therefore is both transcendent and historical, and it is inseparable from the actual struggle of Black people. To speak this truth is to relate it to African American experience across the generations. It is to relate the present struggle to the history of slavery and oppression, and it is to relate it as well to a more humane future.[7]

Reflecting on the moral agency of African American women, Katie Cannon also emphasizes the importance attending to the experience of the marginalized in society as an alternative to dominant perspectives on morality. Cannon finds that African American women have been struggling with two forms of oppression supported by the ideologies both of White supremacy and of male superiority. Their struggle is to "survive in two contradictory worlds simultaneously."[8] Given this twin oppression, Black women's choices have continually been constrained by inimical forces surrounding them.

Cannon attends to the life and works of Zora Neale Hurston as a source for her Black womanist ethics. She finds represented in Hurston's life and in her fictional characters examples of moral agency and virtue. Such agency is represented not only in their ability to survive but also in their capacities to interpret their own situations, to discern choices, to draw on resources for faith and moral action, and to act courageously and compassionately. This moral agency, however, is not trumpeted as the vanguard for the next historical eon; it is instead quietly lived and passed on to the next generation. Truth, in Cannon's treatment of Black women's moral agency, seems more discerned than heralded. Hence, Cannon names some of these womanist virtues as "quiet grace," "unshouted courage," and "invisible dignity."[9]

Feminist Analysis

Feminist theologies are particularly concerned with reclaiming truth by liberating thought from the patriarchal ideologies that have oppressed women and, indeed, all of nature.

Mary Daly, for instance, emphasizes the importance of freeing consciousness through reinterpretation and making new conceptual connections. This reinterpretation is based on women's lived and active experience and includes intuitive experience and ancestral "Memory." For this task, Daly constantly invents, or dis-covers, new words. Patriarchal society is alternately called the *sado*society, *phall*ocracy, and *boreo*cracy. There is a "deep correspondence" between the structures and processes of the mind and reality itself. The sadosociety denies this correspondence and attempts to prevent women from realizing it. The result is that all of nature is reduced to mere matter for use by the phallocracy, and women are mortally wounded on a deep, psychic level. The act of re-membering heals this breach, thereby allowing women to realize their "Elemental" potency.[10] This is not only a cognitive process, but it is energetically emotional. The new consciousness, which is alternative to the necrophilia of sadosociety, Daly terms, "biophilic consciousness."[11]

Similarly, Carolyn Merchant, through careful historical analysis, reveals complex ways in which values and paradigms have served and continue to serve the ends of exploitation and oppression of both women and nature. She hopes the discovery of this truth will be transformative. In *The Death of Nature,* Merchant shows how consciousness both arises from social influence and in turn shapes social institutions. She traces the development of a mechanistic understanding of nature as it develops simultaneously in competition with an alternative, organismic understanding of nature. At the same time, she shows that, because women are associated with nature, attitudes toward nature are reflected in society's treatment of women.

Conversely, attitudes toward women are reflected in society's treatment of nature.[12]

Merchant expresses hope that a recovery of the organismic metaphor may in some way contribute to contemporary restructuring of society. The means by which this may happen is interpretation. History interpreted from feminist and ecological perspectives reveals the biases and values that have led to the denigration of both women and nature. So interpreted, history provides ideas that may then strengthen the feminist and ecological perspectives and contribute to society's transformation.[13] For Carolyn Merchant, as for Mary Daly, truth thus dis-covered is transformative.

Feminist, womanist, and liberationist thought have all emphasized this ability—indeed this necessity—of people to reclaim truth in ways that free them from oppressive ideologies and from abusive categories of thought. This ability to deconstruct false conceptions and to reconstruct more liberating perspectives can be of key importance in pastoral care.

Naming in Pastoral Care

Domestic Violence

We have already seen, in chapter 2 on the subject of nonmaleficence, that naming violence honestly is crucial for finding safety in situations involving domestic violence. Such honest naming of violence is important for a survivor to free herself from any false sense of responsibility for the abuser's violence or any disabling sense of guilt for seeking her own safety. The first chapter in Carol Adam's manual on pastoral care in situations of battering is titled, "Naming." It is important for everyone involved in a situation of battering—including the minister—to name the abuse. The minister must clearly indicate an understanding of the violence in the situation, so that the survivor who is seeking the minister's help will be able to understand that she has been heard. Such honest naming of violence by the minister also helps the survivor and the abuser each to name it as violence, too. A minister or care-provider may need to work with each marriage partner separately for a survivor to find the words to name violence; otherwise the perspective of the batterer is likely to be dominant if the batterer is also present with the survivor during these times.

Carol Adams cites Paulo Freire, "To exist, humanly, is to *name* the world, to change it,"

The power of naming is the power of self-authorization. Ministers must offer both victims and abusers this power because each may minimize the violence, reinterpret what occurred, excuse the battering behavior. She must name her world–including his battering behavior–so that she can be safe; he must name his world–including his battering behavior–as the first step in stopping it.[14]

The minister or care-provider assists in the transition from oppressive silence to naming as an "invitation to healing and liberation."[15] Honest naming is thus a requisite part of addressing the problem of abuse–for the survivor to ensure her own safety, for the abuser to begin to change, and for the pastor to minister effectively to them.[16]

Narrative Techniques

Processes of honest naming and reframing are important in other areas of pastoral care as well. Christie Neuger advocates the use of narrative techniques in pastoral care and, for those properly trained, in pastoral counseling. These techniques help a person to remember or reconstitute stories that may have been lost or denied due to the influences of the dominant discourses of a person's culture, family, etc. In telling the story, a person is able to begin to name the experience as well as to begin to find resources within this story for reframing it or deconstructing it in a liberative way.

Informing Neuger's approach to narrative care is a feminist and postmodern appreciation of epistemology, "that there are multiple and multifaceted angles on truth rather than a single organizing one."[17] Truths are understood to be socially constructed and complicit with the power structures of society. They can be "deconstructed" to reveal these connections with social power and to make possible the construction of alternative, more liberating truths. Narrative pastoral care empowers a person to do this with her or his own narratives and, in so doing, to become more empowered as an agent of her or his own well-being.

Addiction

Twelve-step programs for dealing with addiction also depend on a person being able to truthfully name his or her own reality. These programs begin with Step 1: to admit that one is powerless over the addiction and that one's life has become unmanageable. Such an admission is necessary to begin to disengage from one's self-deception and to start to address truthfully and productively one's addiction. Honesty continues to be a part of a Twelve-step process as a person admits to God, to oneself, and to others the exact nature of one's wrongs (Step 5), as the person seeks God's rectification of these shortcomings (Steps 6 and 7), and as the person seeks to make amends to those whom he or she has harmed (Steps 8 and 9).

In considering all the above examples of truthfulness in context— Bonhoeffer writing in Nazi Germany, Latin American conscientization and need for liberation, Cone and Cannon analyzing African American realities and racism in the U.S., Daly and Merchant as well as Cannon and Neuger freeing thought from the control of patriarchy, pastoral care in situations of domestic abuse, and even the struggle of addicts against the power of their own addiction—a difference in power is a salient part of the situation. Limits in power constrain choice—or at least shape choice in different ways than may be experienced by society's more powerful. Vulnerability makes some choices dangerous or even impossible; it may make other choices possible.

The morality of speaking and acting truthfully is thus also shaped by structures of power in society. Truthfulness in these situations serves a goal of liberation, but such truthfulness may also be dangerous and require prudence or caution in its expression. A difference in power characterizes social relationships. It is within the context of such power differential that we are challenged to broaden our understanding of veracity. We are challenged to move from "not lying" and from silence to a more positive stance of speaking and acting truly. This positive view of veracity should be broad enough to embrace concerns for nonmaleficence, liberation, and justice.

Pastoral Power and Practice

For pastors, though, a word of caution is relevant here. Typically, pastors have considerable power within their congregations, but at the same time they may feel paradoxically vulnerable. This is due, in part, to real ambiguities and balances of power within any given congregational context. Pastors occupy an important and powerful office, but their employment is contingent on both congregational pleasure and denominational structures. Pastors wield considerable interpersonal influence in a congregation, but the pastor may always feel like a marginal newcomer in the midst of families who have their own histories with each other—who may have been "pillars of the church" through generations prior to the pastor's arrival.[18]

Pastors do well, though, not to act out of their own sense of vulnerability—especially with regard to matters of veracity and deception. The harm from a pastor's lies can be great to both sides: first, to congregants who may fall victim to the minister's deception as an abuse of pastoral power, and second, to the minister who may never again recover a sense of trust within the congregation.[19] If a minister is feeling vulnerable within his or her congregation to the point of thinking himself/herself excused in a deception, that minister ought to consult with someone who can function as a professional supervisor or "coach" for the minister. Such a supervisor can help the minister to keep his or own subjective sense of fear in proportion to the actual level of threat. A professional supervisor can also assist the minister in realistically weighing the various options for addressing the problem in question.

At least three reasons might make a minister feel vulnerable and think himself/herself excused in a lie.

First, the minister might be experiencing a heightened emotional reaction to his or her own sense of insecurity—perhaps triggered by someone in, or by some aspect of, the congregation. A supervisor can help the minister to gain perspective on this situation, to reestablish boundaries, or to seek further assistance from a counselor or therapist.

Second, the minister might feel vulnerable because he or she may actually be engaged in criminal or scurrilous activity (sexual abuse, financial embezzlement, etc.), or the minister might want to protect someone else involved in these activities. In these cases, the supervisor can assist the minister in clarifying the minister's own legal and moral duties; the minister might also be further referred to a lawyer or to law enforcement officials.

Third, a minister might feel forced to deceive to protect a relatively legitimate area of privacy in his or her own life. This is the kind of protection from "illegitimate inquiries" discussed by Sissela Bok in the quotation above regarding limits to the duty of truth-telling. In these situations, the minister is challenged to find a proportionate response that maximizes both veracity, on one hand, and privacy or safety, on the other. The United Methodist Church, for example, has a policy against the ordination of "self-avowed practicing homosexuals."[20] Regardless of one's moral reasoning about sexual orientation, it is ethically problematic that a church would so explicitly (even coercively) encourage deception by those whom it has also called to be moral leaders in the congregation and community. Other churches have similar policies that may challenge a pastor to juggle privacy, safety, and veracity in his or her relationships. Again, a trustworthy supervisor or trusted conversation-partner might assist a pastor in making the kind of discernment required in these situations.

To summarize our reasoning about truthfulness up to this point, veracity has been affirmed as a prima facie moral principle. At its most basic, veracity is the idea that people are morally obliged to speak the truth and that lying and deception require justification under special circumstances. We noticed further, however, that the meaning and specific requirements of veracity can be influenced considerably by situational circumstances and especially by the structuring of power within society. The dynamics of power and vulnerability in society, we have seen, shape both moral agency in general and the duty of veracity in particular.

Cultural Meaning

Power inequality, however, is not the only social variable determining the meaning of veracity within a particular cultural context. Sissela Bok has noticed religious and cultural variability with regard to the ethics of veracity. She notes, for instance, a particular Jewish tradition that seeks to "preserve the peace of the household," even if at the occasional expense of strict veracity, although "Jewish texts regard lying as prohibited."[21] She also notices that in early, pre-literate oral culture (in particular, pre-Socratic Greek culture), the stories, songs, and genealogies were memorized and repeated–thus giving them truth:

> In this early tradition, repeating the songs meant keeping the material alive and thus "true," just as creating works of art could be thought of as making an object true, bringing it to life.[22]

An oral culture's "truth" as told in this way can be different than the kind of correspondence theory of truth typical of literate cultures. Western science, in particular, has developed to a high level techniques of verification, validation, and reliability for testing the correspondence between "objective" reality and stated words and theories.

My experience in cultures with a lively oral tradition, however, has impressed on me that "truth" is still understood in some places and by some people as a function of the community's narrative, the culture's living tradition, and the people's memory. In Fiji, for instance, "truth" (*dina*) is very much celebrated. Throughout the Fijian islands (and throughout the neighboring Tongan islands as well), communities celebrate their relatedness through a ritual involving the ceremonial drinking of a native beverage (called *yaqona* or *kava*). One of the forms of ceremonial blessing used at these times employs a call and response; the celebrant shouts, "*Mana!*" (meaning "power"), and the people respond, "*Dina!*" (meaning "in truth").

In a Fijian welcome ceremony, and also in a farewell, the blessing and imbibing would have been preceded by speech-making and perhaps storytelling. The stories affirmed are those that underscore the relatedness between the people gathered–their sense of well-being together as a community inclusive even of the visitors present. Moreover, Fijian villages have an officer in charge of protocol (various individuals may actually serve this role at times), named the *matanivanua*, literally "face of the land."[23] It is this person's responsibility to speak on behalf of visitors during the ceremony and also to present the welcoming face of the land to the newcomers. The *matanivanua* makes sure that the right things are said to establish well-being in the community. Truth here is a function of community and serves a community-building and community-affirming role. One is not under pressure in this situation to lie, but rather to choose the truth to speak that will unite the community. Indeed, withholding of information can be most disruptive to community; as a visitor, one needs to identify oneself fully so that the community is allowed by this knowledge to extend welcome and honor appropriately.

This storied and interpersonal concept of truth also applies to religious life in Fiji. Christian religion there is sometimes termed "true religion" (*lotu dina*), and the title for a Christian minister is "storyteller" (*talatala*). Story, truth, and relatedness in community are all part of the same parcel. Perhaps to some degree this is the case for religious leadership in Western society as well. In addition to speaking truly, veracity can also be a matter of living true in relationship with one another and of being true in relationship to the story of our faith. This kind of truthfulness as integrity within community is particularly relevant to the task of being a pastor. We turn now to the matter of pastoral veracity in greater detail.

Wiest and Smith

Pastoring Truly

For Walter E. Wiest and Elwyn A. Smith, veracity provides both a beginning point and a central emphasis for the professional ethics of clergy. After comparing Kantian absolutism and Bonhoeffer's contextualism, Wiest and Smith affirm a strong moral presumption (though not an absolute principle) for veracity.[24] Their argument moves, however, from a negative presumption against lying to a more positive construction of the implications for truthful pastoring:

> Truth–which includes both truthfulness and being true–is the key both to ministry and the ethics of ministry. Ministers of the gospel have something to be true to. We have a message to proclaim that is given to us, we do not make it up ourselves, and we are to witness to that truth faithfully and with integrity. This is a moral commitment.[25]

They discuss the implications of veracity for pastoral ministry in several areas: preaching and teaching, letters of reference, theological differences, pastoral confidentiality, personal integrity, professional competence, church administration, public witness, and the pastor's vocation.

Veracity is key for pastoral ethics, according to Wiest and Smith, but they do not argue for total and frank honesty at all times. They recognize that discretion requires that to respect the feelings of others the clergy must refrain from always speaking the candid truth. They hold discretion and candidness in tension:

> Discretion is essential to protect privacy—but at an extreme
> it can become secretiveness. Candidness affirms openness
> but unaccompanied by discretion can become offensive.[26]

Nevertheless, they identify aspects of pastoral work that require a greater degree of honesty on the part of clergy than is often practiced. In this, Wiest and Smith move beyond a negative presumption against lying to a positive regard for truthful ministry. In some situations, silence itself can be deceptive. In this vein, Wiest and Smith discuss plagiarism, letters of reference, and theological honesty.

Honest Worship

Wiest and Smith are especially critical of dishonesty in sermons. This can take the form of fabricating stories as sermon illustrations— telling as true an entirely fictitious account. The authors are most critical, however, of preachers who claim, as their own work, that actually done by others. Some preachers use other people's stories, but tell them in the first person as if it is from the speaker's own experience. Many preachers borrow from the writings or sermons of others but fail to ascribe credit to those original authors. This all amounts to plagiarism.[27]

As with Wiest and Smith, I, too, have witnessed rather obvious examples of plagiarism by preachers. I have heard preachers reading directly from a commentary that I recognize—indeed for most of the sermon—without identifying the commentary. I have heard different preachers preach the same sermon—each as if it were original. I have also attended church and found my own prayers and litanies printed without ascription in the Sunday bulletin.

Preachers often simply borrow ideas from others, but sometimes preachers actually read verbatim from others' writings. In either case, ascription of credit to the original source is proper. Such ascription is due whether the original source was a printed text, a spoken sermon, or a Web page. Credit can be given by writing the sources in the Sunday bulletin, by simply stating the sources in the sermon itself, or by mentioning them at another point in the worship service. Parishioners are often interested to hear of the preacher's sources and may want to read these materials themselves. Preachers can nurture this interest by leading study groups that include these materials for parishioners' own reflection.

Honest Qualifications

Clergy are often asked for letters of reference. In writing such a letter, one does not want to unduly prejudice an employer against a parishioner with unnecessary frankness. Nevertheless, the situation calls for honesty in writing the letter concerning the candidate's strengths and weaknesses. Wiest and Smith write, "In any situation, veracity—simply telling the truth honestly and candidly—has the first claim...Exceptions to veracity demand justification, not the other way around."[28] At the same time, a pastor is obligated to one's parishioner as well as to the prospective employer, school, or court requiring a letter of reference. Truth is served by being honest with one's parishioner when the pastor feels uncomfortable with that parishioner's request for a letter of recommendation.

Clergy need to be honest about their own professional competencies and credentials as well. Not only do they need to represent themselves honestly with regard to their competencies for ministry, they also need to be true to the standards of the profession and to truly develop those professional competencies that are expected of the clergy. As I mentioned in the previous chapter on informed consent, such honesty about one's competency in pastoral care is crucial for rendering just care that is in keeping with a person's voluntary consent. Wiest and Smith discuss other areas of ministry as well, such as church administration and the church's public witness, but of paramount importance to Wiest and Smith is the pastor's theological competence and theological honesty.[29]

Theological Integrity in Organizational Leadership

Theological honesty pertains to every aspect of the pastor's work. In church administration, Wiest and Smith advocate honesty and openness in fund-raising and in decision-making. They caution against emotionally manipulative means of raising funds. Instead, they urge honest, straightforward appeals that are consistent with the church's need and are theologically sound. They call for "honest appeals to faith and faith's willingness to deal with the worldly needs of the church without embarrassment."[30] In addition, they suggest that congregations establish clear policies regarding donations if they believe that certain sources of funds might be too inconsistent with the congregation's sense of mission and its understanding of the gospel.

In similar fashion, Wiest and Smith urge honesty in deliberations and caution against manipulation with regard to decision-making in the church:

> An ethical politics of church life is grounded in an honest search for the divine will in group life, full respect for the presence of God's spirit in each believer, and refusal of manipulation of all sorts, including the manipulation of parliamentary order.[31]

They advocate an "openness" in seeking aid and insight from one another to enrich both the work and the worship of the community.[32]

Conversely, Wiest and Smith suggest that constructive church politics can become obstructed by a "failure of trust" that results from "misunderstanding and fear of power." They lament situations in which church officials might abuse power for their own ends. As a corrective, they articulate a theology of stewardship of power and authority—as well as a stewardship of material wealth. Both power and wealth are aspects of God's creation, they affirm, and are intended by God to be employed in mission and service.[33]

Speaking Truth to Power

This theological understanding of rightful power as stewardship extends to the church's work in the world, which should be marked by honesty, much as the church's own internal politics should be marked by openness. "One of the gifts of God is authority," they write—whether that of the church or that of the state. One of the duties of the church and its ministers is to hold the state as well as the church accountable to responsible use of this authority and to the divinely established limits on its use.[34] "The most effective and honest way for the church to affect a whole society," write Wiest and Smith, "is to speak its convictions plainly."[35] To do so well, though, requires that clergy be aware of how the church as an institution intersects with other structures of power within society. They write the following:

> A responsible relationship to established power involves an understanding of how the society functions, where its centers of power lie, and above all a very clear grasp of one's own calling and professional commitments.[36]

Wiest and Smith thus return to one of their central affirmations regarding veracity and pastoral ethics: vocational fidelity for the clergy involves theological honesty. This, as we shall see, is an affirmation shared by other writers as well.

Truthful Teaching

Wiest and Smith emphasize truthfulness as requiring of the clergy both theological competence and theological integrity. It is a fundamental matter of professional ethics, they argue, for a person to demonstrate competence in the skills of the profession–to honestly possess that level of skill that is promised to others when one identifies with the profession. For clergy, this pertains to the disciplines of theological study and reflection as much as it does to the more practical arts of exercising ministry. This is not an elitist function, they insist, but rather clergy bringing their theological skills to work within a congregation as a community of people who are all seeking to live a life of faith and to reflect theologically on that life together. The pastor, as a teacher with specialized theological training, contributes this knowledge to the entire community to equip and enrich the congregation's own theological reflection as well as its ministry of Word and Sacrament.[37]

The fact that theological teaching and preaching occur within a congregational community, however, underscores the need for truthful communication and trust between the clergy and the congregation, as together they are engaged in this theological enterprise. Theological integrity entails at least three dimensions of fidelity:

1. fidelity to the gospel one is called to preach
2. honesty with oneself with regard to theological and vocational discernment
3. honesty with others regarding theological differences and diversity

All three of these dimensions, I would affirm, have to do with one's faithfulness to God as a person called to religious leadership in community.

Wiest and Smith consider the gospel itself to be the "proper center" for Christian ministry. One of the reasons that truthfulness is such an important principle for them in their conception of pastoral ethics is that they identify this gospel with truth. "The message we proclaim," they announce, "is itself the truth we receive in faith by the grace of God." Any authority held by the clergy, they insist, is actually Christ's authority, entrusted to the church, and "conveyed by the gospel." Pastors must therefore be "true to the gospel" in their work of preaching and teaching. It is paramount that pastors also be honest about their own faith as "the first requirement of clerical ministry."[38]

Nevertheless, theological diversity is a fact of life not only in the larger ecumenical church but also in any typical congregation. A pastor is challenged to minister truthfully while recognizing that it is frequently impossible to do so in doctrinal agreement with every single member of a diverse congregation. Often, though, the tension that is felt may be due to theological differences between the congregation as a whole and the pastor. Some degree of difference is to be expected, however, given the different types of education and life situations that pastors and their parishioners have experienced.

As mentioned previously, it is the pastor's responsibility to use his or her professional education to stimulate faithful theological reflection within the congregation as a whole. One would hope that this would include a lively theological discussion between lay members themselves, as well as between the laity and the clergy. Still, clergy are faced with decisions concerning the level of candor with which they should express their theological differences with the congregation. Wiest and Smith are wary of pastors who can be arrogantly and self-righteously honest without regard for the hurt or angry responses that their honesty elicits. While the proper degree of candor may vary with circumstances, a concern for veracity should continue to guide a pastor's communications. Moreover, the pastor should patiently speak in a way that fosters relationships of "love and trust," so that a congregational environment can be created over time in which total truthfulness better flourishes.[39]

Vocational Honesty

There are times when honest self-assessment and vocational discernment may incline a minister to think seriously about accepting a call to a different congregation or even a move to a different denomination. One factor to figure into this process of discernment might be the degree of theological differences the pastor experiences with the congregation. Theological differences might induce a pastor to think of making these kinds of changes in order to be with a congregation that would be more consonant with that pastor's own theological beliefs. This, too, becomes a matter of integrity when a pastor realizes that there may be too great a theological disparity between himself or herself and the congregation to allow effective and constructive ministry to occur.

This is a matter of spiritual discernment. It can be approached not only in private prayer but also in conversation. An honest assessment of theological difference would involve the pastor in conversation with trusted others in the congregation to discern together whether or not the theological disparity is so significant as to justify a change in pastorates. Otherwise, the pastor may be acting out of fear and silence rather than faith and honesty.

Finally, theological integrity and honest vocational discernment may even incline a pastor to think of leaving pastoral ministry and to pursue a different occupation or a different form of service altogether. Again, pastors would do well to bring this kind of vocational questioning into honest conversations with others to discern the Spirit's call together. Methodists are aware of the story of John Wesley struggling with his own faith after having experienced a disappointing ministry in America. Aware of his own lack of faith, Wesley sincerely wondered if he should cease preaching. He brought his question to Peter Böhler of the Moravian Brethren for help with discernment. "Preach faith *till* you have it," Böhler advised, "and then, *because* you have it, you *will* preach faith."[40]

During times of deep doubt, we find it difficult to know with clarity whether we are preaching hypocritically because of our own lack of faith, or if we are preaching faithfully because we persevere in trust. Conversation with spiritual guides, counselors, mentors, supervisors, coaches, or colleagues can help us make this discernment faithfully. A minister might consult one of his or her parishioners. In doing so, it is important to continue to respect the pastor-parishioner relationship, so as not to unduly burden the parishioner at a time when the parishioner is in need of pastoral care from the minister.

A minister visited my office recently with a quandary and a question. After several years in ministry and an untold number of visits to the sick, this minister had become convinced that God does not heal—or at least that God does not answer prayers for health with healing. He was currently seeing an ill parishioner who wanted prayer for healing, but this minister was unsure of what to do or say, given his own belief that God would not grant the petition. "What should I do?" he asked me.

"Well," I asked in turn, "Whose prayer is it?"

For this minister, truthfulness was a matter of personal integrity. He wanted to act in a manner consistent with his convictions, and he wanted to speak in a manner consistent with his beliefs. For him, speaking truly was primarily a matter of personal integrity—of being true to himself. Faithfulness to God was also involved in his thinking about truthfulness, but this was complicated by his suspicion that God might be more fickle than faithful; nevertheless, it was clear that this minister sincerely did not want to misrepresent God's promises.

My question surprised him, though, because he had not been thinking about what it means to give truthful speech to someone else's prayer.

In addition to this minister's own personal and theological integrity, there is also a trust and an expectation established between him and the person requesting prayer. To give true voice to this prayer, the minister must express the petition and the concern of the parishioner–not just his own thoughts, his doubts, and his beliefs. Pastoral care in this situation calls for a priestly ministry as well as a prophetic one. It may not be enough, in a case such as this, to think of theological consistency as the sole guide for pastoral practice. The pastor–like a priest–is in a representative role here. The pastor is called on to represent the parishioner's prayer to God and, conversely, to let this prayer be a means of God's grace to the parishioner in whatever manner God's spirit would determine. To act truly here, the minister must keep faith with the parishioner's trust.

In her books *Dakota*[41] and *Amazing Grace*, Kathleen Norris describes her own experience in moving from her home in New York City to her grandmother's ranch in Dakota after having inherited it. Norris describes this experience as a spiritual pilgrimage in which she learns to embrace, or to be embraced by, wider realities. These include her grandmother's spiritual heritage as well as the physical inheritance, the land itself in its emptiness and richness, the wider landscape of her own faith and doubts, and a church that includes and extends beyond the prairies. As a metaphor for her own experience, she tells the story of a theological student questioning an Orthodox theologian:

> "What can one do," he asked, "when one finds it impossible to affirm certain tenets of the Creed?"
>
> The priest responded, "Well, you just say it. It's not hard to master. With a little effort, most can learn it by heart."
>
> ...the student, apparently feeling that he had been misunderstood, asked with some exasperation, "What am I to do...when I have difficulty affirming parts of the Creed–like the Virgin Birth?"
>
> And he got the same response. "You just say it. Particularly when you have difficulty believing it. You just keep saying it. It will come to you eventually."
>
> The student raised his voice: "How can I with integrity affirm a creed in which I do not believe?"
>
> And the priest replied, "It's not your creed, it's our creed," meaning the Creed of the entire Christian church.[42]

Kathleen Norris was learning to accept her own doubts within the framework of a larger community of faith. Her lesson can be generalized. The creed is more than a personal affirmation. It is the confession of a wide community over centuries of time and across many cultures.[43] To "believe in God…" is more than a personal affirmation; it is to locate oneself within this tradition and within this cloud of witnesses. It is to place oneself into relationship with others who have also struggled with belief. It is to both trust them and to place ourselves accountable to them. We can confess our faith honestly with this creed in the first person plural, "we believe," perhaps more so than with the narrower first person singular as if it were an entirely personal matter.[44]

Wiest and Smith point out that all pastors go through periods of theological wrestling at a deep existential level, as well as at a cognitive intellectual one. This, too, is a part of life in the Spirit and of the development of one's faith over time. It is experiences such as these that allow a pastor to relate empathetically with parishioners who also experience these crises of faith. "Honesty provides for–indeed, requires," Wiest and Smith reassure us, "some wrestling over items of belief."[45] Nevertheless, when one becomes convinced that one can no longer honestly serve this role with integrity, then one might need to find another mode of service and another occupation. I am urging, though, that such vocational decisions should be made in consultation with others. Moreover, I would add, with caution, that such drastic decisions should not be made during times when one's perception of one's own situation is distorted because of suffering from depression. An alternative is to take a sabbatical leave or time off. A sabbatical can give a person a needed chance to rest and renew, and time to reflect on one's call to ministry.

In his book *Surviving Ministry*, Ron Sisk suggests several reasons that a person might want to leave the ministerial occupation. Sisk agrees with Wiest and Smith that ministers who no longer hold the core beliefs of their church are obliged by truthfulness to consider a change of career. Additionally, Sisk suggests, a minister may have simply reached a different assessment of his or her gifts and graces for ministry; a person might honestly notice that he or she is more gifted for a different kind of service or a different kind of job. In some instances, Sisk adds, a minister might want to acknowledge success–the completion of a job well done–and take the opportunity to move on as God's call is being discerned. Also it may be the case, according to Sisk, that the church might narrow its parameters so that a conscientious pastor feels uncomfortably squeezed. In his experience as a Southern Baptist, he finds that many of his colleagues have left the ministry because of a perception of the "narrowing of acceptable theological parameters for ministers."[46] This experience has parallels in other denominations as well.

Because of his strong affirmation of the church as priesthood of believers, however, Sisk reassures his readers that one can feel free to move between various careers and occupations without ever forsaking the church or Christ's service. For Sisk, occupational decisions are a matter of personal integrity:

> Movement back and forth between vocational and non-vocational service becomes a function of circumstance, opportunity, and the immediate leadership of the Spirit in the individual Christian life.[47]

Citing the doctrine of the priesthood of all believers, Sisk insists that "no Christian ever leaves the ministry," regardless of the different career moves one makes and whether or not one is employed by the church.[48]

Examination of Veracity

This chapter and the previous chapter have discussed veracity as it relates to faithfulness. Truthfulness has been examined not only as a matter of personal integrity but also as a need to be both true to God and honest with others. As a principle of professional ethics, veracity is also seen to entail a matter of faithfulness to the implicitly promised standards of the profession.

The previous chapter affirmed with Sissela Bok a moral presumption against telling lies. Several variables were discussed as criteria for determining the stringency of that principle of veracity in varying circumstances. One of these variables had to do with the ways in which culture and social structures—especially differences in power—may shape the meaning and requirements of veracity within different relationships and different circumstances. We noticed, though, that clergy do well to be suspicious of their own subjective sense of vulnerability, lest they underestimate (and abuse) their power and unjustifiably excuse their falsehood.

In this chapter, we have moved from a negative moral presumption against lying to a more positive regard for truth as a value and for honesty as a virtue. We have explored this positive regard for veracity with particular reference to pastoral ministry. In the work of Wiest and Smith we noticed that truthfulness is relevant to several dimensions of pastoral ministry: preaching and teaching, letters of reference, church administration, public witness, professional skill, theological integrity, and vocational honesty.

Wiest and Smith also discuss a tension that can be experienced by clergy between strict veracity and maintaining confidentiality. In the next chapter, confidentiality will be examined in greater detail, including its relationship with veracity. Both veracity and confidentiality, it will be seen, are matters of fidelity and related to the promises we make to God and to each other.

■ ■ QUESTIONS: More Cheese

A. Return to the set of questions labeled "C" in the example of the USDA Cheese given in the last chapter, especially question 6: "How legitimate is the claim of the government agency to normally have accurate information on these forms and an honest response to this particular question about the 'emergency'?" After thinking further about power structures in society, are you now inclined to answer this question any differently?

B. Walter E. Wiest and Elwyn A. Smith have strongly emphasized the importance of "truthfulness to the gospel" for clergy ethics. How is the gospel present or absent in the case about the mission's distribution of cheese? Does Christ seem incarnate or distant in this situation? How is the gospel proclaimed or hidden in this scenario? How might you describe the implicit theology in the mission? How would you begin to write a "theology of cheese" for this mission? Where do you find truthfulness here as well as deception? Are you noticing theological consistency or contradiction? Is such theological consistency or contradiction morally important? If you were Alfred, what might you do that would minister truly in this situation?

6

Confidentiality in Care[1]

"[W]hatever you bind on earth shall be bound in heaven, and whatever you loose on earth shall be loosed in heaven."

MATTHEW 16:19B, 18:18

"Nothing is covered up that will not be revealed, or hidden that will not be known. Therefore whatever you have said in the dark shall be heard in the light, and what you have whispered in private rooms shall be proclaimed upon the housetops.

LUKE 12:2–3

Introduction

A duty of pastoral confidentiality is commonly held by many—clergy and laity alike—to be generally applicable in pastoral relationships and nearly absolute in its moral stringency. This chapter affirms the importance of maintaining confidences in pastoral ministry, but it argues against the elevation of confidentiality as an absolute principle in all pastoral contexts. Instead, three criteria are suggested that can be used to clarify the stringency of confidentiality in particular circumstances. These three criteria are concerned with the "nature of the promise," "ownership," and "vulnerability." Moreover, regardless of the degree of stringency for confidentiality in any situation, this chapter emphasizes that both the keeping of secrets and the sharing of secrets should be done within a context of care—against a backdrop of nonmaleficence.

Definitions

Confidentiality is related to, but distinguishable from, two other concepts: privacy and privilege. Confidentiality occupies a middle area between a rather broad understanding of "privacy" and a narrower legal understanding of "privilege."

Privacy "refers to an individual's right to be left alone and to decide the time, place, manner and extent of sharing oneself…with others."[2] It has been argued that privacy is "an essential component of individuality and selfhood,"[3] and that such selfhood depends on the protection of a person's choices concerning the sharing of information about oneself. A duty to respect confidentiality can be seen as based at least in part on this right to privacy.

Privilege, on the other hand, is specifically the "legal protection against being forced to break a promise or expectation of confidentiality in legal proceedings."[4] It is "an immunity granted to certain people and professionals that exempts them from testifying in court."[5] Legal privilege refers specifically to protection from disclosure in legal proceedings. It is the legal sanctioning and protecting of professional confidences in court. Such legal privilege is established by statute and varies from one state to another. These statutes specify the kinds of professional contexts in which information becomes privileged and the kinds of professions that qualify.

All of the states in the U.S.A. have statutory law protecting legal privilege for clergy, though these statutes vary from one another. In most states, the confessant, rather than the member of the clergy, actually controls the right of privilege. Ronald K. Bullis and Cynthia Mazur note that this is consistent with an understanding of the purpose of privilege being to protect a person's privacy when such a person has confided to a member of the clergy. If, however, the purpose of privilege is seen to be to protect a duty of silence on behalf of the clergy, then the clergy are empowered to invoke or to waive privilege.[6] It is important, though, for members of the clergy to remember that their legal privilege of silence and their moral duty of confidentiality are both related to the dignity and rights of those who have confided in them.[7]

Sissela Bok defines confidentiality and distinguishes it from legal privilege as we have been discussing it, and from privacy (which it can be seen to protect). "Confidentiality," she writes, "refers to the boundaries surrounding shared secrets and to the process of guarding these boundaries."[8] "The principle of confidentiality," she continues, "postulates a duty to protect confidences against third parties under certain circumstances."[9] She raises the question, though, of why we should find such a principle of confidentiality to be morally binding.

Sissela Bok

Sissela Bok provides a philosophical framework for considering duties of confidentiality. She begins with a neutral assessment of the morality of keeping secrets. On the face of it, to have secrets or to share secrets is neither morally good nor bad. She contrasts this moral neutrality of keeping secrets to the negative moral presumption that she attaches to the act of lying or telling falsehoods. A moral difference exists between secrecy and lying, according to Bok. Lying is always prima facie wrong, so that any lie requires justification.[10] In her book, *Lying,* she describes this negative presumption against lying as a basic premise:

> [W]e must at the very least accept as an initial premise...that lying is "mean and culpable" and that truthful statements are preferable to lies in the absence of special considerations. This premise gives an initial negative weight to lies. It holds that they are not neutral...that lying requires explanation...[11]

Stated more positively, she affirms a moral presumption in favor of truthfulness and a principle of veracity. She emphasises the importance of "trust in veracity" not simply as a basic premise for moral argument but as a foundation for society and human relatedness.[12]

Keeping Secrets

Such a moral presumption is lacking, according to Sissela Bok, with regard to the keeping of secrets. Nevertheless, secrecy has potential for both harm and benefit. Secrecy can help people to guard private aspects of their lives from the unwanted intrusion of others. Secrecy can also debilitate judgment and encourage corruption. "Secrecy may prevent harm," writes Bok, "but it follows maleficence like a shadow."[13]

Secrecy is a form of power–the controlling of information and the way one is perceived by others. Bok suggests two moral presumptions to aid in evaluating secrecy: (1) equality and (2) personal control over one's own information. Concerning equality, she writes: "Whatever control over secrecy and openness we conclude is legitimate for some individuals should, in the absence of special considerations, be legitimate for all."[14] The second presumption is for the partial (though not absolute) control by individuals over their own personal or private matters. Individuals are thus empowered with regard to information concerning their own affairs.

Four Premises of Confidentiality

The idea of confidentiality, also, serves to protect the power that individuals might exercise concerning information about themselves. Bok's argument for a presumption to maintain confidence is based on four premises.

The first premise is an affirmation or respect for human autonomy concerning personal information.

The second premise gives respect to those relationships that allow for the sharing of secrets and recognizes the legitimacy of having personal secrets in the first place.

The third premise is related to promise-keeping; it is that a pledge of silence creates an obligation to keep silence.

The fourth premise, concerning professional confidentiality in particular, refers to the utility of such professional confidentiality within society: "the benefits of confidentiality to those in need of advice, sanctuary, and aid, and in turn to society."[15] Society as a whole benefits when its members feel protected in confiding in professionals.

In Bok's argument supporting a presumption for confidentiality, three qualities of confidential relationships appear particularly salient for a discussion about pastoral confidentiality in particular.

The first of these is the obligatory nature of a promise that establishes an expectation of confidentiality.

The second is the importance of confidentiality for protecting elements of a person's privacy; people deserve ownership or control over some kinds of information concerning themselves.

The third is the element of power—that secrecy and confidentiality have to do with an exercise of power over one's own affairs or over others.

The remainder of this chapter evaluates the ethics of pastoral confidentiality with reference to these three dimensions of confidential relationships: promises of confidentiality, ownership of information, and protection of power. Attention will be paid to the contexts in which clergy converse with others: casual conversation as well as counseling situations and sacramental confession. A prima facie duty to maintain confidence will be seen to both strengthen and weaken in relation to each of these variables: promise, ownership, and power.

Promise-keeping in Pastoral Practice

Confidentiality has been defined as a "quality of private information that is divulged with the implicit or explicit promise and the reasonable expectation that it will not be further disclosed except for the purpose for which it was provided."[16] According to this definition of confidentiality, any actual obligation to maintain confidence can be understood as delimited in two ways: (1) the nature of the promise that establishes an expectation or trust to maintain confidence, and (2) the intended or acknowledged purpose for which confidential information is disclosed. For instance, consultation between professionals is often considered a legitimate sharing of confidential information if it is done to serve the purpose for which the information had been conveyed. Also, the sharing of such confidential information is seen as legitimate when this sharing—say, professional consultation—has been communicated and understood within the "promise" made between professional and client.

Ambiguity in Promises

This definition presents confidentiality as a prima facie obligation—delimited on the one hand by the promise that establishes an expectation of confidentiality and, on the other hand, by the purpose intended in the act of confiding. It is already at this point, however, that the problematic nature of pastoral confidence becomes apparent. There is ambiguity in the nature and the content of the promise that typically establishes an expectation of confidentiality outside of the confessional. This ambiguity is due in part to the lack of explicit communication. Most pastoral conversations proceed without written authorization between individuals. The degree of verbal agreement can be both variable and vague. It is based more on implicit role expectations than on explicit agreement.

This problem of vague definition is compounded because of typically inflated expectations of confidentiality on the part of parishioners, if not as well as on the part of the pastor. There is a popular perception that pastoral confidence is held absolutely. That this is actually a misperception is frequently left uncorrected by clergy in their encounters with others. Indeed, many clergy also assume—often uncritically—that all matters communicated to them must remain secret. (A converse problem, of course—and perhaps even more common—is that many clergy are unguarded in revealing conversations and incidents concerning their parishioners.)

The popular perspective's elevation of confidentiality as an absolute principle for pastors would seem to be due to the evolution of confidentiality as a moral principle in two contexts: (1) the inviolable nature of the confessional and (2) the more recent analogy of doctor-patient confidentiality. These two contexts become conflated, though, so that even a tradition such as United Methodism, which does not have a sacrament of confession, nonetheless has a statement about the inviolable nature of pastoral confidences.[17]

Sissela Bok urges her readers "to be quite sparing in one's promises of secrecy about any information, but scrupulous, once having given such a promise, in respecting it."[18] In principle, Bok's advice is sound; it is even implied in the etymology of *confidence* (*con-fidere*, "to keep faith with"). There must be a "with" that links two individuals together in trust, an agreement that obligates the one to keep the confidence of the other. Without such a promise, there is little obligation.

Assumption of Confidentiality

Complicating the matter for ministers, however, is the implicit assumption of confidentiality. People tend to implicitly assume the pastor to be holding their communication in confidence, and they feel betrayed to discover otherwise.[19] Moreover, the pastor is not always aware of this implicit assumption operating outside of such formal contexts as the confessional or counseling sessions.

The misperception that pastoral confidentiality applies wherever parishioners assume it to be applicable is explicitly voiced by H. Newton Malony. Malony defines pastoral confidentiality as "the act of protecting from disclosure that which one has been told under the assumption that it will not be revealed without permission." He emphasizes the importance of this assumption, stating: "If this assumption is not present there is no confidentiality required although certainly discretion should be exercised."[20]

Malony is probably correct in noting that the absence of an assumption of confidentiality would tend to negate a pastor's obligation of confidentiality. However, the converse is not necessarily true. It is not the case that all communications are to be held confidential on the strength of a parishioner's assumption that they should be. Unchallenged assumptions, though, become implicit promises and do become morally binding. It is important, therefore, to clarify the extent and nature of pastoral confidentiality. The minister must explicitly clarify the extent and limits of confidentiality, because in the absence of such explicit clarification, the unstated assumption of confidentiality can in fact function as an implicit promise.

Because of the nature of pastoral work, a strong moral presumption to maintain confidentiality should be kept–even in casual conversation. With regard to the actual sacrament of confession, contextual cues typically indicate that confessant and confessor have entered into their respective roles so that they are both aware that confidentiality applies: "Bless me for I have sinned…" However, people frequently assume that all information shared with a clergyperson will be kept confidential, whether that information is shared in a sacramental or counseling context or otherwise.

Most typically, for Protestant clergy especially, parishioners do not confide so clearly or directly; they tend rather to tack into confidential territory. Confidential information may be preceded by friendly banter about sports or the weather. The conversational context is often fuzzy—failing to provide clear cues that confidentiality is now being invoked. The physical and social context can also be confusing. Information of a confidential nature can be shared with clergy at the ballpark, during the school board meeting, or in the cafe, as well as in the church or the office. H. Newton Malony refers to the "breadth of confidentiality" experienced by the clergy.[21] It is therefore prudent for clergy to assume that nearly everything being told to them may be of a confidential nature.

Confidentiality and "Dual Relationships"

The idea of "dual relationships" is often used to describe the difficulty of discerning the moments in which one is acting in a professional role and bound by the ethics of that profession. If ethical requirements are understood to be at least partly role-specific, and if there is a confusion of roles in a pastor's relationships, how does the pastor then know when the norms of professional ethics are being activated? Other professionals can limit the difficulty of dual relationships by not contracting to provide professional services (e.g., counseling) to close friends or family members. Conversely, they can choose to limit the degree of friendship or intimacy being expected from professional clients. It is difficult in many professions to avoid dual relationships entirely; it is particularly difficult for clergy. This is so not only because we interact with the same people as both parishioners and neighbors, but also because various roles can be operating for us even as we interact in the specific context of church. The context does not mark clearly by time or location or language the lines between our various roles and relationships.

Richard Gula emphasizes that the danger of dual relationships lies not simply in confusion but in differences of power:

> [B]ecause the inevitable inequality of power in pastoral relationships demands clear boundaries, the greater burden of responsibility falls on the minister to keep the boundaries clear. Although dual relationships are not automatically wrong in the pastoral ministry, they do need to be carefully evaluated, and pastoral minsters have the professional duty to make this evaluation.[22]

Given a multiplicity of roles and relationships, Gula urges pastors to "[keep] the pastoral role as the primary one in the relationship."[23] Such primacy of the pastoral role, I am suggesting, implies that pastors assume that confidentiality applies to their conversations unless there is a clear indicator that this is not the case. There is power present for pastors in knowing the private thoughts and concerns of other persons. The general presumption of pastoral confidentiality being advocated here helps to protect people's privacy *from* us as well as *by* us.

Supervision of Clergy

Because of their problematic nature, though, dual relationships require monitoring even if they are not "automatically wrong."[24] Such monitoring might entail the use of professional supervision. Clergy should not be entirely isolated in providing pastoral care. Indeed, such total isolation is not safe practice either for the minister or for those in her or his care. It is a good idea for the pastor to have recourse to someone or some group that can serve as confidant to the pastor. Conversation with such an individual or group can help the pastor to identify his or her own feelings and needs as he or she engages in ministry. It can help the pastor to clarify alternatives for exercising ministry and to deliberate among these options. Ideally, such an individual would be a professional supervisor with whom the pastor has contracted for such services. The individual might also be a mentor, a counselor, or perhaps a spiritual director.[25] It could be a group of individuals such as: a supervisory group that one might experience in a program such as C.P.E.[26], a group of colleagues who covenant together for this purpose, or a group or team of care-providers in one's congregation.

It is important, though, that the pastor clarify with these individuals the degree of supervision that can be legitimately expected and competently offered. It is further advisable to let it be known in one's congregation the manner in which one is receiving such professional support for offering care in matters that are considered confidential. The pastor is, in this way, able to clarify the promise that defines the duty of confidentiality in the first place. At the same time, parishioners are reassured that their pastor acts in keeping with their trust, not only for silence, but also for extending to them competent and safe pastoral care.[27]

Promise-keeping is at the heart of our obligations to keep or share confidences. Confusion about confidentiality can stem from confusion about roles and relationships. It can also stem from a conflict of expectations or a lack of clarity concerning the promise that establishes an obligation of confidentiality and defines the extent of that obligation. Ministers can err by tacitly validating expectations of confidentiality with their silence instead of clarifying their understanding of pastoral confidentiality. They can err secondly, then, when they inadvertently breach these tacit expectations by repeating information that may have been conveyed to them in a rather casual manner. For this reason, I am suggesting a presumption for confidentiality in all circumstances. This presumption heightens when explicit promises are made to clarify such expectations.

Explicit promises clarify our expectations about confidentiality and allow us to mutually commit ourselves to them. Because of their professional context, though, and the multiplicity of roles involved, clergy find the presumption shifting concerning the clarification of a promise of confidentiality. While Bok argues in principle that secrets are not necessarily obligatory unless a promise for such secrecy has been made, pastors must often assume otherwise in practice: that confidentiality is expected of them unless they explicitly clarify otherwise.

Ownership of Information

Gossip

Sissela Bok's argument for a presumption of confidentiality begins with a premise affirming respect for individual autonomy and the legitimacy of personal privacy. The premises that follow build on this. One of the purposes of confidentiality—one of its justifications—is the protection of personal privacy. People own the information about themselves that they are sharing with entrusted others.

Information about someone else, conversely, almost invariably belongs at least in part to that other person. The person being talked about has a legitimate stake in the information conveyed. Pastors should exercise a degree of suspicion regarding information conveyed "confidentially" about third parties who have such a stake in that information. Such "confidential" conversations about others frequently crosses the border from pastoral care to gossip.

Gossip involves secrets shared and kept about other people. Sissela Bok defines gossip as "informal personal communication about persons who are absent or treated as absent."[28] Such gossip, according to Bok, is not morally problematic by this definition, but gossip can be relatively harmful or harmless depending upon other factors. Some gossip is innocuous, according to Bok. But gossip is "reprehensible" in her estimation if it is unduly invasive, if it is a lie, or if it is a betrayal of a promise to secrecy.[29] Moreover, even relatively innocuous gossip can have a trivializing effect on the subject being discussed and a demeaning effect on those being talked about.[30]

Bok's observations about gossip have important implications for the practice of pastoral ministry. Of particular importance is gossip's trivializing effect. Not only does gossip trivialize the content of conversation and demean those being discussed, it also demeans the pastor who participates in gossip and trivializes the pastoral office in general. When people become aware that a pastor participates in gossip, they lose respect for the individual pastor, and they become less trusting of him or her in particular and of pastoral ministry in general.

A Pastor's Inadvertent Gossip

A pastor can inadvertently gossip in both social and professional settings. With regard to professional settings, a pastor can gossip even while conscientiously acting in the role of pastor. A minister might share a "pastoral concern" with a committee or with another member of the congregation to involve others in ministering to the person being discussed. Often pastors do this with the best of intentions and justify it theologically with an understanding of the ministry of the whole people of God. This is one of the ethical hazards of shared ministry or ministry teams. The question is: Do individuals know that their personal concerns confided to a pastor might be shared within such a team?

This question is really of two parts. First, have members of the congregation themselves covenanted together with regard to this sharing of information between the pastor and others so that there is a mutual agreement or perhaps formal authorization for such sharing? Second, are individuals outside of the congregation informed of this arrangement for providing pastoral care when such persons approach the pastor in confidence? It is possible for team ministry to be assumed within a congregation but come as a startling surprise to an outsider in need—especially if a member of the ministry team is also within the circle of that person's acquaintances.

Even if there is an explicit understanding that the pastor may share information of a confidential nature with certain authorized others within the congregation, and even if this understanding of shared ministry has been communicated adequately both within the congregation itself and to those approaching the pastor afresh from without, the pastor should still exercise considerable discretion in sharing confidences with others in ministry. The pastor must be self-correcting in this matter, since members of a ministry team may tend to defer to the pastor's authority.

Even on ministry teams with an egalitarian ethos, three reasons explain why people would be disinclined to correct the pastor for a breach of confidentiality.

First, members of a ministry team are likely to give the minister the benefit of the doubt and to simply assume that a pastor is acting legitimately whenever the pastor communicates pastoral needs.

Second, members of a ministry team are likely to feel responsible once such information has been shared and, conversely, might feel irresponsible by placing the matter back into the pastor's own hands.

Third, members of a ministry team are also likely to feel complimented by being included within the circle of care and would not want to feel excluded by correcting the minister's ethics in this matter.

The subjective feeling of being included or excluded can also influence a minister's desires for collegiality and responsibility. One of the cultural functions of secrecy, according to Bok, is to demark insiders and outsiders.[31]

The gossiper exerts a degree of control in this contest between insider and outsider, as he or she claims the role of insider by virtue of having and conveying information–and by placing others in the role of outsider by talking about them. As ministers, we need to guard against our own desire for community and support as a motive for revealing confidences that have been entrusted to us for safekeeping. It may feel to us like we are empowering others in an egalitarian manner to include them in a ministry that requires the sharing of confidence. At the same time, though, such sharing among comrades in care can be very disempowering to those who have placed their trust and their confidence in us. It may feel to us like a sharing of power, when in actuality we may be baldly exercising power in determining who is insider and who is outsider among us.

Distorting Temptations

Two temptations in gossip can distort our sense of obligation to maintain confidence. The first temptation is that we might draw the circle of confidentiality too widely in our attempt to involve others in our congregations in a ministry of care. The role of confidentiality in such team approaches to pastoral care should be clarified for all concerned.

The second temptation is that we might honor requests for confidentiality when people convey to us information that is actually about third parties–information, in other words, that is not about themselves and that does not carry with it the same need for the protection of their privacy. The temptation in this instance is to promise confidentiality when perhaps we ought not. (Of course, sometimes one should be especially careful to keep information about a third party confidential—when that third party is suspected of being dangerous, for instance.)

Claimants of Information

These temptations indicate the importance of asking, "Whose information is this?" In any communication, there are three possible claimants of that information.

First is the source of the information—its owner whose privacy is at stake. (In an instance of secondhand information, the person whose privacy is at stake might not be the same person supposedly confiding in the pastor.)

Second are those in whom a trust of confidence is being placed—typically the pastor, but possibly broadened to include others who might or might not be necessary for the provision of safe or adequate care.

Third are those who may be mentioned in the communication—those being talked about. Their claim to know might be legitimate as well; this is the logic behind right to know laws that give people access to their own records. All of these individuals might conceivably claim some ownership of the information being conveyed to the pastor with a request of confidentiality.

The obligation of the pastor to maintain confidentiality, I am arguing, strengthens to the degree that the legitimate owners of the information are requesting confidentiality. The pastor's obligation weakens to the degree that the request is made to form an alliance of secrecy about third parties.

Confession

So far, this conversation about confidentiality has been assuming a situation in which a pastor is entrusted with information and is empowered by this trust to respond. We are assuming, in other words, that by virtue of a speaker's confidence in the pastor, the pastor has become a part owner of the information—or at least a trustee of that information and empowered with a degree of agency concerning it. Such agency would be assumed in most instances of professional confidentiality, including pastoral confidentiality. A priest's agency may be different, however, in confidential matters arising from confession during the Sacrament of Reconciliation. A priest may not hold confessional information expressed during the sacrament in the same way as other kinds of confided information. The priest's ownership or agency with regard to information in a sacramental context may be shaped differently by that context.

Sacramental Context

Although Sissela Bok begins her book on *Secrets* by asserting the moral neutrality of secrets outside of a context that gives the sharing of secrets meaning, she does not describe in very much detail the specific sacramental context. This is a peculiar omission, since it is the seal of secrecy in confession that is held in Roman Catholic Canon Law to be inviolable. This inviolability is affirmed in Canon Law apart from considerations of achieving a greater good or even of avoiding abhorrent harm.[32] Bok's fourth premise regarding professional responsibility, however, is a consequentialist appeal for society's overall good. The premise would not continue to be persuasive under weight of evidence that such professional secrecy might contribute more to personal or public harm than to a greater common good.

The context of sacramental confession, however, is concerned primarily with preserving neither public benefit nor even a personal right to privacy. It is primarily prayer. The context is religious and concerns a person's relationship to God. The communication of confession is to God. The priest, and any linguistic interpreters, are bound to secrecy as participants in a communication–confession–between a penitent and God. In a study on the seal of confession in Canon Law, John R. Roos writes that the confessor "actually has no human or communicable knowledge about the information."[33] God is an owner of this information and is understood as being able to act on this information, e.g., by granting forgiveness.

God's putative claim on this conversation is probably of little interest in a courtroom concerned with clarifying questions of clergy privilege. It might be of even less concern to those who might be innocent victims of sins confessed in such a setting. God's claim on this conversation may even be of little concern to many theologians, pastors, and laypeople who would suggest that what God requires is not secrecy, "but to do justice, and to love kindness, and to walk humbly..." (Mic. 6:8c) It is a reason, though, that confessional confidentiality is considered by some to be a sacred trust and not simply a professional obligation.

This distinction is not acknowledged by Bok:

> The sacramental nature of confession is a matter of faith for believers. It may be respected even in secular law on grounds of religious freedom; but it adds no legitimacy to that of the four premises when it comes to what professionals conceal for clients.[34]

It seems to me, however, that the greater stringency afforded to sacramental confession is unavoidably related to this possibility of divine inclusion in the communication. God is being petitioned, and it is God's agency that is being invoked.

God as Stakeholder

In her analysis of applied professional ethics in organized religion, Margaret Battin, like Bok, addresses the issue of clergy confidentiality without considering God as a stakeholder in confessional conversation. On one hand, she acknowledges that doctrine and faith-based claims present methodological issues that make "ecclesioethics" (her word) a "more difficult area of inquiry than secular fields like bioethics or legal ethics."[35] On the other hand, she tries to minimize this methodological problem by approaching her topic with "complete restraint from either affirmation or denial of the traditional metaphysical and religious claims…"[36] She attempts a neutral position that neither accepts nor rejects such religious tenets as "the reality of God or the promise of salvation."[37]

However, by treating God propositionally as a kind of religious hypothesis (and by then remaining sceptical, uncommitted, or disinterested in the propositional question), she does not allow herself to consider God putatively as an agentic participant in the rite of confession. She treats priestly confidential conversation as a subcategory of professional consultation such as that experienced by "doctors, lawyers, psychiatrists, accountants, and other practitioners in the consulting professions."[38] Battin sees "confession" as presenting "the most conspicuous dilemmas in confidentiality" for clergy because, in her words, "confession is a primary mode of conveying personal information from an individual to a religious professional."[39] Battin describes a Roman Catholic position that knowledge from confession is held "in God" rather than in any "ordinary sense" that would allow the confessor to act.[40] Yet, she dismisses this position as an "excuse" which "cannot be accorded status among the premises in the general moral argument concerning confidentiality."[41]

It seems to me, however, relevant to the problem of confidentiality in a sacramental context to take three issues into account. These are

1. God's claim on the information
2. the person's ultimate confidence placed in God rather than human agency
3. the priest's dependent position as conveying and mediating communication between a prayerful penitent and a gracious God

With Battin, I recognize similarities between the ethical dilemmas posed to clergy concerning confidentiality and those posed to other "consulting professions."[42] However, I claim that the confessional context also posits a difference between them. Battin's conceptual framework does not seem to allow her to consider God as stakeholder, agent, participant, owner of information, or moral claimant in a confessional conversation involving also confessor and confessant. It is the religious perception of God's involvement in the sacramental process, and not just the sanctions of canon law, I would suggest, that lends particular stringency to a priestly obligation to maintain confessional confidentiality.[43]

The Seal of Confession

Most writers in pastoral ethics are clear that the language of "absolute" or "inviolable" confidentiality applies only in the context of religious confession, or more particularly in the sacrament of reconciliation and the seal of confession.[44] The "seal of confession" refers to an explicit promise by a priest during the Sacrament of penance that the matter being confessed will not be disclosed to others. This is understood to apply in those churches that practice a Sacrament of penance, such as the Roman Catholic Church and the Episcopal Church. Richard Gula, for instance, writes, "[T]he duty of confidentiality is absolute only in matters pertaining to the sacrament of reconciliation,"[45] and he cites canons 983, 984, and 1388 as binding for Roman Catholics with regard to the absolute confidentiality of sacramental confession.

Similarly in the Episcopal Church, with regard specifically to the "Sacrament of Reconciliation of a Penitent," William Rankin writes, "The term *seal* is an apt indicator of the inviolability of that confidentiality."[46] Arguing that they do not carry the same weight as canon law, Rankin nevertheless quotes the rubrics to the 1979 edition of the *Book of Common Prayer* with approval:

> The content of a confession is not normally a matter of subsequent discussion. The secrecy of a confession is morally absolute for a confessor, and must under no circumstances be broken.[47]

Having affirmed this strict confessional confidentiality, however, Rankin notes that, should the penitent broach the confessed subject again subsequently, the confessor would then be permitted to discuss the matter while still remaining silent about the original confession. Rankin understands the free consent of a penitent to function as at least a partial waiver of strict confidentiality in both Episcopal and Roman Catholic Churches.[48] Rankin also argues that, when necessary, a confessor might withhold absolution from a penitent to urge that person to disclose the matter being confessed or to allow the priest greater freedom to make the necessary disclosure.[49]

Marie Fortune makes very similar points to ensure children's safety from abuse while still respecting the inviolability of confession. A first priority always is to ensure children's safety, but she distinguishes between sacramental confession that represents a "special case" and other situations involving pastoral confidentiality. While she describes "the essence of sacramental confession" as being "secrecy"–"the absolute promise never under any circumstance to share any information that comes to a member of the clergy,"[50] she nonetheless argues that this does not necessarily prevent the reporting of suspected child abuse:

> If an offender confesses…[The clergyperson] can use the occasion to direct the offender to make a report to the authorities as a means of holding the offender accountable. The minister can and should withhold absolution until steps have been taken that clearly indicate the offender's genuine repentance and change.[51]

Fortune's and Rankin's suggestions about the possibility of withholding absolution for the sake of disclosure is also in keeping with my understanding of Roman Catholic practice that the seal of confession should not be given if a confession is insincere or disingenuous.[52]

Protection of Power

This brings us to the third quality of confidentiality that helps to shape its stringency. We can ask the question, "Whose power or vulnerability is being protected by maintaining confidentiality?" It should be apparent that we are more obligated to maintain confidentiality to protect the vulnerable from harm that to protect the machinations of power.

Throughout this chapter, confidentiality has been defined and discussed with reference to power. Sissela Bok describes secrecy as a "form of power–the controlling of information and the way one is perceived by others."[53] Confidentiality then serves to protect that power that individuals exercise concerning information about themselves. Moreover, in building a prima facie case for maintaining professional confidentiality, Bok appeals to the respect owed to people's autonomy or power over their own affairs. The emphasis is placed on the interests of clients rather than protection of the power of the professionals or of other spheres of power:

> Exactly whose secret should it protect? The patient's or client's alone? Or the professional's? Or all that transpires between them?
>
> In principle, confidentiality should protect only the first.[54]

Confidentiality is misapplied when it is used to protect the professional's power rather than the client's vulnerability. Moreover, as Bok notes, confidentiality can be employed as a rationalization to hide information "*from* patients, clients, and the public at large."[55] She concludes that confidentiality should not be used to "undermine and contradict the very respect for persons and for human bonds that confidentiality was meant to protect."[56]

Richard Gula follows Bok in developing an ethical interpretation of confidentiality for pastors. Fidelity is an important value for Gula in grounding his understanding of pastoral ethics in general, and pastoral confidentiality in particular. Fidelity or trust should characterize all pastoral relationships. Pastors should allow fidelity to guide them in their relationships with parishioners. This is particularly important, according to Gula, because of the power differential between pastors and parishioners:

> Everything we do to serve the religious needs of people flows through the pastoral relationship. Its covenantal action of entrusting and accepting entrustment makes fidelity to trust the fundamental moral imperative for the pastoral minister. In professional ethics, this imperative is called the professional's *fiduciary responsibility*. It means that we will exercise our power and authority in ways that will serve their need for seeking our pastoral service in the first place, and that we will not exploit their vulnerability but give greater preference to their best interests over our own.[57]

This trust that characterizes pastoral relationships, according to Gula, "supports a strong presumption in favor of keeping confidences."[58] If there is a need to disclose the information being held confidentially, such disclosure should normally occur with the permission of the confidant if at all possible. In every case, care must be taken to prevent harm to others.

Prevention of harm to others he interprets as a matter of justice:

> Whereas fidelity allows disclosure if permission is given, justice requires disclosure without permission when a serious risk of harm might occur if the information should be suppressed.[59]

Richard Gula contrasts the duty of confidentiality as an expression of fidelity with the duty to prevent harm as an expression of justice. Should they come into conflict in a situation with potential for serious harm, he suggests giving priority to justice. Such risk of harm is present, for instance, in situations involving child abuse. Without necessarily appealing to justice, other ethicists simply give a priority to a duty to prevent harm over confidentiality when the risk of harm is great and when obtaining permission of the one who has confided has first been considered.[60]

Marie Fortune, however, defines confidentiality in a way that avoids conflict with a duty to report child abuse. Like Gula, Fortune understands pastoral confidentiality to be based on a sense of trust. This implicit promise of trust frames the proper limits of confidentiality. Contrasted with absolute secrecy, confidentiality means, according to Fortune, "to hold information in trust." It is within the parameters of such trust to share information with other professionals for the sake of protecting the vulnerable, but not for protecting those in power—whether abusers themselves or even helping professionals.

> Confidentiality is intended as a means to help an individual get help for a problem and prevent further harm to herself or others. Confidentiality is not intended to protect abusers from being held accountable for their actions or to keep them from getting the help they need...In addition, confidentiality is not intended to protect professionals; it is for those whom they serve.[61]

It is consistent with this understanding of confidentiality—consistent with the trust involved—to share information to protect those most vulnerable. It is not that a rule of confidentiality is being broken or even that an exception to the rule is being justified. The principle of confidentiality itself, in this perspective, requires proper use of the information entrusted.

Confidentiality is not violated by such proper consultation; it rather demands that the entrusted information be kept or shared on behalf of those most vulnerable. Fortune does, however, encourage professionals—including clergy—to obtain permission if possible for such sharing of information from those who are confiding their trust. At the very least, though, insists Fortune, "*Do not* use confidentiality as an excuse not to act to protect a child from further abuse."[62]

Children are so vulnerable to their guardians and other adults that arguably they make a special claim for protection from the clergy as well as from all members of society. Even though Ronald Bullis and Cynthia Mazur, for instance, affirm that clergy may breach confidence to prevent harm under a variety of circumstances, they argue that clergy should "make a clear demarcation between disclosing child abuse and disclosing other matters."[63] The prevention of harm to children should receive priority. Some states legally require that members of the clergy report suspected instances of child abuse. All states in the U.S., though, have child abuse reporting laws, and clergy are permitted, even if they are not required, to report suspected instances of abuse.[64]

The severity of harm that can be done to children is probably enough to override even the most stringent duty of confidentiality characteristic, say, even of confessional confidences.[65] In addition to a heightened duty of nonmaleficence or beneficence, however, I am suggesting that the duty of confidentiality is itself shaped by the vulnerability of those who have placed trust in us or whose care is entrusted to us. Confidentiality is based in such trust. Its justification is the protection of that humble power of personal integrity that is called privacy. When the power of secrets turns to protecting or hiding abusive power, confidentiality itself loses much of its justification. Our duty to keep confidence heightens as confidentiality is consistent with the trust of the vulnerable, and it diminishes to the degree that it is not.

Conclusion

In conclusion, I have been suggesting three questions that allow pastors to gauge the strength of a duty of confidentiality as it might apply to their relationships in a variety of situations typical of pastoral ministry. These three questions are with regard to promise, ownership, and power.

The first question has to do with the nature of the promise that establishes or clarifies a duty of confidentiality. Are pastors and parishioners alike clear with each other concerning their expectations and commitments? With the lack of obvious contextual clues or written contracts, are we able to acknowledge with each other how our mutual trust is or is not binding us in confidence? Do we help each other to discern the times of confession, the times of counseling, and the times of casual conversation? Do we acknowledge the limits, as well as the commitments, to confidentiality?

Second, I have suggested that we ponder who are the legitimate owners and claimants of information communicated to us. Who is the source of the information, and whose privacy is being protected? Who is addressed by this communication? Who is its intended recipient? In the situation of the confessional, I have suggested that the priest is probably not the ultimate recipient of the information being confessed.

Third, we need to ask about power and vulnerability if our scruples for maintaining confidence are to be consistent with the trust actually placed in us. Prima facie presumptions remaining, our actual duty to keep confidence, I am saying, is shaped by our answers to these questions. In each relationship and each conversation, as pastors and as persons, it is a matter not just of telling and keeping secrets but of discerning how to keep faith with one another.

Exercise for Reflection: Confidentiality

Think about a situation in which you were being expected to keep some information secret or to hold it in confidence. As you think about that situation, ask yourself the following sets of questions:

1. Was I asked explicitly to keep a secret or was the expectation of secrecy more of an implicit assumption? Was there an institutional policy guiding the expectation of secrecy? Was I serving a particular role that would encourage an expectation of professional confidentiality? Did I have opportunity to voice agreement or disagreement with the request for secrecy? Did I, in fact, voice agreement or disagreement? Did I have opportunity to qualify any agreement to maintain confidence? Did I take advantage of that opportunity and voice qualifications or reservations about keeping confidence? In short, what was the nature of the explicit or implicit promise of confidentiality? After analyzing this promise, how morally binding does it appear?

2. Whose information was this? Was the person confiding something about himself or herself, or was the person talking about other people? If the information is about other people, how are they related to the person confiding? Is this person compassionately concerned for them? fearfully threatened by them? Is this gossip? Does anyone else have a legitimate need to know about this information? If so, what makes that need to know seem legitimate? Does any law require that others (such as child protective services) know? Why was this person confiding in me? Was I expected (implicitly or explicitly) to act on the information in some way? Is this person seeking the Sacrament of reconciliation? Is this information being given as a prayer to God? After analyzing the possible owners or claimants of this information, how obligatory does the request for confidentiality appear?

3. Whose power did secrecy protect? Who was vulnerable to this information? Were the powerful manipulating secrecy in this instance? or was secrecy protecting the vulnerable? Was anyone in danger? Could I assure safety while still maintaining confidentiality? What were my alternatives for acting faithfully with this information? After analyzing power and vulnerability in this situation, how obliged was I to maintain confidence?

4. After analyzing this situation with regard to all three factors of promise, ownership, and power, how am I now understanding a duty of confidentiality in this situation? Is it a strong duty? Are there limiting factors? Which aspects of this analysis strengthen the case for confidentiality? Which weaken it? Are other duties also obliging me in this situation—such as a duty to prevent harm or a duty to be truthful? When I compare and weigh my different obligations in this instance, are they compatible? or do I face trade-offs? If I face trade-offs in this instance, is my duty of confidentiality overridden or does it override other apparent obligations? What seems to be the faithful course of action—accepting such trade-offs if necessary but minimizing them if possible? Which aspects of my analysis of confidentiality have helped me to make this determination?

7

Vocation I

Creation and Community

"Holy, holy, holy is Yahweh of hosts;
the whole earth is full of God's glory."

ISAIAH 6:3B, author's translation

How does the vocation to pastoral ministry relate to the church's ministry as a whole? How do pastor and congregation cooperate for ministry and mission? How do we respond in faith to God who has called us to service? How do pastor and congregation alike relate to the wider society in terms of moral responsibilities and expectations? These questions underlie this book on the ethics of pastoral care and leadership. Previous chapters have examined in greater detail some of the particular moral responsibilities that can be operative in the relationships among pastor, congregation, and the wider community. These final two chapters, however, look more broadly at a theology of vocation that calls us into leadership and service for the glory of God. Here the thesis is that we must see the vocation of the pastor within the wider context of the vocation of the church, of human society, and, indeed, of creation itself. These will be considered in reverse order.

Vocation comes from the Latin word *vocare*, "to call," and literally means "calling." Vocation is a religious idea, turning our attention to the One who calls. It is important to recognize this religious dimension, since the language of a secular culture tends to identify vocation synonymously with one's work, one's job, a career, or a profession. Much of this book, too, has been about ethics on the job–the professional ethics for clergy in their careers of ministry. But it is necessary to affirm this religious dimension to the work of ministry: it is vocation from God.

Creation's Vocation

Theologically, we can begin by recognizing and affirming vocation in creation itself. All of creation is called to give glory to God. Psalm 19 expresses this poetically:

> The heavens are telling the glory of God;
> and the firmament proclaims [God's] handiwork.
> Day to day pours forth speech,
> and night to night declares knowledge.
> There is no speech, nor are there words;
> their voice is not heard;
> yet their voice goes out through all the earth,
> and their words to the end of the world. (Ps. 19:1–4)

Many other Psalms (such as 98; 104; 148) portray creation praising the Creator. The well-known hymn by Saint Francis resounds like these Psalms: "All Creatures of Our God and King, lift up your voice and with us sing Alleluia!"[1] With the psalmist and with Saint Francis, we, too, can sing of this vocation of creation to glorify the Creator.

The Westminster Confession, written in 1647, affirms that God created the world "for the manifestation of the glory of [God's] eternal power, wisdom, and goodness."[2] Humanity's "chief end" is similar– to glorify and to enjoy God.[3] This is our first vocation, with all of creation–to reflect God's glory and to glorify God. Humanity shares this vocation with all other creatures: all animals and plants, air and water, earth and stars.

Jonathan Edwards provided another "classic" theological state- ment of this sense of creation's vocation by in his "Dissertation Concerning the End for Which God Created the World," originally published posthumously in 1765. Edwards argues logically and from scripture that "the glory of God" is the last or "ultimate end" for which God created the world. Edwards argues that God's own glory finds expression within God's creation. God's creatures are moved to express this glory through the love and enjoyment of God. Creation emanates the glory of its Creator. Humanity, as a part of creation, shares in this glorification of God.[4]

The call of the prophet Isaiah is instructive at this point. In Isaiah's vision, the first thing he hears is one heavenly being declaring to another that the "whole earth" is full of Yahweh's glory. Isaiah's response to this is not an immediate recognition and embracing of his own call. Rather, he despairs: "Woe is me! I am lost, for I am a man of unclean lips" (6:5a). Only after one of the heavenly beings in his vision touches his lips with a hot coal is he able to hear God's call, "Whom shall I send…?" and is he able to respond, "Here am I; send me!" (6: 8). Isaiah's call to ministry is set within the whole creation, giving glory to God. This is our first vocation: to glorify God with the rest of heaven and earth.

Note that Isaiah is being formed for ministry even before he is able to hear and respond to God's call. His encounter with the heavenly being and the hot coal prepares him to hear and respond to God's call. For us, too, discernment of our vocation occurs within the wider project of our spiritual formation. This is God's doing–a matter of grace we are to receive with faith. God's spirit does more than simply "call." The Spirit births us, prepares us, forms us, calls us, helps us to hear, empowers our response, and equips us for service. At times we feel very much aware of the Holy Spirit's involvement in this process, but many times we do not. Still, in times of uncertainty, as well as in times of confidence, the Spirit is forming us in love and calling us to some vocation. Whether or not one's vocation is within the institutional church, it will be within creation and to God's glory.

However, having affirmed our vocation with the rest of creation to glorify God, we must admit that we are not always faithful in serving this vocation. We do not act to God's glory when trust is betrayed or when the vulnerable are harmed. We do not act to God's glory

- when parents violate their children
- when clergy abuse those in their charge
- when lawyers betray their clients' interests
- when business leaders embezzle company funds
- when doctors fail to promote life and health
- when scientists apply themselves to destructive technology rather than to enlightening knowledge
- when heads-of-state wage war for self-serving political motives

These activities–destructive to the rest of creation–are not glorious. Regardless of how noble or prestigious the status we gain in society's estimation, such actions are not in service of divine calling. God's call is always a vocation for justice.

Vocation for Justice

Justice, it can generally be said, involves the establishment of right relationship. More particular theories of justice and definitions of "right relation," however, are as varied as the details of our relationships themselves. Justice can be described in terms of the sphere of relationship: ecological justice, political justice, economic justice, justice and gender, etc. Theories of justice can be compared with regard to the different definitions and the relative emphases given to various moral principles or values, e.g., equality, merit, freedom, empowerment, liberation, participation, fidelity, righteousness, individual autonomy, community, etc. Some approaches to justice emphasize process and participation; others emphasize conse-quences—the importance of reaching just results. Some approaches to justice are more traditional or conservative—giving higher priority to the structures that have already been established in society for ensuring a modicum of justice. Other approaches are more visionary or even revolutionary, giving greater attention to present injustice and the need to establish new relationships.

In her books on the subject of justice, Karen Lebacqz acknow-ledges the multiple voices advocating justice. "Justice is elusive," she writes in the preface of one of her books. "I often have the uncomfortable feeling that not all who 'cry justice' mean the same thing by the term."[5] She then approaches the subject of justice by attending to instances of injustice and to biblical themes so she can appreciatively critique certain theories of justice and identify elements that might be required for a more adequate understanding of justice. She concludes by recognizing that both the task of adequately conceptualizing justice and the task of realizing a truer justice in history remain ongoing tasks.[6] In both of her books on justice, Lebacqz offers comparison and critique of six different theories of justice.[7]

This book on pastoral ethics has not attempted to provide a comprehensive definition of justice or to champion a particular theory about justice. We have begun "in the middle" by attending to some of the moral challenges that occur within the relationships that pastors establish between themselves and others. Certain elements of an understanding of justice, nonetheless, have been assumed throughout this discussion. Of primary importance has been a sense of fidelity within these interpersonal relationships. Fidelity can be seen to inform all of the principles here discussed: promise-keeping, truth-telling, keeping confidences, and gentleness. Ultimately, fidelity is the faithfulness we keep—individually and as a community—with God. In the context of professional ethics, it is a matter of establishing and maintaining just relationships with others.

Pastoral relationships, however, exist in a wider web of relation-ship within society and nature. Our participation in the whole web of these relationships should be shaped by our understandings of justice and faithfulness. If the church is to nurture people of virtue, then part of the task of ministry is to encourage people in seeking justice by

1. voicing their perspectives of justice and injustice
2. seeking to establish justice in their own personal and professional relationships
3. empowering their agency more widely within society to work for a more just world

These are tasks pertaining to the role of clergy in moral leadership. The phrase "moral leadership" is not meant to suggest moral superiority; it is, rather, an affirmation that clergy are in a position to embolden others in pursuing justice.

Ecojustice and Imaging God

We have affirmed that all creation serves a vocation of glorifying God. It does this simply as the object of God's creativity and love—thus embodying God's glory. It does this, moreover, by pointing back to God—by reflecting God's glory as a natural act of praise. We participate with all of creation in glorifying God. As creatures, we share in this vocation.

The natural world, however, is also the object of human attention and human endeavors. Rightly or not, people act in the world in ways that use nature for human purposes. For some, an anthropocentric approach to nature has been justified by appeal to the first chapter of Genesis and to the creation of men and women in the image of God:

> God blessed them, and God said to them, "Be fruitful and multiply, and fill the earth and subdue it; and have dominion over the fish of the sea and over the birds of the air and over every living thing that moves upon the earth." (Gen. 1:28)

In 1967, historian Lynn White Jr. published an influential essay in *Science* magazine that argued that the ecological crisis was due in large part to the doctrine of *dominium terrae*.[8] Whether or not White's thesis is correct that a theology of dominion has contributed causally to the ecological crisis, his essay has certainly stimulated theologians to engage in deeper theological reflection about humanity's relationship to the rest of creation.[9]

Larry Rasmussen, who served as the Co-moderator of the World Council of Churches' Commission on Justice, Peace, Creation, noticed that a theology of dominion that some have traditionally used to justify human mastery over nature is now seldom cited for this purpose. He finds that ecumenical theological conversation is increasingly turning to four other metaphors for reflecting on humanity's relationship with nature. One is the image of "stewardship." Dominion is reinterpreted so that humanity is perceived as a trustee or caretaker charged with keeping and maintaining the earth. Another image is that of a "partner" with other creatures. This is an egalitarian image, placing humanity within a kind of creaturely democracy of interdependence and interconnection. A third metaphor is "priest" within and for creation. This image is informed by Eastern Orthodox sacramental theology in which all of creation is understood to participate in the consecration of the elements and in the communion of God's people. Finally, Rasmussen finds many within the church using the image of "prophet" as they urgently proclaim a moral responsibility to care for creation. Some see such care for creation as a matter of covenantal responsibility to God.[10] Rasmussen appeals to these metaphors in defining humanity's proper exercise of dominion and imaging of God:

> [T]he point here is that *imago dei* is understood relationally and dynamically, as human imaging of God's way and as humans turning toward God on behalf of creation as priest, trustee, servant, partner.[11]

All four of these images point in different ways to our human responsibility to seek and maintain right relationships with other creatures and within nature. This, too, is perhaps part of our general vocation—not just to participate with nature in glorifying God, but to participate with God in renewing creation.

Social Justice and Imaging God

The idea of all humanity—male and female—being created "in the image of God" is enormously suggestive. This phrase occurs in the Hebrew Scripture only in Genesis in the story of creation and in the story of Noah (Gen. 9:6). It has nevertheless inspired theological reflection throughout the ages, and theologians have found much to room to ponder. With the psalmist (Ps. 8), we have cause to wonder: What is it about being human that God would be mindful of us and care for us?

The image of God has been a particularly salient image in African American theology and ethics. The image pictures humanity's created equality and dignity under God's love and care. Katie Cannon, for instance, has written that her own understanding of ethics has been shaped by the image of God as interpreted by both Howard Thurman and Martin Luther King Jr. She writes that, for Howard Thurman, the image of God means that "within each individual there is the presence and power of the divine."[12] The beginning of Thurman's ethics, she writes, is this process of divine creation. It arouses potential in every person, which can lead to liberation and transformation. It can inspire liberative actions that destabilize the oppressor and seek to establish a more harmonious community.[13]

Similarly, Martin Luther King Jr. refers to the image of God not only for theological description of humanity's relationship to the Creator but also as a theological grounding for ethical norms to understand human relationships. These norms include human freedom, equality, and an affirmation of God-given human rights. King appeals to the image of God in describing the solid idealistic structure of the United States:

> Its pillars were soundly grounded in the insights of our Judeo-Christian heritage: all men are made in the image of God; all men are brothers; all men are created equal; every man is heir to a legacy of dignity and worth; every man has rights that are neither conferred by nor derived from the state, they are God-given. What a marvelous foundation for any home![14]

King finds consonance between the biblical idea of being created in God's image and Immanuel Kant's categorical imperative, a connection that Cannon developed to the point that she could subsequently write, "The *imago dei* motif gives Black women the divine right 'to be treated as *ends* and never as mere *means*.'"[15]

In other words, by virtue of our common humanity as created by God, we find both the standard of our own ultimate worth before God and the norm by which we can pursue justice in society. Such justice is everybody's right by virtue of the *imago dei,* and the pursuit of justice is everybody's responsibility by virtue of that same image of God. No one is excluded from that blessing of human dignity in the divine image. Moreover, no one should be excluded from common responsibility—which that image entails—to pursue social justice on earth.

African Americans' experience of oppression within the history of the United States surely sharpens the emphasis of this interpretation of egalitarian social responsibility. Peter Paris, writing about African American denominations, similarly identifies an egalitarian "prophetic principle," the "parenthood of God and the kinship of all peoples."[16] This principle has moral, religious, and political implications. It is the point of reference for determining the validity of any form of political engagement–whether party politics, running for office, lobbying, striving for legal guarantees of civil rights, etc.[17] According to Paris, African American denominations have uniquely highlighted this principle, but they have done so with an understanding of its universal validity–that the principle is "theologically correct, biblically sound and morally indisputable."[18]

These ideas, in my opinion, point to an understanding of the human vocation to establish justice in society. Justice is everyone's vocation. The call to justice is a Christian vocation, but it is not exclusively so. It is part of the general vocation for all of humanity. In Genesis 1:26–28, who is created in the image of God and thus charged with the responsibility to exercise rule? Is the church? Are only Christians made in God's image? Of course not! All humans are created in the image of God–male and female according to Genesis– and share in the political responsibility that this entails. All of humanity is represented here.

Everyone is called to justice. All people have the vocation to work for justice in society. Especially in a pluralist society, work for justice involves the establishment of just structures and relationships in every sphere. It includes work for racial justice, economic justice, political justice, just relations between men and women, just relations between generations, justice between human society and the rest of creation. This is not simply a Christian vocation. It is the vocation of all humanity created in God's image and dignified with a share in this responsibility.

The church as a social institution must work with other institutions in society for the public good and to seek a just social order. However, individual Christians participate in public life not primarily as church members. They do so politically as citizens and voters. They do so economically as buyers, sellers, and investors. They do so domestically as parents and as children. They seek justice in each sphere through their participation in that sphere. This is the ministry of the laity. The ministry of the laity is in the world.

Principalities and Powers

In the early centuries of Christianity, the church determined that the "world" is not evil by design and that it does not lie outside the purview of the Creator's sovereign justice. This affirmation of the goodness of creation ran counter to some gnostic understandings that had advocated clearer separation between the realms of God's grace and a purportedly evil world.[19] Overtones of this gnostic worldview seem to sound within the New Testament, especially in the Johannine books with their striking contrast between light and darkness. Notice, too, Jesus' warnings about the world's hatred in his speech prior to his passion in John's gospel. Yet, it is this same gospel of John that affirms Christ as the divine *Logos* (Word) involved in the world's very creation. It is also this gospel of John that affirms God's love for the world to be so deep that God's only beloved Son became Incarnate with us (Jn. 1:1–14; 3:16–17; 15:18–16:11).

New Testament passages that voice suspicion about the world often seem to refer to the structures of authority and rule as a kind of spiritual as well as worldly power. Hence in Revelation, the empire is cryptically and disparagingly called the "harlot" (17:1, RSV) "which has dominion over the kings of the earth" (17:18, RSV). Occasionally, the New Testament refers to "principalities and powers" (*exousiai* and *archai*) over which Christ must claim sovereignty and with which we must now struggle (2 Cor. 15:24; Eph. 1:21; 3:10; 6:12; Col. 1:16; 2:10, 15; 1 Peter 3:22).[20] Ephesians warns, for instance:

> For we are not contending against flesh and blood, but against the principalities, against the powers, against the world rulers of this present darkness, against the spiritual hosts of wickedness in the heavenly places. (Eph. 6:12, RSV)

At the same time, though, Christ's victory is assured over these principalities and powers (Eph. 1:22).[21] Christ's sovereignty over the powers is located at various points theologically: in creation (Col. 1:15–20), on the cross (Col. 1:20; 2:15), in the resurrection and ascension (Eph. 1:20–21), through the church's mission (Eph. 3:10), and approaching the end times (2 Cor. 15:24–25). In all of these moments, God's sovereignty is affirmed within creation–even over those principalities and powers that might seem at times to exercise autonomously their own rule. Even with the otherworldly sound of the apocalyptic language used in Revelation, God's earthly sovereignty is proclaimed in the establishment of a "new heaven and a new earth," with the heavenly city coming down to earth, and with God's dwelling proclaimed to be with God's creatures (Rev. 21:1–3).

Paul's admonition to be subject to the governing authorities can be read in this light. John Howard Yoder, for instance, interprets Paul's admonition not as a relinquishment of divine sovereignty to the empire but rather as a claiming of divine sovereignty over imperial rule. That Paul is not naively optimistic about the empire's justice is apparent, according to Yoder, when he provides justification for Christians to endure persecution from government: that one thereby "heaps burning coals on their heads" (Rom. 12:20d). This is a reference to divine judgment and an affirmation of faith in God's ultimate sovereignty. While Paul urges obedience to the ruling authorities, he recognizes that these authorities are as likely to inflict harm as to promote justice. Nevertheless, he urges Christians not to be overcome by evil, "but overcome evil with good" (Rom. 12:21b). In Yoder's opinion, Paul's confidence is in God's rectitude rather than the government's. His faith is in God's ability to judge human government, whether or not that government "bear the sword" (Rom. 13:4) by faithfully serving its vocation of establishing justice (Rom. 12:19–13:7).[22]

In a contemporary democratic social order, however, sovereignty is shared among the people even while it is centralized among the leaders. Citing Romans 13, Richard John Neuhaus argues that to "be subject to the governing authorities" in the context of a democracy means to justly share in sovereignty with others:

> In a democratic social order, "obedience" does not mean docility or passive compliance but a heightened exercise of individual and communal responsibility. Indeed, if we are to be "subject to the governing authority" in a democratic social order, mere docility must be viewed as disobedience.[23]

Moreover, such public responsibility is not limited to the structures of government. In a democratic pluralist society, life is structured (and authority exercised) "in diverse ways through myriad institutions, economic, political and social."[24]

In 1 Corinthians, Paul addresses the question of Christian responsibility within some of the social institutions of his time. In particular, Paul discusses the institutions of marriage and of slavery. Though it may sound odd to contemporary ears, Paul's reasoning is very similar with regard to both of these institutions. Subsequent theological interpretation (and perhaps misinterpretation) of Paul's reasoning about these social institutions has influenced the development of a secular understanding of vocation.

With regard to marriage, Paul frankly admits at points that he has "no command of the Lord," that he would offer his "opinion," and that he is speaking by "concession, not of command" (1 Cor. 7:6). In the entire chapter, the only point at which Paul is confident to indicate a charge from the Lord is with regard to his discouragement of divorce. Even here Paul recognizes that spouses will indeed separate, and so he provides provisional instruction for that eventuality as well. Actually, Paul expresses a wish: "it is well for them to remain unmarried as I am" (7:8). But he unenthusiastically does endorse marriage, saying: "[I]t is better to marry than to be aflame with passion" (7:9b). One who marries "does well," according to Paul (7:38), but one who refrains from marriage "will do better" (7:38).

Nevertheless, according to Paul, once married, spouses ought to abide by responsibilities entailed in a marital relationship. In Paul's day these responsibilities were framed within patriarchal assumptions that can sound problematic to some contemporary ears. The patriarchal character of heterosexual marriage in Paul's day may have seemed problematic even to Paul himself. He concludes his discussion of marriage in 1 Corinthians 7 by acknowledging a patriarchal assumption: "A wife is bound as long as her husband lives" (v. 39a). She would be free to remarry if widowed, Paul writes, "But in my judgment she is more blessed if she remains as she is. And I think that I too have the Spirit of God" (v. 40). Free of the obligations, distractions, and restrictions of marriage, a person might be able to attend to a life of faith in Christ with a different kind of diligence. My purpose here is not to advocate marriage or singleness or a particular form of either, but rather to simply notice the ambiguity in Paul's letter with regard to marriage, and to further notice an apparent (or at least potential) tension between the call of Christ and one's marital or social status when called.

In the middle of his discussion about marriage, Paul clarifies his reasoning by reference to other inequalities in his society. These are his words pertaining to slavery:

> Every one should remain in the state in which he was called. Were you a slave when called? Never mind. But if you can gain your freedom, avail yourself of the opportunity. For he who was called in the Lord as a slave is a freedman of the Lord. Likewise he who was free when called is a slave of Christ. You were bought with a price; do not become slaves of men. (1 Cor. 7:20–23, RSV)

In all likelihood, Paul is not saying here that people are called by God to particular subservient stations that might be characteristic of such social institutions as slavery or, in the broader context of the chapter, patriarchal marriage. The "calling" to which he refers is the call by God to be saints in and through Jesus Christ.

Thus Paul addresses this letter "to those sanctified in Christ Jesus, called to be saints, together with all those who in every place call on the name of our Lord Jesus Christ..." ((1 Cor. 1:2). This is a call that is given equally and broadly, regardless of a person's status in society. The call is not to a plurality of stations in society but to Christ:

> Consider your own call, brothers and sisters: not many of you were wise by human standards, not many were powerful, not many were of noble birth. But God chose what is foolish in the world to shame the wise; God chose what is weak in the world to shame the strong; God chose what is low and despised in the world, things that are not, to reduce to nothing things that are, so that no one might boast in the presence of God. [God] is the source of your life in Christ Jesus, who became for us wisdom from God, and righteousness and sanctification and redemption. (1 Cor. 1:26–30)

Returning to our discussion of chapter 7, note that Paul refers to slavery, marriage, and circumcision as "the condition in which you were called" (v. 20b). He does not seem to be identifying these conditions with the "callings."[25] Rather, God calls people to life in Christ regardless of their "state" in society. For this reason, Paul can both urge people to "remain in the state" in which they are called and to avail themselves of the opportunity to gain their freedom. Paul's concern is to encourage people–whatever their station in life– in their service to Christ who calls, liberates, and sanctifies people of every station.

Paul is urging people to live in Christ as if their social station or condition did not matter:

> [L]et even those who have wives be as though they had none, and those who mourn as though they were not mourning, and those who rejoice as though they were not rejoicing, and those who buy as though they had no possessions, and those who deal with the world as though they had no dealings with it. (1 Cor. 7:29b–31a)

This is sometimes referred to as an ethic of "*hos me*" because of the Greek words in this passage meaning "as though not." It would seem that in Paul's eschatological perspective God's justice and grace are imminently bringing about a new age and that these distinctions between people shall become either irrelevant or transformed in that process.[26]

Although during the intervening two millennia no abrupt parousia has come that has radically abrogated all worldly inequality, we can still apply an eschatological perspective to our understanding of these stations. Letty Russell says that this ethic of *hos me* sets us free to live in the world as participants already in the new creation in Christ that God is bringing about:

> [I]t is of utmost significance that the message of God's promised liberation be shared with all (1 Cor. 9:19). Without taking ourselves or our roles and status with ultimate importance, we are set free from ourselves, free to risk living out the promised partnership with our neighbors and with God. Yet taking that promise seriously, we are commissioned to work and pray that the liberation of all might be a reality now.[27]

This ethic of *hos me* avoids two temptations. First is the temptation to acquiesce to social institutions and to allow one's limited social status within these institutions to define oneself and to dictate one's sense of responsibility. Second is the temptation to remove oneself from these social institutions and to disengage from the kinds of responsibilities entailed in one's social roles—including the responsibility to participate in the transformation of societal structures.

With regard to the subject of vocation, even Paul's writings express a degree of ambiguity with regard to social institutions and social roles. Paul does not identify these roles with that divine call in Christ that Paul wants to amplify in the ears of his listeners. In other words, the commission or the "call" might be understood as claiming and proclaiming liberation in Christ. Social institutions and our roles within them provide an important arena or context in which we are challenged to follow this call.[28]

Personal Vocation in Historical Perspective

Throughout the centuries, the Christian church has continued to reflect an ambiguity with regard to perceptions of the relative rightness or wrongness of social structures, social power, and social roles. A variety of perspectives can be found—from a general benediction given over society as a whole to a more severe suspicion of social structures and institutions. This is one of the perennial issues in Christian ethics; it occurs over and over again in different guises and in different times and places. Moreover, the degree of trust or mistrust held by Christian communities toward the rest of society at any given time and place bears directly on the development of various understandings of Christian vocation. Is the world trustworthy enough to permit—or even to require—Christians to participate in society's institutions as a way of faithfully serving God? Or is God's "call" to Christians that they should attempt to remove themselves from the rest of society and seek alternative ways of living and serving?

Martin Luther

Martin Luther is often credited with developing a theology of vocation that was inclusive of people's economic labor, their political status, and their family life.[29] He based his argument on passages such as Genesis 1–2 and 1 Corinthians 7. His reading of 1 Corinthians 7 differs from the interpretation of "call" in 1 Corinthians provided above, and has been disputed by some as a misreading of Paul's use of the idea of "call."[30] Unlike the interpretation given above, Luther did apply the idea of "callings" to the particular stations and work of people in the world, though he did so while still prioritizing the broader evangelical call to serve Christ in faith.[31]

Luther's confidence was that one could serve Christ faithfully while attending to one's duties in the world as a "mask" of God. This confidence was based on his understanding of God's work in creation. In his reading of Genesis, Luther understands God to be establishing certain areas of social life within God's good creation: church, family, and labor. Also, the political state is further mandated by God only as a result of the fall.[32] Through such institutions as these, God continues to preserve the world, and within such institutions people find opportunity to demonstrate love for neighbor.

William H. Lazareth explains the relationship in Luther's theology between vocation or calling and these orders or mandates of creation:

> The decisive difference between God's universally mandated and society's officially sanctioned "stations" or "offices" (*Staende*) which all persons hold, and the "callings" or "vocations" (*Berufe*) which only believing Christians acknowledge, is that of the Spirit's motivation, power, and goals. It is not merely what we do or where we do it, but rather why and how it is done, that pleases God.[33]

Luther's understanding of vocation provides a way to conceptualize one's work in the world as an arena in which one can faithfully serve God. Theologically, vocation is linked both (1) to an understanding of God's providence in creation as finding expression in social institutions and (2) to an understanding of God's call to salvation in Christ as occurring within (rather than being hindered by) one's worldly station.

Thomas Aquinas

Prior to Luther, these areas of social life were also affirmed to be a part of creation, but the idea of "vocation" referred more exclusively to the call people might receive to withdraw from worldly activity (be it marriage or occupation) to pursue a religious life. In the system of Thomas Aquinas, social institutions reflect the divine law and are a part of the created order. For Aquinas, however, the conceptual bridge linking social structures with more specifically religious ideas is not vocation, but the use of "law" as a philosophical category. The divine law is all-encompassing. It includes both the "natural law" and the revealed law of scripture. It is also related to human law within society. The natural law is accessible to human reason and is present in the establishing and the ongoing governance of social institutions. Should human institutions deviate from their purposes according to the natural law, they would cease to be just; however, the assumption is that they do reflect this law.[34] For Aquinas, however, one's duty within these structures of society—while both rational and faithful—was not interpreted as a matter of vocation or calling. The idea of divine calling, throughout the Middle Ages, had been largely understood as a call out of the world.

Luther's theology of vocation, however, was linked to his understanding of the priesthood of all believers—that one need not be called out of the world into a religious vocation to serve God faithfully. Rather, one is able to serve God in many capacities of work and service in the world.[35] This was an innovative development in his theological thought—to bridge the divide that had separated the monastic and contemplative life from other "vocations" in society.

Protestant Work Ethic

Luther's theology of vocation became further developed within the context of Calvinism. Two particularly influential thinkers writing at the beginning of the twentieth century—Max Weber and Ernst Troeltsch—have provided historical analyses of this development of a Protestant theology of vocation. Weber's *The Protestant Ethic and the Spirit of Capitalism* remains a classic statement about the worldly importance of the religious doctrine of calling and the development of a "Protestant work ethic."[36] Their analyses continue to be debated, but Weber's and Troeltsch's descriptions of the historical development of the doctrine of vocation are worth our attention both for their continuing relevance as well as for the challenge they present to a contemporary understanding of vocational faithfulness.[37]

According to Weber and to Troeltsch, Calvinism accepted the basic Lutheran understanding of vocation. Within Calvinism's social environment as well as its theological system, however, vocation took on added significance that had repercussions for social ethics. With regard to the social environment, John Calvin developed his theology in the context of Geneva. A city located on a major trade route in the Alps, it had a strong business community and an emerging middle class.[38] Theologically, according to Troeltsch and Weber, Calvin contributed an understanding of election and predestination that became further developed by later Calvinists.[39]

Weber and Troeltsch both argue that a theology of vocation focused people's attention on their work in the world as a service to God in faithful response to divine calling. They argue further that, with its absence of any certainty concerning one's divine election to salvation, the doctrine of predestination provided heightened motivation for people to pursue their work in the world. Their industry itself as well as any success that it might bring could reassure them in their hope to be among the elect.[40] Finally, an ascetic ethos within Protestantism encouraged both diligence and thrift. Unlike earlier forms of asceticism, Protestant asceticism turned a self-denying attitude toward the world rather than away from the world. Such industry and thrift in one's worldly vocation created the conditions for the further accumulation of investment capital and the further development of capitalist economies.

Two ironies are apparent in this thesis. First, it is apparent from a contemporary perspective that the earlier religious and ascetic dimension of vocation is now largely absent (or at least deeply backgrounded) in the ethos of that very Western civilization to which it gave rise. Second, given this original ascetic and world-denying dimension of vocation, it is apparent that the development of a more world-affirming and acquisitive capitalist culture was never actually intended, foreseen, or theologically argued. Weber reminds us that the concern of the Reformers was primarily "the salvation of the soul" and that the cultural and social consequences of their religious ideas may have been "unforeseen and even unwished for results…or even in contradiction to all that they themselves thought to attain."[41]

In short, Weber and Troeltsch each argue that the development of modern capitalist economic society–and Western culture in general–has been shaped by a Protestant understanding of "calling" that emerged with the Reformation. Initially, this doctrine of vocation was not simply world-affirming but rather was shaped by an ascetic ethos that gave rise to industry and thrift. As a result, a religious idea of "calling" as divine service has helped to shape an economy and a culture that are now widely seen as "secular." The doctrine of vocation that gave birth to this economic and cultural result is based on a theology of creation and a faith in God's providence at work in the world.[42]

Orders of Creation

Theological reflection on the orders of creation reached something of a zenith in the mid-twentieth century. The experience especially of German speaking theologians within Nazi Germany provided a troubling challenge for articulating social responsibility within this theological framework.[43] A facile and fatalistic understanding of the orders of creation tended to lend a perception of legitimacy to Nazism in three ways. First, the state, as one of those orders, was assumed to be serving God's purposes even if its policies might appear unjust. Second, the culture (sometimes considered another one of the orders) was also assumed to be serving God's purposes even with its exclusivist support for German culture. Third, some clergy and theologians were hesitant to speak out against the Nazi State because of a perception of the distinctiveness between the orders of the church and the government.

In view of this, many theologians during and after the Second World War worked to articulate a theology of the orders of creation that would not lend a perception of legitimacy to totalitarian government, but would instead encourage greater social and political responsibility among Christians in resisting injustice or in holding the state accountable. As examples, Emil Brunner, Dietrich Bonhoeffer, and Helmut Thielicke each emphasized in their writing about the orders of creation (or divine mandates) that these institutions should not be considered autonomous orders with laws unto themselves. They are meant, instead, to be under the Lordship of Christ and to provide opportunity for people to love and serve their neighbors. These theologians recognized that these institutions are far from perfect and that one serves Christ and neighbor faithfully by seeking justice through one's activity in these areas of social life.[44]

These theological revisions of the orders of creation range, however, from conservative stances to radical ones. Emil Brunner has been criticized as conservative, for instance, for the degree to which he accepts inequality and coercive power in the state[45] (though Brunner argues that the state can exercise an illegitimate, self-serving "daemonic" power as well as the legitimate power of the state that serves community).[46] Nevertheless, Brunner asserts that these spheres of life are called "orders" because in them "God's Will meets us."[47]

In contrast to Brunner, Bonhoeffer refers to "labour, marriage, government and the Church" as "mandates" rather than orders to avoid misperceptions of their autonomy and to emphasize their "divinely imposed task." For Bonhoeffer, one's social duty within these institutions is only "pre-ethical."[48] The ethical arises for

Bonhoeffer when the normal moral course of action according to these social institutions is called into question for the sake of faithfulness to Christ.[49] For Bonhoeffer, the primary ethical requirement is to cooperate with Christ's reality in the world as it is being discerned within a particular time and place.

With regard to a theology of the "orders of creation" in general, several points can be noted. At its best, the idea that society is included within God's creation, God's providence, and God's care encourages Christians to take the world seriously and to be socially engaged in working for justice. This involves a cooperative appreciation between the church and other institutions. It involves, on one hand, the church's own prophetic ministry within society and, on the other hand, the church's respect for the relatively autonomous work of other institutions within society. However, a misinterpretation of the "orders of creation" can actually be counterproductive to this work for social justice in either of two ways. First, a strict division between the "orders" can discourage a process of mutual correction between them. Second, a static interpretation of the will of God at work within society can hinder steps toward a greater justice that might otherwise be inspired by a more dynamic vision of new creation in Christ.

Creation Reconsidered

In the 1960s, Western society as a whole (including the Christian churches) became more aware of environmental degradation and ecological fragility. Rachel Carson published *Silent Spring* in 1962, calling attention to the problem of environmental pollution and its effects on other species as well as humans.[50] As mentioned above, in 1967 historian Lynn White Jr. published his influential essay in *Science* arguing that the ecological crisis was due largely to the doctrine of *dominium terrae*. A study program of the World Council of Churches (WCC) began in 1969 and ended in 1974 on "The Future of Man and Society in a World of Science-Based Technology." One of the inputs to this theological conversation was Lynn White's essay. Other contributors came from both the biological and the social sciences (e.g., Kenneth Boulding, E. F. Schumacher, Herman Daly, Jorgen Randers, Charles Birch). Curiously, even though theological ethics had given a great deal of attention to questions about the "orders of creation" during the preceding quarter of a century, little mention was made of this doctrine in the theological discussions about the natural environment in the five-year ecumenical study program or in the WCC's program emphasis that followed it.

As theological conversation has moved away from a focus on the "orders of creation," the doctrine of creation has also taken on a different emphasis. Creation has always entailed everything created by God—whether human or otherwise, inclusive of but not limited to society. After the Second World War, theologians had been so concerned with articulating an appropriate theology of the "orders of creation" that the word *creation* largely held as a primary referent human society and social structures—at least within this conversation. When the ecological crisis presented its own challenge for theological reflection in the 1960s and early 1970s, theology found itself caught slightly off-guard. The doctrine of creation had been so developed in the direction of theological anthropology and social ethics that it was hard-pressed to address meaningfully the subject of ecological relationships within the natural environment.[51]

Increasingly since the mid-1970s, theologians have responded to the challenge of articulating ecologically informed and environmentally concerned theology. A key category in this project, as one might expect, has been the doctrine of creation. Now the pendulum has swung, however, and the word *creation* is typically used to describe the natural world. While humans are included in creation as God's creatures, the treatment of human institutions is often more vague. Ecotheologians strongly emphasize the importance of human moral responsibility for creation and the need to establish social structures that will allow us to better care for creation's integrity. That society and social institutions are an integral part of God's created order, however, is seldom affirmed strongly. *Creation,* which once seemed to mean society to the peculiar exclusion of nature, now often means "nature" to the conceptual exclusion of society.

Moreover, a trend in contemporary theology has been to voice suspicion with regard to the establishment of all of the traditionally conceived orders of creation. With regard to the state, as we have seen, the experience at mid-century with totalitarianism prompted Bonhoeffer and others to urge caution against seeing the state as a divinely determined and autonomous order of creation. In the 1960s, 1970s, and 1980s, liberation theology applied hermeneutical suspicion to theology in relationship to all structures of social power. Of prominent concern has been a liberationist critique of economic structures that can be seen to create poverty even while creating wealth. With regard to the institution of family, increasingly many forms of family—and even different forms of gender identity and sexuality—are being recognized as legitimate. Suspicion is often voiced toward "essentialist" understandings of gender, sexuality, and family in favor of more open and participatory "cultural constructivist" models of gendering.[52] With regard to the church as a mandate as well, postmodern epistemologies have brought into question "foundationalism" in favor of a recognition of a plurality of truths. For each of these areas of social existence, the trend has shifted to emphasize the importance of human and cultural agency in their construction rather than divine ordering in their creation.

Ironically, though, even as human and cultural agency is affirmed in every area of social existence, the problem of the meaning and importance of individual contributions to social existence comes to the fore. This is part of our vocational crisis within the culture at large. In general, people have little confidence that their work, their recreation, and their family life is in response to God's gracious call or that it is a part of God's blessed creation. We still speak of vocation, and we still hope for fulfillment through our activities in home, workplace, and country. But these loyalties and hopes tend to be separated from a well-articulated theological grounding. This is so for the religious in United States society as well as for the nonreligious. In the absence of a theology that places society within God's creation and God's providence, vocation becomes a more personalistic and privatistic matter. For the religious, it tends to become the individual seeking to hear God's voice. For the nonreligious, it is just as personalistic—a matter of soul-searching and psychometrics.

At the social level, too, without a theological grounding for understanding the importance of family, economy, and country, we can lose one of the vantage points that allows us to critique the family, economy, and country—that allows us to appreciate and to correct these social institutions. Each begins to represent an absolute claim on our loyalty without such critical perspective. Each can become, in short, an idol. The country demands ultimate allegiance from its citizens during a time of war—both in terms of life and in terms of long-cherished liberties. A normative understanding of "family" becomes prominent in political life, prompting particular voting patterns that blur the distinction between private matters and public policy. The economic sphere, too, becomes totalistic. Middle-class workers and professionals all find themselves trapped in cyclic patterns of overworking, overconsuming, and overextending their credit. Sometimes these patterns of all-consuming involvement in state, economy, and "family" are represented even in contradictory ways in the same individuals. Uncritically, yet discontentedly, we find ourselves serving many masters at once.

The very idea of "orders of creation" may sound to postmodern ears as foundationalist, essentialist, and hierarchical. It need not be so, however. The basic tenet is that society is a part of–not apart from–God's creation. This is a tenet affirmed by the church since its earliest struggles with gnosticism. At the same time, however, perhaps as humans we need to take responsibility for our own institutions and to recognize that it is our human project to organize life in society. It is our human task to determine the constitutional structure of government and to utilize that structure in day-to-day governance and policy-making. It is also our human task to determine the shape of an economy and take responsibility for the distribution and the *maldistribution* of goods, services, and wealth throughout the globe. We need to recognize, too, that family structures and familial responsibilities vary between and within societies. If family and gender are culturally constructed, then we have responsibility for helping to shape even our perceptions of biological differences. Within the church, we have a responsibility as well–clergy and laity alike–as "stewards of the mysteries of God," charged with proclaiming the gospel and administering the means of grace.

Conclusion

The final chapter of this book focuses more on the particular vocation of the church to proclaim God's grace and to administer the means of God's grace to the world. Nevertheless, further attention will be given to the ministry of the laity within the various spheres of social life as well as within the church itself. The vocation of the clergy will be discussed with regard to not only the traditional roles of "Word, Sacrament, and Order" but also to the role of moral leadership in concert with the laity's worldly vocation. The clergy's moral leadership, it will be seen, is exercised when the whole people of God are empowered for a life of moral integrity in all of society.

With regard to vocation, we have so far affirmed the following: first, the vocation of creation to glorify God; and second, the vocation of all of humanity to image God by working for justice. Both of these areas of calling are sounded broadly: to all of creation and to all of humanity. With regard to personal vocation, however, we have noticed a challenge. The vocational challenge is due to the moral ambiguity of institutions in society. This moral ambiguity, we have seen, constitutes a perennial issue for theological ethics–that is, the degree to which Christian communities may consider other social institutions as being trustworthy or suspect. The vocational challenge is to conceptualize personal calling in such a way that we recognize realistically the moral ambiguity of social institutions, while at the same time we affirm faithfully that human society is included within God's ongoing love and preservation for this world of God's creation.

Exercise for Reflection: What Are You Doing?

Barbara Smith-Moran suggests an alternative to the Lutheran-Calvinist approach for conceptualizing vocation discussed in this chapter. She relies on the teleological theology of Teilhard de Chardin for her vision. She invites readers to reflect on their own sense of vocation through a series of spiritual exercises. Her entire book (*Soul at Work*) is inspirational as a guide for spiritual reflection on vocation, and can be used to great benefit by both clergy and laity. She begins with this simple exercise that she gleaned from Doris Donnelly's work, *Spiritual Fitness,* another excellent resource for spiritual reflection concerning work:[53]

A story goes like this.

> Three men were breaking up rocks.
> "What are you doing?" a passerby asks.
> "Making little rocks out of big ones," says the first worker.
> "Earning a living," answers the second.
> "Building a cathedral," says the third.
> If a passerby saw you working and asked you what you were doing, what would you answer?

8

Vocation II

Church and Ministry

*Think of us in this way, as servants of Christ and stewards of
God's mysteries.*

1 CORINTHIANS 4:1

All creation is called to glorify God. All humanity is called to
work for justice. The church participates in both of these general
vocations: to glorify God and to seek justice. These tasks are not the
church's exclusive concern or domain, however. The church participates with others in these vocations by virtue of being a part of creation
and a part of human society. In addition, though, the church does
receive its own unique calling. The church has been entrusted with
the gospel for the sake of the world. The Greek word for church
(*ecclesia*) literally means "a calling out"; it comes from the same root
as the word for "calling" (*klesis*). The church has been called and
gathered for the sake of mission and service to the world. This is our
peculiar vocation as Christ's church.

Called and Sent

The church as Christ's body has been called for the purpose of
carrying forward Christ's work in the world. The church's ministry
and mission therefore represents the work and presence of Christ.
As Paul says, "we are ambassadors for Christ," speaking a divine
message of reconciliation on behalf of Christ (2 Cor. 5:20). The church
as a whole, as well as its ordained clergy in particular, serve in this
representative capacity, pointing beyond ourselves to reconciliation
in Christ.

149

One way to think theologically about the church's ministry is to reason by way of comparison with Christ's own anointing for office. According to this logic, Christ was anointed as Prophet, Priest and Ruler; therefore Christ's church will also exhibit ministries in each of these three broad areas. The ordained ministry in particular, by this analogous reasoning, is ordained to the ministries of word, sacrament and order.[1]

I am suggesting that each of these offices or roles makes important contributions to an understanding of the vocation of the clergy, but not *exclusively* to the vocation of the clergy. These roles pertain as well to an understanding of the ministry of the laity. However, the relationship between the clergy and the laity, and the respective roles of clergy and laity in each of these three areas, varies across denominations.

Other metaphors used to describe Jesus Christ can also be applied to the church's ministry on behalf of Christ: Savior, Redeemer, Begotten, Beloved, and others. If we think in terms of the Trinity, still more metaphors come to mind with regard to the Spirit: Comforter, Advocate, Sustainer, Wind, Breath, Dove, Fire, and the list goes on. Sallie McFague's book *Models of God*[2] speaks of God as Mother, Lover, and Friend, and has inspired a generation of theologians and preachers to think more creatively about our images of God.[3] Inspired by McFague, hymnist Brian Wren pens many metaphors:

> Bring many names, beautiful and good;
> celebrate, in parable and story,
> holiness in glory, living, loving God.[4]

All of these metaphors of God's self and God's activity can help us think about our own vocation as God's church, inspired and empowered by God's spirit and ministering on behalf of God to the world of God's incarnate loving.

Using God as an analogy to describe the church's own ministry, however, can be stretched too far. It is not just that we minister on behalf of God, seeking to embody God's grace and to convey God's love to the world. We are not just God's agents in the world. We are the objects—not the subjects—of God's love. We are the Creator's creatures, God's new creation in Christ, and the stewards of this gospel by the power of the Holy Spirit. We experience ourselves as recipients of this message and of the grace to interpret and proclaim it. We are not God, but rather the objects of God's creative, redeeming, and sustaining love.

This caveat concerning reasoning by analogy is especially appropriate when thinking about God's sovereignty and the church's ministry of order. As the Sovereign God's subjects, the Creator God's creatures, and the Redeeming God's new creation, we need to approach the task of decision-making humbly. Arrogance in claiming and exercising power can be a problem; it can interfere with the church's ministry to proclaim grace and to administer the means of grace. The work of "ordering" in the church serves the greater (and humbler) purpose of ensuring that the word of grace is spoken and that the Sacraments and other means of grace are shared.

The moral leadership of the clergy may be thought of as prophetic, but moral leadership can never be simply or only proclamatory. Moral leadership will be integrated into the priestly and pastoral roles as well as the prophetic one. Moreover, the ministry of the Word is concerned with communication and refers to the whole teaching ministry of the church as well as the preaching ministry. Teaching and preaching, though, both involve attending to the listener, the learner, the other. Teaching and learning occur together within a mutuality of speaking and listening. In each of the pastor's roles within a congregation—not just from the pulpit—a pastor will have opportunity to exercise moral leadership. Whenever the pastor is exercising moral leadership, speaking and listening will be proceeding together.

Prophetic and Priestly Ministry

The gospel entrusted to the church is the gospel of Jesus Christ. In whatever manner we may hear this gospel, define this gospel, find ourselves shaped by this gospel, celebrate this gospel, and proclaim this gospel, we hope and pray that our evangelical vocation will be consistent with our human vocation to seek justice and our creaturely vocation to glorify God. Whenever we do find inconsistencies or tensions between our understandings of the gospel, social justice, and God's glory, we have an opportunity to think further about the meaning of our call in society as God's missionary creatures and to deepen our sense of vocational faithfulness to God in the world.

To say that this vocation is "evangelical" is simply to acknowledge that it is concerned with our bearing the gospel (*euangelion*) in the world. "Evangelism" (*euangelizomai*) is the proclamation of this gospel. To say that the church has an evangelical vocation is simply to acknowledge that it carries and proclaims the gospel. It is not necessarily to claim a particular denomination, form of church governance, way of reading scripture, lifestyle, manner of communication, or political party or platform. It is to acknowledge that God entrusts the gospel and its proclamation to the church—however denominated and wherever located.

The church carries the gospel in different ways with different methods, in different styles and with different meanings. Even the

New Testament witnesses a diversity of images to depict this evangelical vocation. One is in the book of Acts. Just before his ascension, Jesus tells a small, young, incipient church, "[Y]ou will be my witnesses in Jerusalem, in all Judea and Samaria, and to the ends of the earth" (Acts 1:8b). The book of Acts unfolds the missionary expansion of the church from these humble beginnings and culminates with the preaching of the gospel in the capital of the Roman Empire. The mission of the church in Acts has a pentecostal empowerment: "and they were all filled with the Holy Spirit and spoke the word of God with boldness" (Acts 4:31b). Even the threats of shipwreck or prison or stoning provided occasions for bold proclamation. Boldness and courage characterize the church's evangelical vocation in the book of Acts.

In 1 Corinthians, Paul provides a different image than that of boldness. He speaks of being "stewards of God's mysteries" and of the trustworthiness required of such stewards (4:1–2). The stewardship of this mystery, though, is to reveal it, to proclaim it rather than to keep it secret. A little earlier, Paul says that his message does not rest on "plausible words of wisdom, but with a demonstration of the Spirit and of power" (2:4b). It is a message of grace in Christ that may be hidden from the "rulers of this age" (2:6), but which is given to the foolish to shame the wise (1:27). The message is mystery as well as proclamation. It is carried with humility as well as with boldness. The stewardship of such a message requires faith and trustworthiness.

In some sacramental traditions, the reference to "stewards of God's mysteries" has been taken to refer to the Sacraments of the church. The Vulgate, a Latin translation of the Bible, translated the Greek word for mystery (*mysterion*) with the Latin word *sacramentum*. In 1 Corinthians, though, the mystery would seem to be the message itself as well as the demonstration of that message. In terms of a more contemporary understanding of the ministry of Word and Sacrament, the mystery would seem to refer to both; it is about the message of Christ crucified *and* the signs and rituals by which that message is celebrated and conveyed.

Moreover, the gospel is entrusted to the whole church—clergy and laity alike—not just to the leaders of the church or to an ordained elite within the church. In 1 Corinthians, Paul speaks critically, even harshly, to the leaders of the church. He is adamant that God chose the foolish, the weak, the low, and the despised to bear God's message of wisdom. This is a peculiar mystery, being so broadly shared. Word and Sacrament, I am suggesting, are given to the entire church, and the entire church is trusted with the stewardship of this mystery and this message. Ordained ministers in particular may be charged with exercising a ministry of Word and Sacrament, but they do so within, on behalf of, and as authorized by the wider church.

With regard to addressing ethical issues through preaching or teaching, pastors can err either on the side of boldness or on the side of tentativeness in their communication with others. We do want to avoid being overly bold as preachers in addressing moral issues. We have heard many who arrogantly proclaim their opinions on sundry subjects without either depth of understanding of the issues or depth of sensitivity to people who are struggling with those issues. Some preachers caricature the difficulties of sin and vice to make rhetorical points. In the process they can trample over people in their congregation who may sincerely desire moral guidance or moral insight. When this happens, rather than providing moral leadership, the preacher has actually missed the opportunity to offer moral guidance.

My experience, however, is that most of us, as preachers, tend to err on the side of tentativeness. This is partly out of respect for parishioners; we are wary of appearing judgmental and overbearing. We can also be timid, though, because of our own insecurities. Such insecurities might include the following: a need to please others and win approval, a fear of controversy and conflict, or uncertainty about our own knowledge on a particular subject or about our ability to address it helpfully.

Richard Bondi suggests several reasons that ministers might fall to a "temptation not to lead."

First are confusing entanglements of local history, local processes, and different expectations of the minister. These confusing entanglements can bind the minister from leading.

Second, some ministers try so hard to stay in the middle on issues without taking sides that they fall into complacency.

Third, wounded pride can motivate ministers to withdraw from leadership.

Fourth, many fears inhibit leadership: fear of conflict especially but also fear of change in general and fear of both failure and success.[5]

Of course, we may consider it prudent to err on the side of timidity rather than arrogance in deciding whether or not to address a complex moral concern or a controversial social issue publicly. This is especially true when that concern or issue seems to lie beyond our particular area of competence or our comfort level. To provide trustworthy moral leadership, however, pastors ought to continue to educate themselves regarding the most important concerns facing their parishioners and regarding the troubling challenges confronting society. Even so, we will seldom be as competent as others within our congregations on many difficult issues, especially with regard to the more technical aspects dealt with by individuals in their different lines of work.

Nevertheless, the pastor is likely to have a better understanding than most congregants of literally thousands of years of a faith tradition and of the intellectual history interpreting that faith. Part of our apostolic heritage is to keep this tradition alive in ways that it can be accessed and critically engaged today. We should not be so bashful about this education that we deny parishioners access to this body of knowledge that we hold. It is a part of our teaching ministry to share that tradition and, in so doing, to invite others to participate in it. Not to do so is to abdicate from our responsibility to be engaged with others in conversation about the moral life.

It is preferable for the clergy to attempt to familiarize themselves with the issues with which their parishioners are engaged and then to open themselves humbly to communicate with their parishioners on these subjects–to offer insight and to allow for correction. Some clergy are very skilled in using the pulpit for addressing difficult moral subjects. But for most of us, the pulpit has a couple of disadvantages in this regard. First, it does not lend itself to two-way communication as well as a class or fellowship group of some kind that allows for a greater degree of mutual communication and interaction. Second, the sermon occurs during the time of worship and is itself a moment in worship–a form of prayer. Since sermons are a form of worship, this shapes the way in which they can also be employed for educational effect.

Sermons are generally best for bringing the moral concern or social issue into a theological context in order to listen for a "word of God" or a transformative meaning that can shift our perspective on the subject and empower our response. We listen spiritually and emotionally to sermons, as well as intellectually. Sermons do not lend themselves as well to the kind of heart-to-heart and give-and-take of more participatory forms of communication. Sermons, though, should be maximized as means of grace and time of prayer in which God is invoked, our concerns reconfigured, our moral character fortified, and our lives inspired. Our deepest moral concerns should, in fact, be addressed in sermons, and in ways that allow for the gospel to inform and transform our whole selves–including our moral sensibilities and resolve.

Sometimes, as preachers, we think that we have preached prophetically, because in our own minds we have been concerned with a controversial political or social issue. We carefully frame the sermon to infer prophetic conclusions for those "who have ears to hear." We are then surprised—and sometimes even resentful—when parishioners have not been astute enough to read our minds and to draw our inferred conclusions. Perhaps we have not been direct enough. Some preachers are so nervous about the strength of these inferences in their own minds that they couch their proclamation with so many caveats that the listener actually thinks the preacher is making the opposite point from that intended.

More likely, however, the sermon will remain vague in the listeners' ears, but they may pick up a tone of passive aggressiveness from the preacher and respond at an emotional level as if they have been antagonized. I am sure, in fact, that this is very common. Whether the preacher realizes it or not, people do listen to sermons at more than one level. They are emotionally as well as intellectually engaged, because they understand (or at least hope) the sermon to be an act of worship and a kind of spiritual exercise. Moreover, whether the preacher encourages it or not (and indeed whether the preacher even desires it or not), the very task of preaching and the person of the preacher are symbolic at a deep level for many listeners.[6]

People are primed (both intellectually and emotionally) to hear and react to words both of grace and of judgment they hear coming from the pulpit. That some of this reaction might occasionally take the form of defensiveness or even cynicism should not fool the preacher into thinking that the sermon has not touched the listeners deeply. As a result, it seems to me that people on both sides of a controversial "issue" can take offence at a preacher who has actually said very little in the sermon, but who has conveyed a generally directed attitude of passive aggression. Rather than addressing an issue indirectly while conveying an implicit attitude of judgment or resentment, in my opinion, it is better to speak directly while conveying to listeners that one is gentle and genuine in doing so.

Worship has its own integrity. Through worship we encounter the Divine and allow ourselves to be formed and reformed by grace. It is fairly common, of course, for the sermon to become exhortation to the listeners rather than a moment of call to the congregation to wait attentively on God. A further temptation faced by preachers of social conscience, however, is to take too much control of the experience of corporate worship so that every moment of the hour of worship becomes a sermon illustration or an object lesson for the points the preacher wishes to make. If worship is to mediate grace for us, as worshipers we each need to be prayerfully engaged in the whole of worship: invocation, praise, confession and pardon, reading and hearing of scripture, proclamation, thanksgiving, acts of response, and signs of renewal.

Consider, for example, the opening to the communion service that is typical in many churches. The leader calls, "Let us give thanks to the Lord our God." The congregation responds, "It is meet and right so to do" (in traditional language), or (in very contemporary language), "We do well to give God thanks and praise." Walter J. Burghardt notices, though, that this is a rendering of the Latin phrase, "*Vere dignum et justum est,*" which he prefers to translate: "It is utterly fitting and a matter of justice."[7] It is a matter of justice to lift the cup.

Ministry of Order and Service

As speaking and listening blend together in this understanding of the ministry of the Word, so too does leading and serving in the ministry of order. In his analysis of professional ethics in contemporary culture, William F. May analyzes the role of the clergy in particular, with reference to the traditional offices of prophet, priest, and ruling/ serving. He defines the ruling function of ministry in terms of service, and he understands this to be consistent with Jesus' inversion of these roles in the gospels. As opposed to traditional exercise of authority, the one who would be great would take the role of a servant. Even the Messiah "came not to be served but to serve" (Mt. 20:24–28; Mk. 10:41–45).[8]

Power is shared, I would add; it involves both clergy and laity. Calvinist thought divides power between the teaching elders and the ruling elders. In Calvin's Geneva, this distinction was particularly important because the authority in question extended beyond the walls of the church to the entire structure of Genevan society. Comments below on the ministry of leadership will refer primarily to the administration of the life and mission of the institutional church, though comparison will be made with theories of leadership that are prevalent in other social institutions (such as business organizations) within the surrounding society. Following this section on church leadership, attention will turn again to the need for moral leadership within society as a whole and the potential for leadership in the church to address that need within the larger society.

Visionary Leaders and Missionary Managers

Some of the literature about organizational leadership–whether for businesses or for congregations–tends to distinguish too neatly between the functions of "leadership" on one hand and "management" on the other. Writing primarily about business organizations, for instance, Stephen R. Covey makes this distinction with an aphorism: "Leadership focuses on doing the right things; management focuses on doing things right."[9] The three jobs of the leader, according to Covey, are pathfinding, aligning, and empowering. Pathfinding is concerned with communicating a "compelling vision and mission" of the organization. One then aligns organizational systems in a manner consistent with that vision and mission, and one empowers those who are so aligned in the synergy of a common mission.

Elsewhere, Covey provides a litany of distinctions between leadership and management.

> Leadership deals with direction...
> Management deals with speed.
> Leadership deals with vision...
> Management deals with establishing structure and systems
>   to get those results.
> Leadership focuses on the top line.
> Management focuses on the bottom line...
> Leadership derives its power from values and correct
>   principles.
> Management organizes resources.[10]

Covey does recognize that both leadership and management are important, that these roles actually overlap, and that individuals may need to exercise aspects of both roles within any given organization. Nevertheless, he celebrates "leadership" as "most important" compared to managers and producers, because of the leader's pivotal role in providing vision and direction.

Literature about church leadership makes similar distinctions between visionary leadership and mundane management, e.g., between maintenance and mission, between institution and movement, between controlling and permission-giving leaders. Kennon L. Callahan, for instance, distinguishes between the church as an institution characteristic of the "past that has been," and the church as a movement characteristic of the "future that has come." He expresses an obvious preference for the latter over the former. The institutional church focuses inward and serves its own institutional needs, he asserts, while the church as a movement focuses outward to the grass roots in mission. The church as movement requires "leaders of the whole," Callahan distinguishes, rather than "leaders of a part." These leaders of the whole work well with "teams" rather than "departments," and they work well with organizational structures that are "flexible" rather than "stiff." They work with a visionary time frame of, say, three years, rather than the annual business cycle. Key also in Callahan's conception is the ability to identify and work with emerging leaders at the grass roots, rather than just those individuals filling traditional offices of the institution.[11]

In a similar vein, William M. Easum contrasts "controlling leaders" with "permission-giving leaders." Easum advocates permission-giving leaders, who are able to equip the laity for ministries that exercise their own spiritual gifts. Permission-giving leaders, according to Easum, are visionary, faithful, in touch with reality, and able to mentor others. They are able to set aside traditional, bureaucratic structures to invite new forms of participation. Easum advocates a "Steering Team," which serves a coordinating function and which helps to clarify the congregation's culture with a mission statement, a vision statement, and a value statement.[12]

Easum, Callahan, and Covey all point to truths pertaining to the exercise of leadership—that visionary leadership inspires and equips others in movements of mission and service. They tend to structure their presentations rhetorically, however, so that all desirable qualities are characteristic of the ideal of the effective leader and are seen to be lacking in the composite of the ineffective leader. (Easum, in considerable detail, presents ten types of dysfunctional leaders in contrast to the permission-giving style that he advocates.) In actuality, of course, there are never such clear distinctions between us. We each exhibit various strengths and weaknesses for leadership, which are both praised and vilified by those around us. We are relatively effective or ineffective at any given time, given the particular circumstances that we are facing. We have successes, and we have frustrations. We have allies, and we have antagonists. We have talents, and we have "growth areas."

The church itself possesses similar complexities and balances. Each and every congregation needs to be "maintained" as well as energized for mission. Each congregation needs to attend to the people in its midst as well as to the surrounding community. It needs to attend to its material resources—buildings and finances—as well as to its human resources and their spiritual gifts. It needs to attend to its past and its present as well as to its future. It needs to attend to its existing legal, financial, and moral obligations as well as to its hopes and vision. In a congregation, people (whether clergy or lay) need to attend faithfully to their relationship with one another, even while together they attend in faith to their mission on behalf of Christ.

Craig L. Nessan provides this kind of balanced perspective in his book *Beyond Maintenance to Mission*. Despite the title, which implies a total transformation from one to the other, Nessan encourages a balance between those activities of a congregation that maintain its identity (fellowship, education, worship, stewardship) and those that propel its mission (evangelism, global connections, ecumenism, and social ministry). In fact, he understands these two areas of church life to be mutually reinforcing of each other.[13] In a similar fashion, Stewart C. Zabriskie states, "there is little mission that can happen without maintenance," which he defines as, "keeping a local congregation or a diocese *centered* so that its members are sent with common purpose and energy."[14]

An older resource also outlines the very helpful balance between maintenance and mission. In fact, James D. Glasse's *Putting It Together in the Parish* in 1972 may have originally contrasted "maintenance" with "mission" in describing the program of the church and the use of the pastor's time. Glasse encourages pastors to become "change agents," but he advises them to "count the costs" realistically (in terms of members, financial support, etc.) to decide prudently whether a particular course of change is advisable or not for a given congregation. With regard to the pastor's time, Glasse recognizes the many demands for "maintenance" within a congregation. He advocates that pastors attend intentionally, and "pay the rent," to these demands for maintenance, so that the pastor can then be free for other missional pursuits.[15] Glasse may seem reticent compared to Easum, who provides emboldening aphorisms like, "If it ain't broke, fix it."[16] However, I find that Glasse's more careful and calculating approach actually works for many people. It allows pastors to place the demands for maintenance and the risks for change into perspective. Realistically assessed in this fashion, mission and change become less frightening and more inviting as courses of action.

Moreover, I would add, there is a moral value to "counting the costs" and "paying the rent." Actually, two sets of moral issues need to be considered. One moral consideration has to do with "proportionality" with regard to consequences—a kind of utilitarian concern. The other is a more deontological consideration of the mutuality of faithfulness between people (clergy and lay) both within a congregation itself and beyond the congregation—within the wider community. Each shall be discussed in turn.

Proportionality

Iconoclasm is not necessarily constructive activity. Iconoclasm is the destruction of images and icons. It assumes that the symbol of the Holy is an impediment or distraction from true worship of that which it represents. It assumes, further, that destruction of the symbol will promote truer worship. Sometimes, though, destruction is simply that—destruction—despite our best intentions or envisionings. Iconoclasm has been one of the tendencies within English-speaking Christianity since at least the time of the English Reformation. William Easum appeals to our iconoclastic tendencies even in his humorous title, *Sacred Cows Make Gourmet Burgers*. Until its end, the book maintains the assumption that the destruction of bureaucratic structures will produce more creative possibilities. The very end of the book, though, urges more caution in the degree of change likely to be actually helpful for a congregation given its "readiness."[17]

Proportionality, as a moral principle, is much like the principle of utility; it asks whether the benefits are worth the risks. It is important, I think, in initiating change, that we do attempt to "count the costs" and strategize realistically to achieve a balance of benefit over harm. We can ask: Will these changes allow ministry to occur effectively or beneficially within this congregation and community? Or, will these changes hurt or frustrate people to the point that good will is undermined, resources reduced, and the change becomes counterproductive to its intended benefits?

Of course, facing change will always bring hurt feelings and fears. The point being made here is not that those who are most fearful or displeased with change should have veto power over a congregation's processes. Such displeasure and resistance is to be expected. But if it is to be expected, then it can also be realistically anticipated and weighed against the probability and desirability of the goals of the new direction being contemplated.

Often, clergy as leaders want to have it both ways: they want to be out in front as "change agents," but at the same time they want to empower egalitarian and participatory patterns of decision-making by consensus. In actuality, these two patterns of leadership can work against each other. A strategy for combining them is to try to build teams of people who share a vision with one another and with the pastor and who, together, can help lead the congregation in the direction of that vision. Again, though, pastors should be aware of whether the team approach to ministry is actually facilitating the fellowship and mission of the congregation as a whole, or whether it is inadvertently introducing cliquishness and division between those who are "on board" and those who are not.

Conflict is one of the costs of change. This is not necessarily bad, but it never feels good. Some observers of adaptive congregations have noticed that conflict is a necessary part of congregations dealing constructively with diversity. Charles Foster has observed that the members of multicultural congregations constantly have to negotiate differences in cultural expectations between themselves, but the result of such conflict and negotiation is a better understanding between people and a deepening sense of fellowship.[18] Nancy Ammerman also observed that conflict and a healthy approach to conflict were necessary ingredients in those congregations that were able to adjust to social and demographic changes in their neighborhoods and within their own fellowship.[19]

As a seminary intern, I was fortunate to have been placed in an urban, multicultural church that was experiencing change in the cultural constellation of its constituency. The pastor advised me, "choose your fights." I still think it is good advice. Sometimes conflict may be necessary to negotiate or settle differences that will then allow for a fellowship to be formed across cultural barriers. Also, sometimes conflict may be necessary and proportionate to the benefits envisaged—in order, for instance, for the gospel to be proclaimed within a community.

Most often, though, church conflict is about relatively trivial matters that seem to carry considerable symbolic weight. Frequently, turf wars are fought using whatever issue is at hand. These church fights can become destructive. It is good if a minister can avoid becoming embroiled in these symbolic conflicts—at least until such time as the minister's involvement can actually prove helpful. Most ministers, though, find it difficult not to become involved in church disputes. Sometimes, though, one can expedite resolution of the conflict by keeping a degree of engaged distance.

Perhaps even more destructive, however, are pastor-initiated symbolic conflicts. These force people to take sides in support of or in opposition to the pastor's agenda. This can take an emotional toll on the laity, especially if they find themselves torn by disagreement with a pastor whom they love and want to support. A pastor might actually think that the laity are being empowered when the pastor brings conflict-laden decisions before a governing board, although the pastor could decide these items directly. Sometimes this strategy does, indeed, serve to galvanize support for the decision and to let people "own" the decision. However, if the procedures that are in place force people to take sides, many people can eventually tire of fighting and exit the church. Even win-win strategies that aim at communication and reconciliation rather than competition can become wearying, as they require a commitment of energy from participants in the conversation. Within a denomination's polity, the pastor should know which kinds of decisions are legitimately the pastor's own, and which belong to the particular boards or committees of the congregation. Pastors should not make people take sides over an issue unnecessarily; pastors can, instead, allow people to conserve their emotional energy for those decisions that are rightfully theirs to make.

Proportionality has to do with minimizing harm from conflict or change and maximizing the benefit. This is a matter of discerning the times and occasions to become engaged in potentially conflictual change for the sake of a greater benefit, e.g., to promote the mission of the church, maintain the health of the congregation, or protect the well-being of its members. This is a ministry of "order"—to use the pastoral office in such a way that people are productively and satisfyingly engaged in the work of mission and in the joy of fellowship. To put the question of "order" theologically: how best can a congregation proclaim a salvific word and administer the means of God's grace both to the people within its walls and to those outside? What changes might help this to happen? What traditions might help this to happen? What structures might help this to happen? What loosening of structure might help this to happen?[20]

Mutual Faithfulness

In addition to proportional weighing of the consequences of envisioned change, another set of moral issues has to do with keeping faith with one another. Theologically, this has to do with the nature of covenant and the question of what it means to be related to one another as church. When they are in need, people should be able to expect that their congregation will provide the services of the church as appropriate. Such ministries of the church include the Sacraments and other rites: baptisms, weddings, funerals, etc. It would also include pastoral care if desired or needed. Actually, by virtue of one's baptism, a person is incorporated into the church universal and might justifiably expect this kind of welcome and access to the ministries of the church in any congregation.

The nature of our vocation, though, is that we are called together in Christ's mission for the sake of the world. Each member of a congregation is a minister and not just a recipient of ministry. One might hope that members of a congregation would be supportive of the mission of Christ's church as exercised by the congregation. They would not be acting in a manner consistent with this missiological perspective, however, if they were to make the choice of turning a congregation into a private club to meet their own needs exclusively. There are tendencies in this direction, though, in many congregations.

Pastors as leaders find themselves obliged to be faithful in two directions at once and are confronted with a discerning choice to make. They are obliged to keep faith with their congregants by providing to them pastoral care, sacramental ministry, and the teaching/preaching ministry of the church. This is in keeping with those ecclesial traditions that ordain to Word, Order, and Sacrament. As such, these duties of the pastor can be seen to be faithful at once not only to the pastor's own congregants, but to the larger church. The church has ordained the clergy in trust that these services will be rendered on behalf of Christ, whose service and church and flock we tend.

Pastors are obliged as well, though, to challenge their congregants to be engaged in ministry themselves. Pastors can help congregants to utilize their own gifts and the congregation's resources in outreach and mission. Formally, at least, and in so-called "healthy congregations," these two directions of a pastor's attention—in toward the congregation and out toward the wider community—are not conflicting or mutually exclusive loyalties. Pastoral care and meaningful worship that are provided to the congregation should prove, in turn, to be empowering to the members of the congregation for mission and ministry in the world. In actuality, however, pastors sometimes experience tensions between these two directions of pastoral priorities. Care for the congregation itself can become an exclusive concern for a pastor—either because of the pastor's need and desire for the congregation's approval, or because of the congregation's demands for the minister's time.

One potential solution to this problem is to work toward a shift in the model of ministry operating within the congregation to provide more emphasis on the contributions of the laity in ministry. Many models of ministry currently being promoted seek to bridge the divide between clergy and laity and to emphasize the ministry of the laity. This is certainly the case for William Easum's model of permission-giving churches; everyone who wants one has a ministry! Easum and others emphasize the looser structure of teams in which laypeople, encouraged and resourced by the clergy, support one another in ministry.[21] Another similar inspiration is that of "total ministry," which emphasizes the participation of all the baptized in the work of the church.[22] These approaches to ministry as lay enablement are utilized in variously sized churches, and they can be prompted by various motivations. One might hope that the primary motivation for ministry would be mission itself—a sense of vision of God's call to a congregation to be engaged in caring for its community. Other practical motives also enter in, such as the availability or affordability of fulltime clergy to serve as pastors.

At the meeting of my United Methodist Conference each year, the Conference Lay Leader gives a "Laity Address." One year, the Lay Leader decided to share the spotlight with three others, each of whom spoke about a different aspect of the ministry of the laity—four lay addresses in all. I listened to them all and was surprised to hear them each talk about the institutional church. No one talked about their work in their homes or their gardens, their labor or their investments, their political commitments or their school boards. They all talked about the importance of the laity for the institutional church!

Surely, there would be no church at all without the laity. With regard to priestly ministry in particular, most Protestants follow the tradition of Martin Luther in acknowledging the priesthood of all believers. The book of 1 Peter makes no distinction between clergy and laity when inviting people to come to Christ to be "a holy priesthood" (1 Pet. 2:4–5), and when declaring that having attained mercy we are now "a royal priesthood" (1 Pet. 2:9–10). But the ministry of the laity is also in the world. Congregations and denominational bodies need not only to open themselves to the support of the laity and to the contributions of lay ministry, they also need to empower the laity for their ministry outside of church.

William H. Lazareth relates Luther's doctrine of the priesthood of all the baptized to Luther's theology of vocation. Lazareth observes that the church can be described as "a baptized priesthood that also has an ordained ministry." While all may be priests, only some exercise priesthood primarily within the rites and rituals of the church; others exercise their priesthood within other institutions of society. Lazareth explains: "the laity's primary duty is not worship leadership but societal service, that is, not as cultic but as ethical priests." The laity exercise their priesthood within the context of their respective "callings" as opportunities for conveying God's sanctifying love to their neighbors.[23]

The irony is that the church is in danger of usurping for itself the energy that laypeople might otherwise apply to their vocational faithfulness in the world. This may be a temptation that is inherent in some of the models of heightened lay ministry. However, this is neither the intent of many of these models, nor is the usurpation of lay energies a logical necessity of them. For instance, Stewart C. Zabriskie understands vocation to embrace every sphere of activity in the world:

> Vocation is then our acceptance of the Spirit's coordination of our gifts, and the Spirit provides the energy, the momentum, and the context to live out the promise and to extend

the center in whatever arenas may be offered—whether that be workplace, home, school, or play environments. There is no recognizable limit to viable vocational expression so long as we remember that vocation is a community enterprise...

To "have a vocation" is to be baptized. To "go into the ministry" is to be baptized.[24]

In other words, it is a matter of vocational faithfulness to be in ministry, whether through church activities or through other aspects of one's life in society.

Vocational Struggles

However, as noted in the previous chapter, the very social institutions that we want to support—which promote peace, justice, material prosperity, and ecological health—also and ironically support war, inequality, poverty, and environmental damage. It is hard to be a layperson—one whose ministry is "in the world"—under these conditions. Many people genuinely do pray and seek to discern their vocation in the world—a way to be of service, to help others, to participate in the healing of creation, to glorify God. Some are fortunate to find a satisfying niche in which they feel they can both earn a living *and* be of service to God and neighbor. Others, though, can become frustrated or cynical when they discover that their ideals are compromised within the practical institutional realities of "making a living." Many who enter some form of social service (social workers, teachers, healthcare workers, religious workers, park naturalists) are vulnerable to burnout when they find themselves disillusioned by these institutional realities.[25]

The idea of work as calling may seem to hold out a promise that our work should be meaningful, even though we may experience it in actuality as meaningless drudgery or as stressful burden. The very hope that work might be existentially fulfilling sets us up for disappointment when our labor proves instead to sap life's energies. In suggesting that we need to recover a sense of vocational faithfulness within society, we must recognize that such an understanding of vocation has been severely fractured in Western culture and that its recovery is no easy task.

Ironically, the more our hope for fulfillment may be placed in our labor, the more we may find ourselves disappointed. It has been suggested that the church holds potential for fostering a greater sense of vocational commitment to community and mutual responsibility. This role of the church, and of the clergy in particular, for offering moral leadership and guidance will be discussed further below. The clergy, though, also face the challenge of avoiding the problem of burnout. Disillusionment can be a problem, especially for those serving their first pastorate and suddenly confronted with a disparity between their hopeful ideals and the toilsome reality. The clergy are not immune from vocational disillusionment any more than are the members of other hopeful professions.

■ CASE FOR DISCUSSION: Taking Account

Lydia has had a career as a mother and as an accountant, and now teaches accounting to business students in a small Midwestern university. Some of her students are motivated to study business because it seems to be a practical major that offers the promise of a well-paying career after graduation. Some of them, however, become frustrated to discover that they may have little actual aptitude for the particular mathematic and analytical skills needed in accounting. Some of these students have other talents, but feel that they have to get a practical degree from four years of college.

One particular student became distressed about the consistently poor grades he had been achieving in his business classes and consulted with his teacher about it. Having had this student in more than one class and thus able to evaluate his performance, Lydia was sympathetic concerning his current distress. But she was not optimistic that he could successfully complete this program in accounting.

She reassured him, saying: "You know, Jim, accounting is not the 'be all and end all' of the whole world. You could do many other things to earn a living if you are able. I, for one," she confessed, "would rather be able to sing."

■ ■ QUESTIONS

Discuss this case from four standpoints.

1. If you were Jim, what do you imagine you are expecting from your course of study? from yourself? from your teacher? from this particular visit with your teacher? How do you imagine hearing and responding to her advice?
2. If you are the teacher, how do you imagine your own vocation? How do you imagine your student's vocation? Is Lydia being wistful? frustrating to Jim? helpful to him? Would you consider her role here to be pastoral? a moral guide? just a teacher? an antagonist?
3. If you were Jim's pastor and he raised this concern with you, how might you respond to him? If you were Lydia's pastor and

she told you this story, expressing concern for Jim, how might you respond to her? Would you consider your responses to be moral guidance? pastoral care? How so?

4. As you read this story, are you facing anything like Jim's business course? What? Are you able to sing? What are you able to do? If you were to choose a song to sing, what would it be? Can "calling" ever be discerned through these kinds of encounters? If so, how? Or, conversely, why not?

The church, like other social institutions, does not provide a guaranteed safe haven from vocational disillusionment. This is so not only for so-called dysfunctional congregations, but it is true for so-called "healthy congregations" as well. A pastor can become tired and disappointed even while serving in a congregation that may embody a salvific gospel in whole and healthy ways. I do think that most congregations are sincerely seeking to exhibit an ethic of love and justice in their organizational life as well as in the lives of their individual members. In many congregations, the members may genuinely seek to nurture one another in the faith, to encourage one another in living well, and to relate to one another honestly and transparently. A pastor can find himself or herself disappointed and disillusioned even in these congregations, however, if the congregation's life does not fit with the pastor's own personal expectations. This is especially common for ministers in their first pastorate after seminary.[26]

When a person shifts her or his status from that of a layperson to that of an ordained pastor, a shift in roles and expectations takes place. This shifting seems to occur regardless of a person's or a congregation's explicit ecclesiology or theology of leadership. A newly ordained pastor finds that leadership is now expected from him or her in ways that were not expected prior to ordination—even if that leadership is to be exercised within an egalitarian framework of mutual ministry. Pastors whose preparation for leadership has occurred within the classrooms of a seminary may find that—despite their own best intentions as well as the intentions of the seminary curriculum—they are more prepared for the liminal status of a student than the central status of a pastoral leader.[27]

Moreover, prior to ordination, many seminarians have had good experiences of congregational life in which they felt themselves nurtured within community. Such an experience can be a strong motivator for seeking a career in the church. Seminarians frequently hope to be called by such a nurturing congregation, to lend their own efforts in promoting such a community of nurture, and in turn to enjoy life within such a community—nurturing and being nurtured by it in kind. This seldom happens. Congregations do look to the pastor for nurture and emotional support, but it is not always reciprocated. This can frustrate a pastor who may be expecting his or her own needs for nurture to likewise be met by the congregation. As Scott Walker warns in his essay for first-time pastors, "You Can't Get Your Blessing from a Church."[28]

John Snow's book about pastoral ministry deals very realistically with different sets of competing and even conflicting expectations that impact pastors' self-perceptions.[29] At an emotional level, he notices that a pastor must often deal with people's deep insecurities as they face life's many uncertainties, and death's single certainty. The typical pastor is ill-equipped, he contends, to address these emotional needs and can become overwhelmed by them. The gospel, he affirms, promises salvation rather than survival. This gospel speaks to the core of human need, he contends. In a secular culture, however, and in the absence of wide moral consensus, it becomes difficult for the clergy to apprehend for themselves—let alone interpret for others—the deeply meaningful significance of this salvific message. Proximate as well as ultimate worries become all-consuming—for both the clergy and the laity—even as the words of this gospel of peace resound around us.

Moreover, a new pastor can begin to think of even a healthy congregation as needy, because the pastor is now experiencing a different set of expectations and is being exposed to a different layer of people's emotional vulnerability. If the pastor's own needs for nurture remain unfilled, the pastor may then be less equipped emotionally to provide the emotional nurture as well as organizational leadership that are being expected.

Furthermore, newly ordained pastors are often hoping for reassurance that they are doing well in their new pastorate in the many and various duties required of them. This is a most natural and expected tendency for anyone in a new job. We all want positive feedback that assures us that we are both productive and appreciated. Some people in the congregation will delight in giving this reassurance to the minister (and a pastor in need of such reassurance may be tempted to spend a disproportionate amount of time ministering to these particular individuals). Other parishioners will be oblivious to this need in the pastor for reassurance, because they simply see the pastor occupying a strong role as leader (and this, too, can lead to miscommunication). Still others—perhaps a small but vocal minority—will actively criticize the new pastor. This can be very distressing to the pastor, who may be particularly sensitive to even a minority's criticism during the early months of a new pastorate.

All of these dynamics can provoke a vocational crisis for a pastor. Especially powerful is the combination of (1) disappointment when a congregation does not provide emotional nurture to the pastor, and (2) the pastor's sensitivity to criticism from members of the congregation. In these situations, however, a greater degree of sensitive and caring leadership is called for from the pastor. In the case of the pastor's own disappointment, the pastor is challenged to hear constructive criticism well and not to overreact to criticism even when it may seem picky or unconstructive. The pastor is further challenged to rely on friends and family for emotional support rather than on parishioners who may themselves be relying on the pastor for strength, pastoral care, and leadership.

Leadership in Society

The moral leadership of clergy, we have said, should be seen in relationship to the vocation of the laity. The ministry of the laity is "in the world." Their participation in church should empower them for faithful life and witness outside of church–in the home, the market, and the polling booth. Several recent observers of the role of religion in public life have emphasized the importance of a recovery of a sense of vocation in society. We will briefly discuss three here: Robert Bellah and his associates, Robert Putnam, and William F. May. All three criticize a culture of individualism that diminishes a sense of mutual responsibility within contemporary civil society. Also, they each point to the potential for the church to exercise leadership in drawing people toward a greater degree of responsibility in community, though this potential is not unambiguous.

Robert Bellah

Robert Bellah and his associates decry the degree to which individualism has eroded a sense of moral commitment to community within American society. They suggest that a "reappropriation of the idea of vocation or calling" might contribute to the reconstruction of a sense of community and commitment to the common good. Moreover, they understand that a more traditional understanding of professionalism as "calling" may have implications for the public responsibility of professionals. One of the contributions of the church to public life, they notice, is to encourage this sense of vocation as public responsibility.[30]

Robert Putnam

In a similar vein, Robert Putnam addresses the problem of the disintegration of community in American society. Putnam notices that some people expect the workplace to provide an increased sense of meaning and that many people tend to rely on work-related personal relationships to form an important community for them. Some people do find a high level of personal satisfaction in their employment and in their relationships established in the workplace. However, a number of job-related pressures tend to work against the formation of significantly meaningful community or intimate relationships in places of employment. Moreover, increased pressures on people to earn a living competes for time that might otherwise be given to volunteering or engaging in meaningful activities in the wider civil society.[31]

To the church's credit, according to Putnam, members of congregations are actually more likely to be involved in various ways and at various levels of community life. Putnam uses the phrase, "social capital"" to refer to the relationships people have with one another in society as a resource for society's well-being:

> Faith communities in which people worship together are arguably the single most important repository of social capital in America…As a rough rule of thumb, our evidence shows, nearly half of all personal philanthropy is religious in character, and half of all volunteering occurs in a religious context.[32]

Religious institutions support a wide range of social activities in addition to charity. Moreover, by participating in the life of a congregation, people develop skills for communication, cooperation, and leadership that allow them to contribute constructively in other organizations and civic groups as well.

However, according to Putnam, not all religious organizations provide this social benefit to the same degree. Putnam distinguishes between "bridging social capital," which facilitates wider networking within society, and "bonding social capital," which concentrates relationships more intensely within a particular group. That which promotes civic responsibility and the health of society as a whole is bridging social capital, whereas bonding social capital can exhibit more exclusivist tendencies. Putnam notes that some religious organizations are more conducive to such bonding rather than bridging.[33]

William F. May

William F. May attends to professionals in relation to the rest of society. He analyzes the public role of society's professionals, including the clergy, with reference to leadership and moral responsibility. May argues for the recovery of a sense of professionalism as vocation, that is, as a calling to public service and as a responsibility for the common good. This runs counter to more individualist "careerist" trends shaped by the dominant influence of the economic marketplace on the professions. The professional's covenant with society, in May's opinion, has intellectual, moral, and organizational dimensions. A professional should not only be competent in the body of knowledge of one's profession, but should also demonstrate the virtues of fidelity and public spiritedness.[34]

The clergy, May hopes, will demonstrate these virtues themselves. In addition, the church has a role in encouraging the development of a sense of vocational faithfulness and public spiritedness within society as a whole. The church can effectively serve this public role in three ways:

1. by organizing and encouraging forms of charity and service
2. by promoting and equipping the laity's vocational faithfulness within society
3. by engaging in a public witness for justice

With regard to the ministry of the laity, May writes, "lay people can minister to others through their services as doctors, lawyers, engineers, accountants, corporate and union leaders, politicians, journalists, and teachers." In addition to their jobs, however, people are also called both to acts of charitable service and to political action, May says:

> [O]ne's calling includes not simply occasional works of personal charity and steadfast service to others through one's job, but also through one's duties as a citizen. The church, as well, must accept its institutional duties of citizenship and serve as a public within the public at large.[35]

May's position is consistent with that being articulated here–that our vocation includes a universal call to seek justice and to serve the public good. This call may be pursued through many and various forms of individual participation in economic life, political life, family, and community.

The church's particular vocation of Word, Order, and Sacrament should be exercised in such a way that it empowers rather than distracts from the vocational faithfulness of the church's members in society—in their homes, their employment, their recreation, their communities. The clergy can promote this worldly faithfulness through every aspect of their work in congregations: through teaching, preaching, worship, administration and enablement of others, social witness, pastoral care, and ministries of service.

Moral Guidance and Pastoral Care

Rebekah Miles has described our dilemma concerning the value of work well. According to Miles, we both overvalue and undervalue work. "We need greater idealism and greater realism about work," she writes.[36] It is not only that we must recover a sense of vocation—to raise our hopes, if you will—we also must accept the fact that work tends to be drudgery. Thus, citing Ecclesiastes, Miles explains:

> We need to lower our sights and recognize that all work has limited value. We aren't called to like it, just to do it. In short, we value work too much and too little. We expect too much of it when we look to it for ultimate meaning or when we forget that it is toil and vanity. Remembering God and the larger purposes of life, we are reminded of work's important but secondary role. We need a hopeful realism and a chastened idealism about work.[37]

The pastor as a "moral guide," according to Miles, can help people think realistically and reflect theologically about the significance of their work. Pastors can do this through worship and the study programs of their congregations. They can also do this within both casual conversations and counseling sessions with parishioners.

In counseling sessions, Miles advises that pastors attend to work-related issues in several ways. She suggests that pastors be attentive to the role that work or work-related stress might play in any given problem and to take initiative, when appropriate, to encourage parishioners to describe their work history and to reevaluate their relationship to work. She suggests that issues related to work might be an important part of people's relationships and should be examined, for instance, in premarital counseling sessions. She urges that pastors be sensitive to different personal needs as well as cultural expectations pertaining to work. Finally, she urges that special care be offered to those who have recently become unemployed—with attention given both to their material and their emotional needs.[38]

Miles provides a model for combining the roles of pastoral care and moral guidance. "A primary task of moral guidance," she suggests, is simply "to be with parishioners in crises," and she urges pastors to remember that people are free and responsible to "make their own decisions."[39]

Because the clergy do many things, we often describe and contrast these discrete tasks with reference to areas of the seminary curriculum. *This* is pastoral care, and *that* is prophetic ministry. This is church administration, and that is a teaching ministry. This is exegesis, and that is homiletics. Our experience of ministry, however, is that we find ourselves moving quickly between these different roles and even doing them simultaneously. We find opportunities for teaching throughout the life of the church. We find a need to extend pastoral care at any given moment in our various duties. Church meetings become a time for worship and reflection as well as for conducting business.[40] This book has consistently attempted to present the professional ethics of clergy within the full and fluid scope of this experience in ministry, leadership, and fellowship.

Some people set two areas of pastoral work in tension: the provision of pastoral care and the offering of moral guidance or instruction. The former tends to proceed with a premise of nonjudgmentalism and acceptance, while the latter posits a need to deliberate and to make right judgments. Indeed, the helpfulness of pastoral care for people has surely increased as it has been liberated from an excessive and judgmental moralism. People need to feel accepted as a precondition for nearly any kind of helpful relationship.

Nevertheless, some pastoral theologians, such as John Snow, confess that a therapeutic model of pastoral care, which a generation of clergy nearly universally adopted, did not always provide the tools for facilitating moral discernment, for resourcing critical ethical analysis of society, or for encouraging social engagement.[41] Other pastoral theologians have argued similarly for a recovery of ethics in the practice of pastoral care. John C. Hoffman and Geoffrey Peterson, for instance, each propose that the development of a healthy moral conscience should be one of the goals of counseling, psychotherapy, and pastoral care.[42]

More recently, Sondra Ely Wheeler has written about the intersection of bioethics and pastoral care. She suggests four roles of the pastor "in a medical crisis," which seem to me generally applicable for relating moral leadership to pastoral care:

1. a "ministry of presence" of companionship and fellowship during times of trouble, recognizing that Christ too is present in this fellowship

2. the "minister as interpreter," facilitating communication and understanding between parties

3. the minister as "partner in discernment," which, for Wheeler, combines both spiritual discernment and moral deliberation as people face difficult times and difficult decisions

4. the minister as "witness to the gospel," for which she notes that this "vocation has a special urgency" in the hospital setting that may appear alien to the symbols and stories of the faith tradition

Ministry of word and worship, pastoral care and ethics all proceed together in these moments of ministry.[43]

This book has proceeded on assumptions that pastoral care and moral empowerment can work together–and do even coalesce–in the course of offering pastoral ministry. At this point, we need to make these assumptions explicit and discuss the possibilities of the compatibility of these two functions in the vocation of ministry. The assumptions of compatibility in this book so far have been two: the first concerning listening and the second, agency.

Listening

Listening well is central to both pastoral care and moral guidance. Most pastors have been educated or at least familiarized with the insights of Carl Rogers about reflective listening. The basic approach was described earlier in the chapter on nonmaleficence. In that context we recognized times in which a person's safety requires a more interventionist approach than is typical in Rogerian nondirective counseling. This is not to diminish the importance, however, of listening carefully to parishioners as a mode of pastoral care and help.

Theologically, one can find in this nondirective approach to listening as care an affirmation–or at least an assumption–of God's presence, providence, and care. We assume that a person has access to healing resources as that person works through his or her own situation in conversation with the counselor or pastor. The pastor's listening allows the person to explore and express his or her own situation. In the process he or she opens to healing and grace.

As the chapters of this book have illustrated, listening well is also deeply important for the pastor's role as a moral guide. One must listen attentively to parishioners at every step of the process of moral guidance. One must listen to gauge the degree of danger that might be present in a troubling situation. One must listen to determine the nature of a parishioner's need, request, or expectation for care. One must listen to know whether confidentiality is called for. One must listen truly if one is to speak truthfully as well. In moral guidance, one must listen to discern a parishioner's deepest moral values or how the parishioner is thinking about his or her options. If a reader receives assistance from these pages to facilitate his or her role as a moral guide, it will likely be related to this emphasis on listening. Listening allows us into the moral world of others. When people know that we listen with respect, they extend that invitation to us.

Agency

This leads to the second area of fundamental commonality between the roles of pastoral care and moral guide. Both helpful pastoral care and empowering moral guidance have as a common goal the strengthening of a person's own agency. That is, they each seek to assist the other person in affirming his or her own ability to reflect, decide, and act. Agency as reflecting, deciding, and acting involves a person's personality or character in every way. It includes thoughts and reasoning, feeling and emotion, likes and dislikes, values and loyalties, relationships and sense of self. Agency is a matter of being able to reflect, decide, and act in the present, while taking account of the past and anticipating a future.

A pastor might be inclined to attend to different aspects of a person's situation depending on whether the pastor understands himself or herself as being engaged in pastoral care or in offering moral guidance. Different aspects of the pastoral role, though, become contextually salient in different situations. The circumstances themselves suggest that which is more important for our attention. Some situations suggest themselves to us immediately as requiring pastoral care, and some situations present us immediately with a moral quandary. Many situations, of course, entail elements of both–both a need for care and a need for responsibility.

Jackson Carroll suggests that reflective practitioners (or reflective practical theologians) conduct "frame experiments" as they find themselves engaged in ministry.[44] That is, one considers a puzzling situation from different standpoints to free oneself from one single way of viewing it. One can examine a situation first from the standpoint of pastoral care, then from the standpoint of ethics, then from the standpoint of organizational leadership, and finally from the standpoint of being a teachable moment. One has innumerable possible standpoints from which to view any given situation.

The point is to give oneself the opportunity to challenge one's own assumptions so as to expand one's options for interpreting a situation and responding appropriately to it. This is a helpful skill that can be practiced and developed. At first, one may need to take reflective time out to write up a case study and to examine it–perhaps with a supervisor, colleague, or mentor–from within different frames.[45] With practice, though, one begins increasingly to reframe on the spot and to simultaneously see different ways of interpreting a situation and responding pastorally. One can invite others into this process as well–whether in the context of study programs, business meetings, counseling sessions, or times of ethical consultation.

When the agenda of a consultation with a parishioner is explicitly about a moral dilemma, reframing can occur with reference to different moral frameworks for analyzing the problem at hand. Many such frameworks have been suggested in the pages of this book. Shall we look at a moral quandary in terms of consequences or in terms of duties? Shall we examine it in terms of loyalties or with reference to virtue? What are the risks of harm in a situation, and how shall we weigh those risks? Is rescuing required, and can it be done safely? How is the truth at stake? To what degree is confidentiality required? All of these moral questions allow for the ethical reframing of a problem as pastor and parishioner view it together.

Most often, a parishioner will have a preferred way of thinking about moral issues. It may be consequentialist, or it may be more deontological. It may be more directed to the future, or informed by the past. It may be logically structured, or it may flow in a more narrative pattern. A discerning pastor can help a person to identify his or her own moral commitments and to reason further with them. We can "think with" a person to some degree if we can understand their moral assumptions and the pattern of their reasoning. In a situation of moral quandary, however, when a person is unable to reach a satisfactory conclusion, the pastor as moral guide might suggest reframing the question so that other, alternative moral frameworks are employed to provoke further insight.[46]

People talk to their pastors about ethics with different expectations or agendas in mind; sometimes these expectations and motives are complexly mixed. Only occasionally will a parishioner deliberately approach the pastor and expressly communicate a moral question and genuinely request help with the task of discernment. Gaylord Noyce enumerates from one pastor's notebook the variety of difficulties parishioners might bring to their pastor's attention but without necessarily emphasizing moral dimensions to these difficulties:

> a sense of drivenness; a sense of guilt–over broken relation-
> ships, in another case over feeling so much hate, in yet
> another case over being too self-centered; an inability to cope

because of too many pressures; being depressed, feeling suicidal, experiencing marital problems,[47]

The list continues. Some of these issues have been discussed previously with regard to pastoral ethics and safe practice. All of these issues have elements related to mental health and to moral agency. The pastor chooses how to respond to a parishioner's concern in a manner that might be most helpful. A clarifying discussion will then likely ensue between pastor and parishioner. Reframing the problem is always possible so that a pastor can shift between one mode of care and another. Pastoring is an art more than a technique; its medium is the relationship itself rather than a particular science.

Rebekah Miles is even clearer with regard to the motives of parishioners for approaching pastors with moral issues. Although some do have an explicit ethical quandary, many come to the minister because they have already made a decision and it proved to be a wrong one. They are in trouble and trying at one level or another to deal with that trouble. Others are contemplating a decision they already know to be morally problematic and are seeking justification for it. It is the more rare event, she indicates, when a parishioner has something of a classic two-sided moral dilemma to contemplate. Still, the pastor converses with the parishioner to raise to consciousness those values and principles that allow that person to reflect on the morality of the matter at hand.[48]

When people do approach the minister with a moral quandary, they may be interested in engaging the minister with one of at least four possible intents.

1. They may be seeking moral advice in a rather straightforward manner.
2. They may have already thought of a course of action and are hoping for confirmation about the rightness of this action from the minister.
3. At another level, they may want emotional affirmation rather than cognitive confirmation concerning the matter.
4. Some people have neither made up their own minds on a question nor are they really asking for advice; instead they tend to think out loud. They want to verbally test out their own ideas in conversation together. This may be more typical than atypical in pastoral conversations; use of nondirective counseling techniques can sometimes help these individuals to further clarify their own hearts and minds.

A fifth agenda is always possible in these types of encounters when people seem to be approaching the minister for advice. Since ministers tend to be interested in morality and in theology, both subjects can become bait on the hooks of a more hidden agenda. An example is the "game" Eric Berne described once as "Why Don't You–Yes But."[49] In this "game," one person manipulates another into endlessly offering advice by alternately asking for and then rejecting that advice. The game provides a certain level of social gratification to the individual while reinforcing that person's sense of self-pity. The minister should not immediately assume that such a manipulation is occurring. Once aware of the dynamics of such a game, however, the minister can decide how much he or she wants to play and whether or not to try to engage the person in a different activity. However, ministers should probably not be too preoccupied about this kind of game or hidden agenda.

These subtle manipulations are not always totally bad. Hidden agendas are a part of life, and it can be counterproductive to the minister to form a habit of constantly resenting them. Also, while it is helpful for the minister to converse with eyes open to the different possible meanings–honest or hidden–within a conversation, it is not helpful for the minister to substitute an attitude of cynicism for an attitude of caring. A modicum of caution mixed with care, though, can help focus the minister's attention. Even a manipulated conversation is a request for care (albeit on its own terms), and the minister must decide then whether to play along with the game or to offer an alternative kind of care. If the minister's offer of a different kind of care is rejected, the minister should accept the rejection.

Conclusion

Pastors need not become too distracted by the mixed messages and the moral foibles, by the ambiguities and the ambivalence of the members of their congregation. We are each of us in the process of learning to rely on grace, to be transformed by grace, and to live in grace. When we look for the glory of God in one another–in the joy of our successes and in our struggles with failure, in our certainty and in our confusion, in our faith and in our doubting, in our compulsiveness and in our growth–we can begin to take delight in all of it. We can begin to notice and affirm the heroism in each of us, which is there despite our shortcomings as surely as grace is there despite our sins. It is always a miracle, I think, to find people persevering in faith and seeking to grow in love. Our call as pastors is to encourage the moral life and the faithful life through the means that are at our disposal: through preaching and teaching, through worship and sacraments, through caring and serving, through leading and empowering. As pastors, our hope is to strengthen those around us who, in turn, can be faithful witnesses to God's love, and faithful servants of God's justice in our homes, our jobs, our communities, our many nations and cultures, our single home on earth.

Exercise for Reflection

The quotation from Gaylord Noyce above begins to list various kinds of experiences that would lead a person to seek help from the pastor. Think of a particular instance of one of these situations, or think of the last time a parishioner approached you for help of some kind. Be sure to imagine a particular situation. Then reflect on the following questions.

1. What are the needs for pastoral care for this person that you are remembering or imagining? Are you able to address these needs for care, or would you need to refer?

2. What are the moral issues or the moral questions that come to mind as you contemplate this person's situation? How might you guide this person to reflect on the moral questions or moral patterns? Would such reflection be consistent with or counterproductive to the pastoral care you would want to provide?

3. How does this issue or concern involve a wider community? Is this person's family involved? this person's place of work? this person's municipality? Are there social issues or matters of justice to be addressed? Who should be attending to these wider issues (e.g., this person asking for help, another person, yourself, the church, another organization or agency)?

4. Are there implications here for the worship or the study life of your congregation? How might this concern be brought through ministry of word or worship into the fellowship of the congregation while still respecting this person's privacy?

5. Can you help this person explore her or his relationship to God while still honoring the intensity of this person's thoughts and feelings in the moment? Can you help this person in a process of discerning God's call? How can you do so without pushing your own voice into that call? Can you help this person in discovering God's glory in some of this? How can you do so in a truly pastoral or priestly manner without becoming too preachy or instructive? Can you discover the glory of God in this situation yourself? How do you find yourself glorifying God as you minister with this person?

Conclusion

I attended church one morning with my sister-in-law, Margie, and my eight-year-old niece, Caitlin. Caitlin likes church. The pastor had preached that morning on discerning vocation. He had emphasized that people should prayerfully consider a religious vocation for themselves, and that parents should encourage their children to consider a religious vocation. It had seemed to Margie that he had pushed this point strongly, and we were discussing it after church. I had just been reading John Snow's book *The Impossible Vocation,* which makes vivid some of the emotional challenge of pastoral ministry, and I was relating some of this in my conversation with Margie. Caitlin listened, and then asked,

"What's an impossible vocation?"

"The work of the pastor," I replied.

She pondered briefly, thinking of her own pastor, I imagine, and visualizing the pastor leading worship, preaching, attending meetings, and interacting with the people of the parish in various ways, including her own relationship as a member of the congregation. "That's not impossible," she observed simply.

In fact, she is right. I have been reassured ever since.

This book has attended to the actual work of clergy and to the kinds of relationships that we establish in order to reflect faithfully on our obligations as professionals. Keeping ministerial practice in mind, we have attended to both theological and philosophical categories of analysis to display aspects of our moral responsibility. We began with a discussion about character and virtue in chapter 1, and moved from there into a consideration of the "ethics of doing" in subsequent chapters. Virtue, though, has remained at least implicitly integral to this treatment of pastoral ethics, and we now focus directly on it again in this brief conclusion.

Indeed, nonmaleficence as a duty is predicated on gentleness as a virtue. Beneficence can be seen as a duty that is predicated on love. Truth-telling, promise-keeping, and confidentiality are all predicated on virtues of fidelity, honesty, and trustworthiness. In each area of professional life, inward virtue and outward action are united.

The vocation of the clergy is essentially spiritual as well as relational, social, and institutional. We need spiritual resources that help us to live a moral life in relationship to others. We also need occasional reassurances that we ourselves are cared for—that we are held within God's care even while we extend care to others. Saint John of the Cross wrote that there are three virtuous effects on the soul that can keep one's soul secure against any attack; they are: peacefulness or tranquility, gentleness or meekness, and strength.[1]

Citing John of the Cross, Evelyn Underhill finds these three benefits of God's spirit to provide a reassuring indicator of one's spiritual life:

> [A] consideration of the tranquillity, [*sic*] gentleness and strength with which we deal with the circumstances of our outward life will serve us better than anything that is based on the loftiness of our religious notions, or fervour [*sic*] of our religious feelings. It is a test that can be applied anywhere and at any time. Tranquillity, [*sic*] gentleness and strength, carrying us through the changes of weather, the ups and downs of the route, the varied surface of the road; the inequalities of family life, emotional and professional disappointments, the sudden intervention of bad fortune or bad health, the rising and falling of our religious temperature. This is the threefold imprint of the Spirit on the souls surrendered to [God's] great action.[2]

Tranquility, gentleness, and strength are not just subjective or inward indicators of one's spiritual well-being; they are outwardly evident in action, and they are produced by the Spirit's work in one's life.

This book has not discussed tranquility, but such tranquility is surely important for us in exercising caring and effective ministry. We need tranquility to be centered ourselves as we live and work amid the many entanglements of agendas and anxieties that are found within the web of relationships surrounding us. We need tranquility as well as strength to persevere in caring for others over time—through periods of both joy and sorrow, both faith and doubt.

We need tranquility in our public witness as well, if we are to be effective in our vocation of pursing peace and justice in our world. A martial culture threatens to overwhelm both the church and society, as people's fears provide fuel for war. Tranquility is needed again in people's souls if peace is to return to society, and tranquility is required of the church's leaders if we are to inspire peace in others.

Gentleness, I suggest, refers to the minister's own integrity in working with others. It refers to the minister's own character and a disinclination to abuse pastoral power. Gentleness also refers to the process of shepherding itself, of offering spiritual and moral guidance and counsel. This book has urged ministers to show respect for the moral agency of the people with whom we interact. Our own moral judgment should not overwhelm the other's struggle for moral discernment. Gentle ministers facilitate that struggle for discernment.

Similarly, within a congregation as a whole, ministers are called to empower the ministry of the group. This facilitates the congregation's own spiritual presence within its neighborhood. It inspires the congregation's mission that might expand beyond the geographic and cultural confines of the parish itself. Gentleness includes this empowering of others rather than self-promotion. Gentleness involves respect for others and faithfulness in our relationships. Gentleness seeks others' good and avoids harming.

At each step of the progression of thought in this book, it has become apparent that strength is needed as well as gentleness. It was noted in chapter 1 that merely refraining from harming is not always sufficient for ensuring safety. Sometimes, such as in situations involving violence, a pastor might need to intervene in ways that require courage and strength as well as gentleness and prudence.

Concerning the duties of fidelity, strength of character is needed as well as trustworthiness. Veracity sometimes requires more than simply refraining from lying, but to speak and act truly requires courage and strength. Confidentiality also requires moral strength to hold fast a secret entrusted (as well as wisdom to know how tightly to hold it).

In sum, vocational faithfulness requires strength and gentleness. Strength is necessary–both in order to exercise leadership in congregations and to pursue justice in society. Gentleness displaces arrogance and allows us both to encourage others for ministry, and to participate humbly with the rest of creation in giving glory to God.

Notes

Chapter 1: Moral Self in Community

[1]Bruce C. Birch and Larry L. Rasmussen, *Bible and Ethics in the Christian Life,* rev. ed. (Minneapolis: Augsburg, 1989), 39–43.

[2]The two are related to each other variously in ethical systems as well as in "real life." For Immanuel Kant, as an example, an ethics of doing very strongly involves a duty to oneself—one's own integrity and autonomy as a rational moral agent. The distinction between "being" and "doing," though, provides a good beginning point for noticing how they can be related to each other in both theory and practice.

[3]Thomas Aquinas, *Summa Theologica: Complete English Edition in Five Volumes,* trans. Fathers of the English Dominican Province (Westminster, Md.: Christian Classics, 1981) First Part of the Second Part, Question 64, p. 857, citing Aristotle, *Ethic,* ii 6. Thomas cites Aristotle in arguing that virtue follows the mean, but does make exception for the theological virtues of faith, hope, and charity.

[4]Katie Cannon, *Black Womanist Ethics* (Atlanta: Scholars Press, 1988), 5.

[5]Ibid., 104.

[6]Ibid., 105–43.

[7]Alasdair MacIntyre, *After Virtue: A Study in Moral Theory* (Notre Dame: University of Notre Dame Press, 1984).

[8]Benjamin W. Farley, *In Praise of Virtue: An Exploration of the Biblical Virtues in a Christian Context* (Grand Rapids: William B. Eerdmans, 1995).

[9]James F. Keenan, S.J., and Joseph Kotva Jr., *Practice What You Preach* (Franklin, Wis.: Sheed & Ward, 1999).

[10]Stanley Hauerwas, *The Peaceable Kingdom: A Primer in Christian Ethics* (Notre Dame: University of Notre Dame Press, 1983); *Vision and Virtue* (Notre Dame: Fides Publishers, 1974); *Character and the Christian Life* (San Antonio: Trinity University Press, 1975).

[11]MacIntyre, *After Virtue,* 178.

[12]B. F. Skinner, *Beyond Freedom and Dignity* (New York: Bantam/Vintage, 1972), 191.

[13]Herbert Ginsburg and Sylvia Opper, *Piaget's Theory of Intellectual Development: An Introduction* (Englewood Cliffs: Prentice-Hall, 1969), 18–19; Jean Piaget, *The Moral Judgment of the Child* (London: Routledge & Kegan Paul, Ltd., 1968).

[14]Lawrence Kohlberg, "The Child as a Moral Philosopher," *Psychology Today* 2, no. 4 (Sept. 1968), reprinted in *Readings in Developmental Psychology,* ed. Judith Krieger Gardner (Boston: Little, Brown and Company, 1978), 349–57.

[15]J. R. Snarey, "Cross-cultural universality of social development: A critical review of Kohlbergian research," *Psychological Bulletin* 97 (1985): 202–32, cited by David Matsumoto, *People: Psychology from a Cultural Perspective* (Pacific Grove, Calif.: Brooks/Cole Publishing, 1994), 76–77.

[16]Carol Gilligan, *In a Different Voice: Psychological Theory and Women's Development* (Cambridge: Harvard University Press, 1982); experiments attempting to replicate Gilligan's work, however, have yielded mixed results with regard to gender difference. See L. J. Walker, "Sex differences in the development of moral reasoning: A critical review," *Child Development* 57 (1984): 522–26, discussed by Matsumoto (in *People: Psychology from a Cultural Perspective,* 76), who with his colleague, Margaret Lynch, suggest that some gender differences in moral reasoning observed by Gilligan may be due to cultural relativism, since Kohlberg first developed his theory by studying primarily Midwestern males in the 1950s and 1960s.

[17]Hazel Rose Markus and Shinobu Kitayama, "Culture and the Self: Implications for Cognition, Emotion, and Motivation," *Psychological Review* 98 (1991): 224–53; Hazel

Rose Markus and Shinobu Kitayama, "A Collective Fear of the Collective: Implications for Selves and Theories of Selves," *Personality and Social Psychology Bulletin* 20 (1994): 568–79; Alan Page Fiske, Shinobu Kitayama, Hazel Rose Markus, and Richard E. Nisbett, "The Cultural Matrix of Social Psychology," in *The Handbook of Social Psychology*, ed. Daniel T. Gilbert, Susan T. Fiske, and Gardner Lindzey, 4th ed. (Boston: McGraw-Hill, 1998), 915–81.

[18]Matsumoto, *People: Psychology from a Cultural Perspective*,23–24, citing M. H. Bond and C. Tak-Sing, "College students' spontaneous self concept: The effect of culture among respondents in Hong Kong, Japan, and the United States," *Journal of Cross-cultural Psychology* 14 (1983): 153–71; also citing H. C. Triandis, "The self and social behavior in differing cultural contexts," *Psychological Review* 96 (1989): 506–20; also citing S. D. Cousins, "Culture and self-perception in Japan and the United States," *Journal of Personality and Social Psychology* 56 (1989): 124–31; also citing R. A. Shweder and E. J. Bourne, "Does the concept of the person vary cross-culturally?" in *Culture Theory: Essays on Mind, Self, and Emotion*, ed. by R. A. Shweder and R. A. LeVine (Cambridge: Cambridge University Press, 1984), 158–99.

[19]Ethical relativism can be generalized from the mere matter of cultural variability to view the subject of truth itself as relative. Such epistemological relativism has been important in the development of postmodern thought. Several types of truth-claims might be fundamentally questioned: that language refers to external reality, that language reveals the intent of the speaker, and even that language can be rationally analyzed as meaningfully self-referential. Such epistemological relativism is not necessarily a requirement of postmodern thought, but these epistemological challenges do constitute a necessary part of the intellectual context that marks postmodernity. Nancey Murphey, a philosopher of religion, has suggested, however, that the choice is wrongly conceived as an either/or—either extreme skepticism and relativism on the one hand, or epistemological absolutism on the other. Rather, she sees the challenge being to locate one's own thought and the thought of others along a spectrum between absolutism and relativism. She finds "degrees of relativism" that depend on the extent to which one recognizes epistemological systems competing with one's own. The difficulty, then, is in finding a way to meaningfully compare or arbitrate between competing epistemological systems. "The worry is," she says, "that there may be a number of competing wholes (webs of belief, paradigms, total sciences, worldviews, traditions) and no nonarbitrary way to choose among them." Murphey affirms, however, that communication occurs within communities in which people are able to share meaningfully in the interpretation of their traditions and texts. This brings a stability of meaning (as well as an epistemological dynamism, I might add) to the task of interpretation and meaning-making. Nancey Murphy, *Anglo-American Postmodernity: Philosophical Perspectives on Science, Religion, and Ethics* (Boulder: Westview Press, 1997), 3, 49, 136–37, 151.

[20]Ruth Fulton Benedict, "Anthropology and the Abnormal," *Journal of General Psychology* 10 (1934): 59–80, reprinted in *The Problems of Philosophy,* 2nd ed., ed. William P. Alston and Richard B. Brandt (Boston: Allyn and Bacon, 1974), 136–37.

[21]H. Richard Niebuhr, "Moral Relativism and the Christian Ethic," presented at a Conference on Theological Education at Drew Theological Seminary, Nov. 30–Dec. 1, 1929. Published by the International Missionary Council, p. 9

[22]George Herbert Mead, *Mind, Self, and Society from the Standpoint of a Social Behaviorist,* ed. Charles W. Morris, Works of George Herbert Mead, vol. 1 (Chicago: University of Chicago Press, 1934), 135–226.

[23]H. Richard Niebuhr, *The Responsible Self* (New York: Harper & Row, 1963), 65.
[24]Ibid., 125.
[25]H. Richard Niebuhr, "The Center of Value" from *Moral Principles of Action*, ed. Ruth Nanda Anshen (Harper & Brothers, 1952), reprinted in *Radical Monotheism and Western Culture* (San Francisco: Harper & Row, 1970), 112.

[26]Bruce C. Birch and Larry L. Rasmussen, *Bible and Ethics in the Christian Life,* 1st ed. (Minneapolis: Augsburg, 1976), 127–32; see also revised and expanded edition, 66–84, 120–26.

[27]Character, according to Hauerwas, is the "qualification or determination of our self-agency, formed by our having certain intentions (and beliefs) rather than others." Hauerwas, *Peaceable Kingdom,* 39, quoting Stanley Hauerwas, *Character and the Christian Life* (San Antonio: Trinity University Press, 1975), 115.

[28]This is as opposed to grounding character on an abstract notion of transcendence (Hauerwas, *Peaceable Kingdom,* 43).

[29]Ibid., 89–90.

[30]Tom Sine, *Mustard Seed versus McWorld: Reinventing Christian Life and Mission for a New Millennium* (Great Britain: Monarch Books, 1999), 197.

Chapter 2: Working Gently

[1]*The Book of Discipline of the United Methodist Church* (Nashville: United Methodist Publishing House); in the 2004 edition, the General Rules are found in para. 103, pp. 73–74.

[2]Hippocrates, ca. 400 B.C.E.; cited by Ronald Munson, *Intervention and Reflection: Basic Issues in Medical Ethics,* 6th ed. (Belmont, Calif.: Wadsworth, 2000), 34.

[3]Tom L. Beauchamp and James F. Childress, *Principles of Biomedical Ethics,* 5th ed. (New York: Oxford University Press, 2001), 113–64.

[4]Karen Lebacqz and Joseph D. Driskill, *Ethics and Spiritual Care: A Guide for Pastors, Chaplains and Spiritual Directors* (Nashville: Abingdon Press, 2000), 102.

[5]Ibid.

[6]Munson, *Intervention and Reflection,* 12–13.

[7]W. D. Ross, *The Right and the Good* (London: Oxford University Press, 1965; also Indianapolis: Hackett Publishing Company, 1988), 18.

[8]Ibid., 21.

[9]Ibid., 21n.

[10]J. Philip Wogaman, *Christian Moral Judgment,* (Louisville: Westminster John Knox Press, 1989), 60, 62; this is largely a revision of his earlier *A Christian Method of Moral Judgment* (Philadelphia: Westminster Press, 1976). Unless otherwise indicated, all references are to the 1989 edition.

[11]Wogaman, *Christian Moral Judgment,* 72–115; Wogaman also discusses ideological presumptions, presumptions about authority, and presumptions about dialectical values (pp. 116–68). With regard to presumptions about moral authority, the first area of authority that Wogaman discusses is "the Biblical witness," which he describes as "the quintessential starting point" (p. 133). Throughout the book, Wogaman makes reference to scripture. With regard to the goodness of creation, for instance, he cites Genesis 1, Colossians, and 1 Timothy 4:4. Similarly, with regard to the value of individual life, he makes reference to the "image of God" in Genesis. With regard to the unity of the human family in God, he makes reference to Ephesians 2, that Christ "has broken down the dividing wall of hostility" (p. 83). With regard to the presumption of equality, he refers to Romans 5:8 and Mark 10:44. With regard to human finitude, he cites 1 Corinthians 13:12, "Now we see in a glass darkly," and with regard to human sinfulness, Romans 3:23, "all have sinned and fallen short of the glory of God." Wogaman resists citing scripture, however, in a way that could be interpreted as prooftexting. With regard to his use of scripture, he writes:

"Inevitably we have been selective. I do not think this merely means choosing those biblical passages we find most useful in buttressing view points derived from nonbiblical sources. Rather, it is selection of the points at which biblical words are most illuminating of the problem at hand" (p. 133).

Consistent with his "Christian method of moral judgment," Wogaman assigns strong presumptive (but not absolute) weight to scriptural teaching concerning any moral problem being considered which scripture itself seems to address (p. 134).

[12]Arthur J. Dyck, *On Human Care: An Introduction to Ethics* (Nashville: Abingdon Press, 1977).

[13]William K. Frankena, *Ethics,* 2nd ed. (Englewood Cliffs: Prentice-Hall, 1973), 47; quoted in Dyck, *On Human Care,* 72, and in Beauchamp and Childress, *Principles of Biomedical Ethics,* 5th ed., 114.

[14]John Snow, *The Impossible Vocation: Ministry in the Mean Time* (Cambridge, Mass.: Cowley Publications, 1988).

[15]Tom L. Beauchamp and James F. Childress, *Principles of Biomedical Ethics,* 4th ed. (New York: Oxford University Press, 1994), 113–16, 165–76.

[16]Ibid., 167; the phrase, "minimally decent Samaritan" is from Judith Jarvis Thomson, "A Defense of Abortion," *Philosophy and Public Affairs* 1 (1971): 47–66, quoted by Beauchamp and Childress in the 4th edition of *Principles of Biomedical Ethics,* (New York: Oxford University Press, 1994), 271 but omitted from the 5th edition (2001).

[17]Beauchamp and Childress, *Principles of Biomedical Ethics,* 5th ed., 170–71 [4th ed., 266], citing Eric D'Arcy, *Human Acts: An Essay in Their Moral Evaluation* (Oxford: Clarendon Press, 1963), 56–57; also citing Ernest J. Weinrib, "The Case for a Duty to Rescue," *Yale Law Journal* 90 (December 1980): 247–93; and Joel Feinberg, *Harm to Others,* vol. 1 of *The Moral Limits of the Criminal Law* (New York: Oxford University Press, 1984), chapter 4.

[18]David K. Switzer, *Pastoral Care Emergencies* (Minneapolis: Fortress Press, 2000), 127; citing Norman L. Farberow, Samuel M. Heilig, and Robert Litman, *Training Manual for Telephone Evaluation and Emergency Management of Suicidal Persons* (Los Angeles: Los Angeles Suicide Prevention Center, (1972); Paul W. Pretzel, *Understanding and Counseling the Suicidal Person* (Nashville: Abingdon Press, 1972); Howard W. Stone, *Depression and Hope* (Minneapolis: Fortress Press, 1998); and Switzer, *The Minister as Crisis Counselor,* revised and enlarged (Nashville: Abingdon Press, 1986), chapter 9, "Intervening in the Suicidal Crisis."

[19]Switzer, *Pastoral Care Emergencies,* 128.

[20]FBI statistics cited by Carol J. Adams (*Woman-Battering,* Creative Pastoral Care and Counseling Series [Minneapolis: Fortress, 1994], 7) indicate that 95 percent of the victims of battering are women. This book will therefore use the feminine gender to refer to survivors of domestic violence and the masculine gender to refer to batterers. Boys and men, however, can also become the victims of domestic violence. Conversely, women, too, can be abusers. The incidence of males being abused may even be under-reported because of their experience of shame. The principles advocated in the pages that follow should be understood to promote safety for the victim of violence–whether male or female–and accountability for the perpetrators of violence–again, whether male of female.

[21]Marie M. Fortune, *Violence in the Family: A Workshop Curriculum for Clergy and Other Helpers,* The Center for the Prevention of Sexual and Domestic Violence (Cleveland: Pilgrim Press, 1991), 76.

[22]Ibid., 82.

[23]Ibid.

[24]Carl R. Rogers, *Client-Centered Therapy: Its Current Practice, Implications, and Theory* (Boston: Houghton Mifflin Company 1951); Rogers, *Counseling and Psychotherapy* (Boston: Houghton Mifflin, 1942).

[25]Seward Hiltner, *Pastoral Counseling* (Nashville: Abingdon Press, 1949).

[26]Carol J. Adams, *Woman Battering* (Minneapolis: Fortress Press, 1994), 53, quoting David K. Switzer, *The Minister as Crisis Counselor* (Nashville: Abingdon Press, 1986), 54–55.

[27]Adams, *Woman Battering,* 56–59, 67.

[28]Lebacqz and Driskill, *Ethics and Spiritual Care,* 140–44, citing Walter E. Wiest and Elwyn A. Smith, *Ethics in Ministry: A Guide for the Professional* (Minneapolis: Fortress Press, 1990), 64, that clergy sometimes have a responsibility to see that the congregation "stays on track" by judging or correcting parishioners' behavior.

[29]Ibid., 105.

[30]Ibid., 103.

[31]Matthew Fox, *Original Blessing* (Santa Fe: Bear & Co., 1983), 119.

[32]Matthew Fox, *Sins of the Spirit, Blessings of the Flesh* (New York: Harmony Books, 1999), 191.

Chapter 3: Permission for Mission

[1]This chapter was originally delivered as part of the Fall Convocation address at United Theological Seminary of the Twin Cities, 19 September 2002. Portions were subsequently published as Joseph E. Bush Jr., "Informed Consent and Parish Clergy," *The Journal of Pastoral Care and Counseling* 57, no. 4 (Winter 2003): 427–36.

[2]The topic of efficiency in ministry is frequently ignored in writings about both pastoral care and pastoral ethics, though it is discussed in writings about church administration and time management. An exception is John Snow, who discusses efficiency briefly in both *The Impossible Vocation: Ministry in the Mean Time* (Cambridge, Mass.: Cowley Publications, 1988), 109, and *A Vocation to Risk: Notes on Ministry in a Profane World* (Boston: Cowley Publications, 1992).

[3]Karen Lebacqz and Joseph D. Driskill, *Ethics and Spiritual Care: A Guide for Pastors, Chaplains and Spiritual Directors* (Nashville: Abingdon, 2000), 27.

[4]Ronald Munson, *Intervention and Reflection: Basic Issues in Medical Ethics,* 6th ed. (Belmont, Calif.: Wadsworth, 2000), 473–74, citing "Special Supplement: Biomedical Ethics and the Shadow of Nazism," *Hastings Center Report* 6 (August 1976): 5.

[5]Munson, *Intervention and Reflection,* 476–77; Barbara S. Anderson, *The Counselor and the Law,* 4th ed. (Alexandria: American Counseling Association, 1996), 12.

[6]Elizabeth Reynolds Welfel, *Ethics in Counseling and Psychotherapy: Standards, Research and Emerging Issues,* 2nd ed. (Pacific Grove, Calif.: Brooks/Cole, 2002), 105.

[7]Anderson, *The Counselor and the Law,* 13. Margaret P. Battin, *Ethics in the Sanctuary: Examining the Practices of Organized Religion* (New Haven: Yale University Press, 1990), 116, also refers to three rather than two conditions for valid informed consent. According to Battin, "[T]he conditions for autonomous choice involve three criteria: (1) the decision must be uncoerced, (2) it must be rationally unimpaired, and (3) it must be adequately informed." "Rationally unimpaired" refers to the individual's own mental competency and autonomy—his or her internal capacity to freely make a rational decision. The "person in question" refers to the client, patient, or—in a pastoral context—parishioner. The criterion of rational unimpairment functions largely as a qualifier of the other two conditions of informed consent. For a person's consent to be freely given, not only must that person be informed and uncoerced in making a choice, but he or she must also be capable of understanding the information given and competent to make a responsible choice.

[8]Even for professional counselors, according to Elizabeth Reynolds Welfel, informed consent with clients can be established verbally rather than in writing, though a lack of a written agreement can make counselors more vulnerable in litigation. Regardless of the degree of written documentation, though, Welfel argues that conversation between counselor and client is always necessary in the process of establishing informed consent and that this conversation should be an ongoing one. She states, moreover, that any documentation should be written so as to facilitate rather than hinder this conversation. Welfel, *Ethics in Counseling and Psychotherapy,* 111–15. Such ongoing conversation, I am arguing, is even more important for parish clergy, who, as a general rule, do not rely on written forms or contracts.

[9]Margaret P. Battin, *Ethics in the Sanctuary: Examining the Practices of Organized Religion* (New Haven: Yale University Press, 1990).

[10]Ibid., 129.

[11]Ibid., 132.

[12]Ibid., 141–47, 184–87.

[13]http://www.scriptureunion.org.nz/camps/about_camps.htm

[14]"Winter Camps 02" brochure, Scripture Union, P.O. Box 760, Wellington, N.Z.

[15]Keith Nisbet, in a conversation with author, 5 June 2002.

[16]Battin, *Ethics in the Sanctuary,* 93–101, 116.

[17]Ibid., 82.

[18]Ibid., citing Jim Quinn and Bill Zlatos, in a series of stories beginning 2 May 1983, in the *Fort Wayne News-Sentinel,* Indiana; also citing Ron French, in the *News-Sentinel,* 25 Aug. 1987 and 8 June 1989.

[19]Battin, *Ethics in the Sanctuary,* 82–128, 235; citing Karen Lebacqz, *Professional Ethics: Power and Paradox* (Nashville: Abingdon Press, 1985), 119.

[20]InterChurch Commission on Genetic Engineering, "Closing Submission" to the Royal Commission on Genetic Modification, 15 March 2001, p. 3, reproduced at http://www.casi.org.nz/gecommission/gesubmission.html; see also Joseph Bush, "Rhetoric and Risk in Genetic Modification," *Crosslink* (November 1999), 5, available at http://www.casi.org.n2/ge/gebush.htm.

[21]Snow, *The Impossible Vocation,* 51–72, has argued that a legalistic appropriation of Elisabeth Kübler Ross's "stages" from *On Death and Dying* (New York: Macmillan, 1969) has led to a trivializing of ultimate loss and grief by a generation of clergy.

[22]Quoted in Munson, *Intervention and Reflection,* 136. For an explanation of the distinction between ordinary and extraordinary means, see Richard J. Devine, *Good Care, Painful Choices: Medical Ethics for Ordinary People,* 2nd ed. (Mahwah, N.J.: Paulist Press, 2000), 96–97, 211–14.

[23]Father Thomas Trapasso, quoted in Joseph and Julia Quinlan with Phyllis Battelle, *Karen Ann: The Quinlans Tell Their Story* (Garden City: Doubleday, 1977), 90–91.

[24]"In the Matter of Karen Quinlan, an Alleged Incompetent," *Supreme Court of New Jersey, 70 N.J. 10, 355 A. 2d 647*; reprinted in Munson, *Intervention and Reflection,* 138–40.

[25]Ibid., 140.

[26]Tom L. Beauchamp and James F. Childress, *Principles of Biomedical Ethics,* 5th ed. (New York: Oxford University Press, 2001), 125–26.

[27]Relevant sections of these codes of ethics are cited in Welfel, *Ethics in Counseling and Psychotherapy,* 108–109; the codes in their entirety are reproduced in Welfel's Appendices. See also Barbara S. Anderson, *The Counselor and the Law,* 4th ed. (Alexandria: American Counseling Association, 1996), 12–13, 115–49.

[28]Aaron Liberman and Michael J. Woodruff, *Risk Management,* Creative Pastoral Care and Counseling Series (Minneapolis: Fortress, 1993), 57. Writing for individual counselors and pastoral counseling organizations rather than for pastors of congregations, Liberman and Woodruff urge the use of three types of consent forms: (1) consent to counseling itself, (2) authorization for the disclosure of information, and (3) agreement to payment for services.

[29]Alan C. Tjelveit, "Psychotherapy and Christian Ethics," in *Christian Counseling Ethics: A Handbook for Therapists, Pastors & Counselors,* ed. Randolph K. Sanders (Downers Grove, Ill.: InterVarsity Press, 1997), 35.

[30]Horace C. Lukens, Jr., "Essential Elements for Ethical Counsel," in *Christian Counseling Ethics,* 49–51. See also the Appendix, 391–400.

[31]Thomas E. Rodgerson, M.S., "Pastoral Counseling and the Informed Relationship," *Journal of Pastoral Care,* vol. 45, no. 4 (Winter 1991): 389–98, citing Andrew Thompson, *Guide to Ethical Practice in Psychotherapy* (New York: John Wiley and Sons, 1990), 219. An even more complete list of topics for consideration by professional counselors in establishing consent is provided by Welfel, *Ethics in Counseling and Psychotherapy,* 109–111.

[32]I am indebted to my colleague, Rev. Ian Robertson, with whom I have team-taught in New Zealand, for defining professionalism with such simple clarity for me.

[33]Joe E. Trull and James E. Carter, *Ministerial Ethics: Moral Formation for Church Leaders* (Grand Rapids: Baker, 2004), 103–104, citing Wayne Oates, ed., "Editor's Preface," in *An Introduction to Pastoral Counseling* (Nashville: Broadman, 1959), vi.

[34]Ronald D. Sisk, *Surviving Ministry* (Macon: Smyth & Helwys, 1997), 99–108.

[35]Paul Roth, "The Privacy Act and the Church's Ministry," Public lecture at Knox College, Dunedin, New Zealand, 11 April 2001.

[36]Roth, e-mail communication with author, 24 June 2002.

[37]This statement is assuming a Western cultural context. In other cultural contexts, the reverse is the case. In Fiji, for instance, silence on the part of a minister would indicate a reluctance to comply with the request. In either case, though, explicit communication helps to clarify the obligation that the minister is undertaking in response to another's expectation.

[38]Bill Blackburn, "Pastors Who Counsel," in *Christian Counseling Ethics*, ed. Randolph K. Sanders, 80.

[39]Ibid., 81. A parishioner would bring a personal problem to the attention of the pastor for one of two reasons. It is best to assume straightforwardly that the parishioner is requesting pastoral care. It is also possible, of course, that titillating or shocking information is being conveyed to the pastor for the sake of some other kind of personal gratification or manipulation. Sometimes the two motives are mixed. Experienced pastors learn to be on the lookout for such bait, but it is best not to become cynical and to always listen compassionately for a parishioner's genuine concern.

[41]Snow, *The Impossible Vocation*, 106–109.

[42]Lebacqz and Driskill, *Ethics and Spiritual Care*, 67.

[43]Christie Cozad Neuger, *Counseling Women: A Narrative, Pastoral Approach* (Minneapolis: Fortress Press, 2001), 87.

Chapter 4: Keeping Faith I

[1]W.D. Ross considers both truth-telling and promise-keeping to be duties of fidelity. W.D. Ross, *The Right and the Good* (London: Oxford University Press, 1965), 21. Sissela Bok notes that philosophers may disagree on the exact relationship between these duties while still agreeing that they are related to each other. She writes:

"Many philosophers have regarded promise-keeping as revealing the truth about what one promised. This would make promises one part of veracity. Others, such as Ross, have looked at veracity as part of promise-keeping as a 'general undertaking to tell the truth'–a promise of a kind. But all see the two as closely connected." Sissela Bok, *Lying: Moral Choice in Public and Private Life* (New York: Vintage Books, 1999), 152n.

[2]*The Book of Discipline of The United Methodist Church 2004* (Nashville: The United Methodist Publishing House, 2004), para. 340, 2532.1, pp. 238–41, 689.

[3]Karen Lebacqz, *Professional Ethics: Power and Paradox* (Nashville: Abingdon Press, 1985), 87–88, 90, 96, citing Talcott Parsons, *Essays in Sociological Theology*, rev. ed. (Glencoe, Ill.: Free Press, 1954), 372.

[4]Richard M. Gula, S.S., *Ethics in Pastoral Ministry* (Mahwah, N.J.: Paulist Press, 1996).

[5]William W. Rankin, *Confidentiality and Clergy: Churches, Ethics and the Law* (Harrisburg, Pa.: Morehouse Publishing, 1990).

[6]Walter E. Wiest and Elwyn A. Smith, *Ethics in Ministry: A Guide for the Professional* (Minneapolis: Fortress Press, 1990)

[7]Arthur J. Dyck, *On Human Care: An Introduction to Ethics* (Nashville: Abingdon Press, 1977), 97–98.

[8]Dyck, *On Human Care*, 156–57, citing J. Bronowski, *Science and Human Values* (New York: Harper & Row, 1972), 65–66.

[9]Wiest and Smith, *Ethics in Ministry*, 21.

[10]Dyck, *On Human Care*, 53.

[11]Ibid., citing J. A. T. Robinson, *Christian Morals Today* (London: SCM, 1964), 16–18.

[12]Sissela Bok, *Lying: Moral Choice in Public and Private Life* (New York: Vintage Books, 1999), 18–29.

[13]Ibid., 31.

[14]Ibid., 13, 30.

[15]Ibid., 31, 140.

[16]Ibid., 92–106.

[17]Immanuel Kant, *The Metaphysics of Morals*, ed. and trans. Mary Gregor (New York: Cambridge University Press, 1996), 182–83; Kant, "On a Supposed Right to Lie from Altruistic Motives," in *Critique of Practical Reason and Other Writings in Moral Philosophy*, ed. and trans. Lewis White Beck (Chicago: University of Chicago Press, 1949), 346–50, reproduced and discussed in Bok, *Lying*, 37–39, 267–72.

[18]Jeremy Bentham, *The Principles of Morals and Legislation* (New York: Hafner, 1948), 2; see also John Stuart Mill, *Utilitarianism* (New York: Bobbs-Merrill, 1957), 10. Both are discussed in Karen Lebacqz, *Six Theories of Justice: Perspectives from Philosophical and Theological Ethics* (Minneapolis: Augsburg, 1986), 15–32.

[19]Bentham, *Principles*.

[20]Joseph Fletcher, *Situation Ethics: The New Morality* (Philadelphia: Westminster Press, 1966), 95, 115.

[21]"The Theological Declaration of Barmen," (1934), 8:11, 8:23–24, in Arthur C. Cochrane, *The Church's Confessions Under Hitler* (Philadelphia: Westminster Press, 1962), 237–42, reprinted in *The Book of Confessions*, Part I of The Constitution of the Presbyterian Church (U.S.A.), (Louisville: The Office of the General Assembly, 1996), 257–58.

[22]Eberhard Bethge, Foreword to Dietrich Bonhoeffer, *Letters and Papers from Prison*, trans. Reginald H. Fuller (New York: Macmillan, 1953), 10–14.

[23]Dietrich Bonhoeffer, "What Is Meant by 'Telling the Truth'?" in *Ethics*, ed. Eberhard Bethge, trans. Neville Horton Smith (New York: Macmillan, 1955), 363–72, reproduced in Bok, *Lying*, 286. Bonhoeffer's christocentric ethic and his understanding of the "orders" will be discussed further in chapter 7, on the subject of vocation.

[24]Bonhoeffer, as quoted in Bok, *Lying*, 282; for personal insight about the high value placed on truth in the Bonhoeffer family, see Larry Rasmussen with Renate Bethge, *Dietrich Bonhoeffer–His Significance for North Americans* (Minneapolis: Fortress Press, 1990), 22–24.

[25]Bok, *Lying*, 37–38, 268.

[26]Bok, *Lying*, 150, citing Bonhoeffer, "Telling the Truth," 367.

[27]Sissela Bok is careful to distinguish between two questions: the larger, epistemological question, "What is truth?" and the ethical question concerning the morality of intentionally deceiving another. Bok, *Lying*, 6–16. Each question raises a different but related set of concerns. Each is also important for the ethics of pastoral practice. It is my intent in this and the next chapter to treat each question separately so as not to conflate them. At the same time, they should be seen to be related to each other in order to highlight the mutual challenge they present to clergy in seeking to be faithful to the principle of veracity.

Chapter 5: Keeping Faith II

[1]*Faith and Science in an Unjust World: Report of the World Council of Churches' Conference on Faith, Science and the Future: Massachusetts Institute of Technology, Cambridge, U.S.A., 12–24 July 1979*, vol. 1: *Plenary Presentations*, edited by Roger L. Shinn; vol. 2: *Reports and Recommendations*, edited by Paul Abrecht; 2 vols. (Geneva: Church and Society, WCC, 1980), 1:373.

[2]Ibid., 1:41.

[3]Rubem Alves, "Marxism as Scientific World View–The State of the Debate About Science and Ideology in Latin America," *Anticipation*, no. 25 (January 1979): 13.

[4]Paulo Freire, *Pedagogy of the Oppressed* (New York: Continuum, 1984).

[5]James H. Cone, *God of the Oppressed* (New York: Seabury Press, 1975), 30.

[6]Ibid., 17.

[7]Ibid., 29.

[8]Katie G. Cannon, *Black Womanist Ethics* (Atlanta: Scholars Press, 1988), 6–7.

[9]Ibid., 17, citing Mary Burgher, "Images of Self and Race in the Autobiographies of Black Women," in *Sturdy Black Bridges*, ed. Roseann Bell, et al. (New York: Anchor Books, 1979), 113.

[10]Mary Daly, *Pure Lust: Elemental Feminist Philosophy* (Boston: Beacon Press, 1984), 152–53.

[11]Ibid., ix; Mary Daly, *Gyn/Ecology: The Metaethics of Radical Feminism* (Boston: Beacon Press, 1978), 23.

[12]Carolyn Merchant, *The Death of Nature: Women, Ecology and the Scientific Revolution* (San Francisco: Harper & Row, 1980), 168.

[13]Ibid., xv–xix, 290–95.

[14]Carol J. Adams, *Woman-Battering*, Creative Pastoral Care and Counseling Series (Minneapolis: Augsburg Fortress Press, 1997), 28, citing Paulo Freire, *Pedagogy of the Oppressed* (New York: Penguin, 1972), 61 [1984 Continuum edition, p. 76].

[15]Adams, *Woman-Battering*, 29.

[16]Ibid., 53.

[17]Christie Cozad Neuger, *Counseling Women: A Narrative, Pastoral Approach* (Minneapolis: Augsburg Fortress Press, 2001), 6–7.

[18]George B. Thompson Jr. makes the point that even a well-accepted and well-respected pastor may be suddenly marginalized by the congregation's "cultural insiders" when important decisions have to be made. Thompson advocates that pastors work deliberately to develop their own "cultural capital" within their congregations, so that they are better trusted and empowered to exercise leadership. At the same time, Thompson urges ministers to be sensitively aware of the limits to their cultural capital and to not feel overly threatened whenever their relatively marginal status does come to the fore. In the toughest decisions about a congregation's life, Thompson suggests, it may be the true cultural insiders within a congregation rather than the pastor who are in the best position to exercise influential leadership. George B. Thompson Jr., *How to Get Along with Your Church: Creating Cultural Capital for Doing Ministry* (Cleveland: Pilgrim Press, 2001).

[19]An abhorrent example of the damage due to deception is apparent in recent scandals involving the sexual abuse of children by clergy and the consequent deception by these members of the clergy, as well as by their church superiors, in attempting to cover up the abuse. This deception has allowed the abuse to go unchecked so that increasing numbers of children, whose abuse could have been prevented, have tragically fallen victim. It has also--perhaps incurably and even rightfully--damaged the trust between the church and both the churched and unchurched members of society.

[20]*The Book of Discipline of The United Methodist Church 2000* (Nashville: The United Methodist Publishing House, 2000), para 304.3, p. 185.

[21]Bok, *Lying*, 45, citing Lewis [sic] Jacobs, *Jewish Values* (London: Vallentine, Mitchell, 1960), 145–54. See Louis Jacobs, *Jewish Values* (Hartford, Conn.: Hartmore House, 1960).

[22]Bok, *Lying*, 5.

[23]Ilaitia Sevati Tuwere, *Vanua: Towards a Fijian Theology of Place* (Suva, Fiji: Institute of Pacific Studies, 2002).

[24]Walter E. Wiest and Elwyn A. Smith, *Ethics in Ministry: A Guide for the Professional* (Minneapolis: Fortress Press, 1990), 30.

[25]Ibid., 21.

[26]Ibid., 189.

[27]Ibid., 37–41.

[28]Ibid., 43.

[29]Ibid., 21–23, 72–74.

[30]Ibid., 151.

[31]Ibid., 154.

[32]Ibid., 155.

[33]Ibid.

[34]Ibid., 165.

[35]Ibid., 172.

[36]Ibid., 163.

[37]Ibid., 63–64, 73–75.

[38]Ibid., 22–23, 63.

[39]Ibid., 44–46.

[40]Peter Böhler, as quoted in A. Skevington Wood, *The Burning Heart: John Wesley: Evangelist* (Minneapolis: Bethany Fellowship, 1978), 62, who is citing John Wesley, *The Journal of the Rev. John Wesley A.M.*, ed. Nehemiah Curnock (London: The Epworth Press, 1938), vol. 1, 442, entry for 4th March, 1738.

[41]Kathleen Norris, *Dakota: A Spiritual Geography* (Boston: Houghton Mifflin, 1993).

[42]Kathleen Norris, *Amazing Grace: A Vocabulary of Faith* (New York: Riverhead Books, 1998), 65.

[43]Actually, the creeds serve different functions historically within the church. The "Apostles Creed" developed as a baptismal formula from an interrogative form: "Do you believe...?" "I believe..." This creed begins with personal affirmation, "I believe" (*credo*), being placed within the context of the trinitarian belief of the community. The Nicene Creed begins, rather, in the first person plural, "We believe" (*credemus*), and grows out of polemic debate with the church concerning christological controversies. The Nicene Creed symbolizes the ecumenicity of the church; it is the last and most developed theological statement before the church divided between East and West, and it is still recited by Catholic, Protestant, and Orthodox. However, the Nicene Creed can also be seen to sadly symbolize the division out of which it developed and the many groups of heterodox Christians who were thus excluded from the church by this development.

[44]Curiously, in American culture, more liberal Christians with an ecclesiology informed by an understanding of cultural constructivism seem able to be most zealous for individual integrity in belief and also most suspicious of tradition as an invitation to participation in historical community. Traditionalists—ironically, it seems to me—tend more toward personalistic and fideistic frames of reference, even when they are seeking to locate themselves within the wider and deeper tradition of the diverse Christian community through the ages.

[45]Wiest and Smith, *Ethics in Ministry,* 48.

[46]Ronald D. Sisk, *Surviving Ministry* (Macon: Smyth & Helwys, 1997), 26–27.

[47]Ibid., 27.

[48]Ibid., 25.

Chapter 6: Confidentiality in Care

[1]An earlier version of this chapter, titled "Keeping Secrets and Telling Truth: Fidelity in Pastoral Ethics," was presented in Pittsburgh at the Annual Meeting of the Society of Christian Ethics, 10 January 2003, subsequently published as "Pastoral Confidentiality," *Business & Professional Ethics Journal–Incorporating Professional Ethics: A Multidisciplinary Journal* 22, no. 4 (Winter 2004).

[2]Horace C. Lukens Jr., "Essential Elements for Ethical Counsel," in *Christian Counseling Ethics: A Handbook for Therapists, Pastors & Counselors,* ed. Randolph K. Sanders (Downers Grove, Ill.: InterVarsity Press, 1997), 44, citing C. D. Stromberg, D. J. Haggarty, R. F. Leibenluft, M. H. McMillian, B. Mishkin, B. L. Rubin and H. R. Trilling, *The Psychologist's Legal Handbook* (Washington: Council for the National Register of Health Service Providers in Psychology, 1988), 371–72; also citing C. D. Stromberg, D. Lindberg, B. Mishkin, and M. Baker, *The Psychologist's Legal Update: Privacy, Confidentiality and Privilege* (Washington: Council for the National Register of Health Service Providers in Psychology, 1993).

[3]L. Newton, *Ethics in America Study Guide* (Englewood Cliffs, N.J.: Prentice Hall, 1989), quoted by Elizabeth Reynolds Welfel, *Ethics in Counseling and Psychotherapy: Standards, Research, and Emerging Issues* (Pacific Grove, Calif.: Brooks/Cole, 1998), 84.

[4]Lukens, "Essential Elements," 44.

[5]Ronald K. Bullis and Cynthia S. Mazur, *Legal Issues and Religious Counseling* (Louisville: Westminster/John Knox Press, 1993), 69.

[6]Bullis and Mazur, *Legal Issues,* 71, 75–76; a helpful table enumerating each state statute is provided on pp. 82–85. With regard to professional identity, Bullis and Mazur

note that the Supreme Court of Iowa has also applied clergy confidentiality to Presbyterian elders (p. 72).

[7]Ibid., 86–89.

[8]Sissela Bok, *Secrets: On the Ethics of Concealment and Revelation* (New York: Random House, 1984), 119.

[9]Ibid.

[10]Ibid., xv.

[11]Sissela Bok, *Lying: Moral Choice in Public and Private Life* (New York: Vintage, 1999), 30.

[12]Ibid., 31.

[13]Bok, *Secrets*, 28.

[14]Ibid., 27.

[15]Ibid., 119–20, 122.

[16]Horace C. Lukens Jr., "Essential Elements for Ethical Counsel," 44, citing *The Psychologist's Legal Handbook*, 371–72, and *The Psychologist's Legal Update*.

[17]"All clergy of the United Methodist Church are charged to maintain all confidences inviolate, including confessional confidences, except in the cases of suspected child abuse or neglect or in cases when mandatory reporting is required by civil law," *The Book of Discipline of the United Methodist Church* (Nashville: United Methodist Publishing House, 2004), 241, paragraph 341.5.

[18]Bok, *Secrets*, 95.

[19]In a survey including both laity and clergy of the Congregationalist Christian Churches, 82 percent of respondents believed that "anything told to a minister under any circumstances is confidential." Susan E. Fox and Judith Trott Guy, eds., *A Handbook on Legal Issues in Theological Field Education* (Richmond: Presbyterian Field Educators, 2000), ch.2, p.9, found at www.atfe.org, and citing Elizabeth D. Audette, "Does Only Your Minster Know? Religious, Legal Confidentiality Differ," *The Congregationalist* (April-May 1998): 18.

[20]H. Newton Malony, "Confidentiality in the Pastoral Role," in *Clergy Malpractice*, ed. H. Newton Malony, Thomas L. Needham, and Samuel Southard (Philadelphia: Westminster Press, 1986), 111.

[21]Malony writes: "[Pastors] assume a lifelong, broad, interpersonal, and familial responsibility for persons. Thus, they should treat all that they hear as confidential, because by divulging it they may endanger or make more difficult the lives of those entrusted to their care.

This is a much broader concern than most other professionals assume in regard to those with whom they work. It also makes the keeping of confidences a much more serious issue, because much that a pastor hears is not in a private office but is communicated as the pastor fulfills the day-to-day parish duties of ministry and administration." Malony, "Confidentiality," 118.

[22]Richard M. Gula, S.S., *Ethics in Pastoral Ministry* (Mahwah, N.J.: Paulist Press, 1996), 81–82.

[23]Ibid., 81.

[24]Ibid.

[25]Ibid.

[26]Clinical Pastoral Education (C.P.E.) is an organized program of training and supervision in pastoral care. See more at www.acpe.edu

[27]Problems of dual relationships and role confusion are not confined to parish clergy. People in specialized ministries (e.g., chaplains) in other institutional settings have to exercise similar care to maintain confidentiality, because they see people in a variety of roles even within a singular institutional context. Karen Lebacqz and Joseph Driskill remark that the power differential held by chaplains in such settings can be even more pronounced than for parish clergy in congregations. This has implications for confidentiality. They write:

"One implication of this for clergy serving in these settings is maintaining strict confidentiality, often treating as confidential information shared in settings that are not typically associated with requirements for confidentiality…This ability to cross social, power, class, and rank boundaries will often place the clergyperson in a privileged position of knowing information that will affect those at other levels. Information learned in these often social or casual exchanges must often be treated with great discretion or those who have shared the information may be hurt.

"As with parish clergy, the importance of maintaining confidentiality for people in specialized ministries heightens as a result of (1) the professional's relative power both structurally in the organization and interpersonally as a confidant and (2) the potential for confusion caused by a fluidity of roles within the institution." Karen Lebacqz and Joseph D. Driskill, *Ethics and Spiritual Care: A Guide for Pastors, Chaplains and Spiritual Directors* (Nashville: Abingdon Press, 2000), 115.

[28]Bok, *Secrets*, 91.

[29]Ibid., 95–98.

[30]Ibid., 99–100.

[31]Ibid., 40: "[T]he conflicts between insider and outsider about control over secrecy and openness arise in every form of human encounter. And within each perspective, the same tensions are felt: for outsiders, between seeking to probe secrets and refraining therefrom, and between accepting and avoiding what is revealed; and for insiders, between keeping secrets and divulging them."

[32] *Code of Canon Law: Latin-English Edition* (Washington, D. C., 1983), Can. 983.1–2, 984.1–2.

[33]John R. Roos, *The Seal of Confession*, Catholic University of America Canon Law Studies No. 413 (Washington: Catholic University of America Press, 1960), 73, quoted by Margaret P. Battin, *Ethics in the Sanctuary: Examining the Practices of Organized Religion* (New Haven: Yale University Press, 1990), 58.

[34]Bok, *Secrets*, 123.

[35]Battin, *Ethics in the Sanctuary*, 4.

[36]Ibid., 16.

[37]Ibid.

[38]Ibid., 20.

[39]Ibid., 26.

[40]Ibid., 58, 273 23n., citing *New Catholic Encyclopedia*, vol. 4 (New York: McGraw Hill, 1967), s.v. "confession, seal of," 134. ; also citing Roos, *The Seal of Confession*, 73.

[41]Battin, *Ethics in the Sanctuary*, 59. Battin's method of analysis distinguishes four levels of authority for religious practices or doctrine: (1) 0–level mandates, (2) first-order doctrines, (3) second-order doctrines, and (4) excuses. She explains as follows:

"0–level foundational mandates of a religious tradition are to be regarded as initially immune to ethical scrutiny, while increasingly higher levels—first-order doctrines that specify practices typically identificatory of a group, second-order doctrines and policies that serve to resolve the ethical issues, and 'excuses'…for residual moral problems—are to be seen as increasingly vulnerable candidates for ethical critique." Ibid., 47.

This unique approach to the analysis of religious ethics, in my opinion, is in keeping with neither an *emic* appreciation of religious self-understanding nor with more *etic* sociological approaches that view doctrine as emerging and developing in concert with praxeological realities. Battin assumes for her own analysis a fundamentalism, a legalism, and a lexical organization in the traditions she examines that may not be assumed by the religions themselves or by other interpreters of those religions.

[42]Those similarities are: (1) that client and professional typically have "sustained, direct personal contact"; (2) that in the "usual course of professional practice" the professional makes use of the information confided; (3) that "disclosure is unidirectional"; and (4) that problems can become more acute when confidential disclosure becomes more central to the professional relationship or where there may be important consequences to confidential disclosure or to the lack of it. Ibid., 20.

[43]The question is that of who counts as a moral person—as one claiming another's moral regard or as one capable of acting responsibly. The question is at the heart of many contemporary ethical issues that stretch a humanistic framework. Examples are: (1) the putative moral rights of *gaia*, ecosystems, animals, plants, or microbes; and (2) the putative moral rights of human fetuses, embryos, zygotes, or stem cells. The question of whether or not these moral rights can also be represented in some fashion in a courtroom as legal rights is secondary. In court, corporations, for instance, may count as legal persons while these other entities usually do not. It is a religious perspective, I am arguing, that God is a moral person, even if this language may sound odd to the ears of both the religious and the nonreligious. Moreover, if it is a premise of religious logic to assume God to be agentic, then it is courteous for philosophical analysts to accept this premise at least provisionally for the sake of argument.

[44]Battin, *Ethics in the Sanctuary*, 48; William W. Rankin, *Confidentiality and Clergy: Churches, Ethics and the Law* (Harrisburg: Morehouse, 1990), 34–45; Mary Angela Shaughnessy, S.C.N., J.D., *Ministry and the Law: What You Need to Know* (Mahwah, N.J.: Paulist Press, 1998), 54; Richard M. Gula, S.S., *Ethics in Pastoral Ministry*, 122, 135.

[45]Gula, *Ethics in Pastoral Ministry*, 122.

[46]Rankin, *Confidentiality and Clergy*, 47.

[47]Ibid., 34; quoting the *Book of Common Prayer*, (Greenwich, Conn.: Seabury Press, 1979).

[48]Rankin, *Confidentiality and Clergy*, 35, citing Marion J. Hatchett, *Commentary on the American Prayer Book* (New York: Seabury, 1981), 454, and Brice Schratz, "Seal of Confession," in *The Encyclopedia of Religion*, ed. Vergilius Ferm (Secaucus: Poplar Books, 1945, 1987), 698. Rankin does make this claim of "waiver," though a more accurate interpretation might be that the priest is able to discuss the matter as it is revealed subsequently but should let the original confession stay under a seal of secrecy. My thanks to Sondra Wheeler of Wesley Theological Seminary for this observation.

Rankin also cites Francis J. Hall's earlier teaching about four areas of possible exception to the strict confidentiality of confession: (1) when a priest needs to consult with another priest on the matter, but in which case should nonetheless protect the identity of the penitent, (2) when a priest already has prior knowledge of the matter confessed, (3) "when the good of others can be promoted and the penitent freely consents; the seal may be broken for such good, but not further," and (4) "when the confession clearly reveals intention to commit in the future a crime that endangers others..." Rankin, *Confidentiality and Clergy*, 36, citing Francis J. Hall, *The Sacraments* (New York: Longmans, Green, 1921), 24, 242.

[49]Rankin, *Confidentiality and Clergy*, 37; citing *Doctrine in the Church of England: The Report of the Commission on Christian Doctrine Appointed by the Archbishops of Canterbury and York in 1922* (London: SPCK, 1938), 197.

[50]Marie M. Fortune, "Reporting Child Abuse: An Ethical Mandate for Ministry," in *Violence in the Family: A Workshop Curriculum for Clergy and Other Helpers*, ed. Marie M. Fortune, The Center for the Prevention of Sexual and Domestic Violence (Cleveland: Pilgrim, 1991), 231.

[51]Ibid., 81.

[52]Roos, *The Seal of Confession*, 61, and Battin, *Ethics in the Sanctuary*, 57, citing *New Catholic Encyclopedia*, s.v. 'confession, seal of'" vol. 4, 134.

[53]Bok, *Secrets*, 27.

[54]Ibid., 133.

[55]Ibid.

[56]Ibid., 135.

[57]Gula, *Ethics in Pastoral Ministry*, 74–75.

[58]Ibid., 122, 130.

[59]Ibid., 131.

[60]Walter E. Wiest and Elwyn A. Smith, *Ethics in Ministry: A Guide for the Professional* (Minneapolis: Fortress Press, 1990), 49–54; Rankin, *Confidentiality and Clergy*, 22, citing

LeRoy Walters, "Confidentiality" in *Westminster Dictionary of Christian Ethics*, ed. James F. Childress and John MacQuarrie (Philadelphia: Westminster Press, 1986); Malony, "Confidentiality," 116–17; Battin, *Ethics in the Sanctuary*, 24.

[61]Fortune, *Violence in the Family*, 231.

[62]Ibid., 82.

[63]Bullis and Mazur, *Legal Issues*, 111.

[64]Ibid., 90, 96–97. Bullis and Mazur provide a helpful list of questions for members of the clergy to determine their legal responsibilities given their particular state's child abuse reporting laws:

1. How does your state define clergy?

2. Are you a mandatory or permissive child abuse reporter under the laws of your state?

3. Are there other laws that require you to report suspected abuse, such as elder abuse or abuse of the mentally ill?

4. Who must you report to?

5. How quickly must you report?

6. Does the statute specify what type of evidence the report is to be based upon?

7. Do the reporting laws conflict with your state's clergy privileged communication law? If so, how would you resolve the conflict if you were required to report suspected abuse and were required to maintain confidences?

8. Suppose you are a permissive reporter and are required to maintain confidences. Is there a way to make a report?

[65]According to Patrick J. Schiltz, "The Impact of Clergy Sexual Misconduct Litigation on Religious Liberty," *Boston College Law Review* 44, no. 4 (2003): 971n61 the mandatory reporting law in Texas requires clergy to report information about child sexual abuse even if learned during confession. He is citing Tex. Fam. Code Ann. 261,101(c) (Vernon 2002). Also in agreement with this interpretation is Norman Abrams, "Addressing the Tension Between the Clergy-Communicant Privilege and the Duty to Report Child Abuse in State Statutes," *Boston College Law Review* 44, no. 4 (2003): 1127–1166.

Chapter 7: Vocation I

[1]Francis of Assisi, "All Creatures of Our God and King," trans. William H. Draper, *Chalice Hymnal* (St. Louis: Chalice Press, 1995), 22.

[2]"Of Creation," chapter 4 of "The Westminster Confession of Faith," in *The Constitution of the Presbyterian Church (U.S.A.), Part I Book of Confessions* (Louisville: Office of the General Assembly, 1996), 6.022, p. 130.

[3]"The Shorter Catechism," Q. 1 and "The Larger Catechism," Q. 1, 7.001 and 7.111 in *Presbyterian Book of Confessions*, 181, 201.

[4]Jonathan Edwards, "Dissertation I: Concerning the End for Which God Created the World," *Works of Jonathan Edwards*, vol. 8 *Ethical Writings* (1776; reprint, New Haven: Yale University Press, 1989), 403–63.

[5]Karen Lebacqz, *Justice in an Unjust World: Foundations for a Christian Approach to Justice* (Minneapolis: Augsburg, 1987), 7.

[6]Ibid., 155.

[7]Ibid., 156–60; Karen Lebacqz, *Six Theories of Justice: Perspectives from Philosophical and Theological Ethics* (Minneapolis: Augsburg, 1986). The six theories of justice that are compared are: (1) utilitarianism as represented by John Stuart Mill, (2) John Rawls's contractual theory of justice as fairness, (3) Robert Nozick's minimalist understanding of justice as entitlement, (4) Roman Catholic social teaching about economic justice, (5) Reinhold Niebuhr's realism characterized by a balance of power, and (6) a liberationist perspective represented by Jose Porfirio Miranda.

[8]White writes: "Especially in its Western form, Christianity is the most anthropocentric religion the world has seen…Man shares, in great measure, God's transcendence of nature. Christianity…not only established a dualism of man and

nature but also insisted that it is God's will that man exploit nature for his proper ends." Lynn White Jr., "The Historical Roots of Our Ecologic Crisis," *Science*, 155 (1967): 1203–7, reprinted in *Readings in Ecology and Feminist Theology,* ed. Mary Heather MacKinnon and Moni McIntyre (Kansas City: Sheed & Ward, 1995), 31.

⁹Actually, even the verses of Genesis that follow verse 26 make it evident that "dominion" does not involve *carte blanc* license over nature, for the newly created humans are not even permitted to eat meat (Gen. 1:29–30). Rather, humans–together with all the other land animals–are given plants to eat. In the Noah story, God finally gives humans permission to eat meat (Gen. 9:2–4) as a kind of compromise to the fact of violence within creation. Nevertheless, humans are charged not to "eat flesh with its life" in it, but rather to pour out the life-containing blood before consuming the flesh. See Odil Hannes Steck, *World and Environment,* Biblical Encounters Series (Nashville: Abingdon, 1980), 57–113.

¹⁰Larry L. Rasmussen, *Earth Community, Earth Ethics* (Maryknoll: Orbis, 1997), 228–44.

¹¹Ibid., 280.

¹²Katie G. Cannon, *Black Womanist Ethics* (Atlanta: Scholars Press, 1988), 160–61, citing Howard Thurman, *Jesus and the Disinherited* (Nashville: Abingdon-Cokesbury Press, 1949), 21.

¹³Ibid.

¹⁴Martin Luther King Jr., *Where Do We Go from Here: Chaos or Community?* (Boston: Beacon Press, 1968), 84.

¹⁵Cannon, *Black Womanist Ethics,* 163, quoting King, *Where Do We Go from Here,* 97.

¹⁶Peter J. Paris, *The Social Teaching of the Black Churches* (Philadelphia: Fortress Press, 1985), 10.

¹⁷Ibid., 16–17.

¹⁸Ibid., 10.

¹⁹Tim Dowley, ed., *Introduction to the History of Christianity* (Minneapolis: Fortress, 1995), 96–105.

²⁰Werner Foerster, "*exousia,*" *Theological Dictionary of the New Testament,* ed. Gerhard Kittle, vol. 2, (Grand Rapids: William B. Eerdmans, 1985), 566–74.

²¹John Howard Yoder, *The Politics of Jesus* (Grand Rapids: William B. Eerdmans, 1972), 147–50, citing Hendrik Berkhof, *Christ and the Powers,* trans. John Howard Yoder (Scottdale, Pa.: Herald Press, 1962), 30f.

²²Yoder, *Politics of Jesus,* 144, 193–214; Yoder also makes the point (p. 206) that the short sword mentioned in Romans 13 is the "*machaira*" used ceremoniously as a symbol of ruling authority rather than a weapon for warfare or capital punishment.

²³Richard John Neuhaus, *Christian Faith and Public Policy: Thinking and Acting in the Courage of Uncertainty* (Minneapolis: Augsburg, 1977), 29.

²⁴Ibid., 30.

²⁵The distinction between calling and one's role in society, especially with reference to Paul, is emphasized by Dietrich Bonhoeffer, *Ethics,* ed. Eberhard Bethge (New York: Macmillan, 1965), 254–56. For a contemporary analysis of Paul's use of "calling" in 1 Corinthians with reference to Hellenistic philosophical categories, especially pertaining to marriage and sexuality, see Will Deming, *Paul on Marriage and Celibacy: The Hellenistic Background of 1 Corinthians 7* (Grand Rapids: William B. Eerdmans, 2004), 163–69; Deming's analysis places Paul "before and outside" the tradition of Christian asceticism rather than as one of the founders of that tradition (p. 208).

²⁶Günther Bornkamm, *Paul,* trans. D. M. G. Stalker (New York: Harper & Row, 1971), 196–216.

²⁷Letty M. Russell, *The Future of Partnership* (Philadelphia: Westminster Press, 1979), 175.

²⁸Ibid.; Yoder, *Politics of Jesus,* 185–92.

²⁹*The Encyclopedia of the Lutheran Church,* vol. 3 (Minneapolis: Augsburg, 1965), 2504.

[30]Rupert Davies, "Vocation," in *The Westminster Dictionary of Christian Theology,* ed. Alan Richardson and John Bowden (Philadelphia: Westminster Press, 1983), 601–2.

[31]William H. Lazareth, *Christians in Society: Luther, the Bible, and Social Ethics* (Minneapolis: Fortress, 2001), 221–22.

[32]Ibid., 65–71; 81.

[33]Ibid., 165.

[34]Thomas Aquinas, *Summa Theologiae,* I–II. Questions 90–97, presented in R. J. Henle, S. J., ed., *St. Thomas Aquinas: The Treatise on Law* (Notre Dame: University of Notre Dame Press, 1993); Edward LeRoy Long Jr., *A Survey of Christian Ethics* (New York: Oxford University Press, 1982), 180–90; Clifford G. Kossel, S.J., "Natural Law and Human Law (Ia IIae, qq. 90–97)," in *The Ethics of Aquinas,* ed. Stephen J. Pope (Washington: Georgetown University Press, 2002), 169–93.

[35]Lazareth, *Christians in Society,* 220–21; Max Weber, *The Protestant Ethic and the Spirit of Capitalism,* trans. Talcott Parsons (New York Charles Scribner's Sons, 1958), 80.

[36]Ernst Troeltsch, *The Social Teaching of the Christian Churches,* trans. Olive Wyon, 2 vols. (Chicago: University of Chicago Press, 1981); Weber, *The Protestant Ethic.*

[37]Both Troeltsch and Weber emphasize the conservative dimension of Luther's ethic of vocation. "Thus for Luther the concept of the calling remained traditionalistic," Weber states succinctly; it is a divine ordinance which one must accept and to which one must adapt. Weber, *Protestant Ethic,* 85; see also Troeltsch, *Social Teaching of Christian Churches,* 2:570–73. Some Lutheran scholars have challenged this conclusion, stated as it is in such a seemingly fatalistic way. William H. Lazareth, for instance, argues that Luther never posited autonomous orders of creation that might "claim to be a naturalistic 'law unto itself.'" Nevertheless, with greater nuance, Lazareth explains:

"[T]he divinely ordained mandates of humanity *are* institutionally accountable to the moral direction (not legislated directives) of the universal will of God the Creator and Preserver for the common good, as revealed in Holy Scripture…"Lazareth, *Christians in Society,* 71.

Moreover, in Lazareth's interpretation of Luther, humans are responsible not simply to maintain a static order, but to realize a life of faith and an ethic of love in accordance with scripture even within these institutions: "to image God's holy and loving will for societal peace, justice and freedom…in the 'obedience of faith' (Rom. 1:5)." Ibid.

[38]Williston Walker, *A History of the Christian Church* (New York: Charles Scribner's Sons, 1970), 346.

[39]Weber, *Protestant Ethic,* 106–12; Troeltsch, *Social Teaching of Christian Churches,* 2:581–87.

[40]Troeltsch and Weber present this second point (regarding the influence of a theology of predestination and election) as more of an unintended consequence of the doctrine. Weber states plainly that Calvin himself was little concerned with evidence of election, that he rejected the assumption that one can determine whether people are chosen or damned by observing their conduct, and that he contended that "we should be content with the knowledge that God has chosen and depend further only on that implicit trust in Christ which is the result of true faith." Weber, *Protestant Ethic,* 110. Nevertheless, Weber argues that later Calvinists found here a motivation to work and a reassurance in their work that they may be among the elect.

[41]Weber, *Protestant Ethic,* 89–90. In Troeltsch's interpretation, it was an accidental fit involving the mutual influence between the religious teaching itself and the economic conditions in history, Troeltsch, *Social Teaching of Christian Churches,* 2:644, n. 915, citing Weber.

[42]Weber, *Protestant Ethic,* 120–21, 180, citing Troeltsch; Troeltsch, *Social Teaching of Christian Churches,* 2:645–46, citing Weber.

[43]Lazareth, *Christians in Society,* 7–10.

[44]Emil Brunner, *The Divine Imperative: A Study in Christian Ethics,* trans. by Olive Wyon (London: Lutterworth Press, 1953), 291ff.; Bonhoeffer, *Ethics,* 207–13; Helmut

Thielicke, *Foundations,* vol. 1 of *Theological Ethics* (Grand Rapids: Eerdmans, 1966), 359–82.

[45]Long, *Survey of Christian Ethics,* 191–92.

[46]Brunner, *Divine Imperative,* 446.

[47]Ibid., 291.

[48]Bonhoeffer, *Ethics,* 207–8, 283.

[49]Larry Rasmussen, *Dietrich Bonhoeffer: Reality and Resistance* (Nashville: Abingdon, 1972), 30.

[50]Rachel Carson, *Silent Spring* (Greenwich: Fawcett Publications, 1962).

[51]I discuss this from another angle in chapter 1 of my dissertation, "Social Justice and the Natural Environment in the Study Program of the World Council of Churches, 1966–1990" (Ph.D. dissertation, Drew University, 1993), 25–97; I am reminded, though, of a comment Charles West, retired professor of social ethics at Princeton, made to me about the social categories employed by ecumenical theology during the late 1960s–including by himself in *The Power to Be Human* (New York: Macmillan, 1971)–"This was all in response to Bonhoeffer's challenge to do theology in 'a world come of age.'" conversation.}

[52]For a discussion about essentialism and social constructivism in sexuality, see James B. Nelson and Sandra P. Longfellow, eds., *Sexuality and the Sacred: Sources for Theological Reflection* (Louisville: Westminster John Knox Press, 1994), 3–8.

[53]Barbara Smith-Moran, *Soul at Work: Reflections on a Spirituality of Working* (Winona, Minn.: Saint Mary's Press, Christian Brothers Publications, 1997), 15, quoting Doris Donnelly, *Spiritual Fitness* (HarperSanFrancisco, 1993), 83. See also Donnelly, ch. 4 "Working," in *Spiritual Fitness,* 45–89.

Chapter 8: Vocation II

[1]Curiously, John Calvin popularized this threefold formulation of Christ's office, but his instruction about ordained ministry distinguished between the two offices of ruling elders, on one hand, and ministers of Word and Sacrament who were teaching elders, on the other; see the relevant sections of John Calvin, *Institutes of the Christian Religion,* trans. Ford Lewis Battles (Philadelphia: Westminster Press, 1960), 2:15 (pp. 494–503), 4:3.4–4:4.4 (pp. 1056–72), 4:11.1–6 (pp. 1211–18) as well as historical interpretation of these passages by John Frederick Janson, *Calvin's Doctrine of the Work of Christ* (London: James Clarke & Co., 1956), 23–59.

[2]Sallie McFague, *Models of God: Theology for an Ecological, Nuclear Age* (London: SCM, 1987).

[3]See, e.g., Sue Swanson, ed., *Bless Sophia: Worship, Liturgy and Ritual of the Re-Imagining Community* (Woodbury, Minn.: Re-Imagining Community, 2003).

[4]Brian Wren, "Bring Many Names," in *What Language Shall I Borrow? God Talk in Worship: A Male Response to Feminist Theology* (London: SCM, 1989), 143.

[5]Richard Bondi, *Leading God's People: Ethics for the Practice of Ministry* (Nashville: Abingdon Press, 1989), 88–106.

[6]John Snow, *The Impossible Vocation: Ministry in the Mean Time* (Cambridge, Mass.: Cowley Publications, 1988), 28–50, interprets this symbolic power of the office of the minister both theologically and psychologically in terms of transferential dynamics.

[7]Walter J. Burghardt, S.J., "Worship and Justice Reunited," in *Liturgy and Justice,* ed. Anne Y. Koester (Collegeville: Liturgical Press, 2002), 39.

[8]William F. May, *Beleaguered Rulers: The Public Obligation of the Professional* (Louisville: Westminster John Knox Press, 2001), 234.

[9]Stephen R. Covey, "Three Roles of the Leader in the New Paradigm," in *The Leader of the Future: New Visions, Strategies, and Practices for the Next Era,* ed. Frances Hesselbein, Marshall Goldsmith, and Richard Beckhard (San Francisco: Jossey-Bass, 1996), 154.

[10]Stephen R. Covey, *Principle-Centered Leadership* (New York: Simon & Schuster, 1992), 246.

[11]Kennon L. Callahan, *The Future that Has Come* (San Francisco: Jossey-Bass, 2002), 182–202.

[12]William M. Easum, *Sacred Cows Make Gourmet Burgers: Ministry Anytime, Anywhere, by Anyone* (Nashville: Abingdon Press, 1995), 31–37, 71–96, 131–40, 147–50.

[13]Craig L. Nessan, *Beyond Maintenance to Mission: A Theology of the Congregation* (Minneapolis: Fortress Press, 1999), viii, 6–9.

[14]Stewart C. Zabriskie, *Total Ministry: Reclaiming the Ministry of All God's People* (Bethesda, Md.: Alban Institute, 1995), 41.

[15]James D. Glasse, *Putting It Together in the Parish* (Nashville: Abingdon Press, 1972), 33–39, 53–61.

[16]Easum, *Sacred Cows,* 149.

[17]Ibid., 170–72.

[18]Charles R. Foster, *Embracing Diversity: Leadership in Multicultural Congregations* (Bethesday, Md.: Alban Institute, 1997), 36–48.

[19]Nancy Tatom Ammerman, *Congregation and Community* (New Brunswick, N.J.: Rutgers University Press, 1997), 310–70.

[20]A helpful resource for determining the right balance for a congregation between tightening and loosening within the structures of organization and leadership is George Parsons and Speed B. Leas, *Understanding Your Congregation as a System,* 2 vols.: *Congregation Systems Inventory* and *The Manual* (Bethesda, Md.: Alban Institute, 1993).

[21]See also George Cladis, *Leading the Team-Based Church* (San Francisco: Jossey-Bass, 1999).

[22]Zabriskie, *Total Ministry,* 9. Curiously, it seems that some of the church organizations with a traditionally hierarchical and clerical polity (such as the Episcopal Church and other Anglican churches, the Roman Catholic Church, the Uniting Church in Australia) have been moving in directions such as "total ministry," which make better use of lay leadership and lay ministry. Some other denominations that are traditionally accustomed to strong lay leadership (Society of Friends, Disciples of Christ, Unitarian Universalists) have been exploring the virtues and possibilities of stronger pastoral leadership and professionalism. Paradoxically, though, the two models can actually work together—strong leadership finding a niche in encouraging and coordinating others and facilitating teams. In fact, one can find some very strong, charismatic leaders turning to the team-building approach, in part because people look to these individuals for leadership and are motivated by these leaders to contribute to the congregation's ministry.

[23]William H. Lazareth, *Christians in Society: Luther, the Bible and Social Ethics* (Minneapolis: Fortress Press, 2001), 217.

[24]Zabriskie, *Total Ministry,* 9.

[25]An excellent resource for use by lay and clergy alike for exploring vocation given the ambiguities of economic life is David A. Krueger, *Keeping Faith at Work: The Christian in the Workplace* (Nashville: Abingdon Press, 1994).

[26]I am emphasizing here the case that clergy can experience burnout in even "healthy congregations." There are also dysfunctional congregations that will accelerate burnout. G. Lloyd Rediger, *Clergy Killers: Guidance for Pastors and Congregations Under Attack* (Louisville: Westminster John Knox Press, 1997), describes some of these. With less hyperbole, Karen Lebacqz and Joseph D. Driskill helpfully summarize and discuss the literature about abusive churches in *Ethics and Spiritual Life: A Guide for Pastors, Chaplains, and Spiritual Directors* (Nashville: Abingdon Press, 2000), 127–46. Even the hyperbole of "clergy killers" contains some truth. Such difficult parishes can be extremely challenging to the emotional well-being of even the most experienced minister. Clergy do need to be able to recognize when they are in such a situation and find the professional support they need to avoid being "burned." At least as common as clergy internalizing other people's negativity, however, is the tendency of the clergy themselves to externalize their own anxiety and to blame others. My comments here about clergy burnout are directed at fellow members of the clergy in the hope that we

can own our sense of responsibility when we experience dissonance between our expectations and congregational realities. Resources that apply "family systems" theory to congregational life can be of particular help to clergy in identifying systemic dysfunction without either fixing the blame for such dysfunction on troubling individuals or taking too much of the blame oneself. See, especially, Ronald W. Richardson, *Creating a Healthier Church: Family Systems Theory, Leadership, and Congregational Life,* Creative Pastoral Care and Counseling Series (Minneapolis: Fortress Press, 1996).

[27]James D. Glasse, *Putting It Together,* 47–52.

[28]Scott Walker, "You Can't Get Your Blessing from a Church," in *No One Told Me! An Honest Look at Ministry,* ed. James E. Hightower Jr. (Macon: Smyth & Helwys, 1997), 1–9.

[29]Snow, *Impossible Vocation.*

[30]Robert N. Bellah, Richard Madsen, William M. Sullivan, Ann Swidler, and Steven M. Tipton, *Habits of the Heart: Individualism and Commitment in American Life* (Berkeley: University of California Press, 1985), 218, 242, 287–88, 300.

[31]Robert D. Putnam, *Bowling Alone: The Collapse and Revival of American Community* (New York: Simon & Schuster, 2000), 85–92, 203.

[32]Ibid., 66. Putnam provides statistics as follows: "about 75–80 percent of church members give to charity, as compared with 55–60 percent of nonmembers, and 50–60 percent of church members volunteer, while only 30–35 percent of nonmembers do." Ibid., 67.

[33]Ibid., 75–77.

[34]William F. May, *Beleaguered Rulers: The Public Obligation of the Professional* (Louisville: Westminster John Knox Press, 2001), 7–22.

[35]Ibid., 229.

[36]Rebekah L. Miles, *The Pastor as Moral Guide,* Creative Pastoral Care and Counseling Series (Minneapolis: Fortress Press, 1999), 68.

[37]Ibid., 69.

[38]Ibid., 73.

[39]Ibid., 7, 9.

[40]See, e.g., Charles M. Olsen's suggestions for "worshipful work" in his *Transforming Church Boards into Communities of Spiritual Leaders* (Bethesda, Md.: Alban Institute, 1995).

[41]Snow, *Impossible Vocation,* 1–27.

[42]John C. Hoffman, *Ethical Confrontation in Counseling* (Chicago: University of Chicago Press, 1979); Geoffrey Peterson, *Conscience and Caring* (Philadelphia: Fortress, 1982).

[43]Sondra Ely Wheeler, *Stewards of Life: Bioethics and Pastoral Care* (Nashville: Abingdon Press, 1996), 93–112.

[44]Jackson Carroll, *As One with Authority: Reflective Leadership in Ministry* (Louisville: Westminster / John Knox Press, 1991), 129, citing Donald A. Schön, *The Reflective Practitioner* (New York: Basic Books, 1983), 145.

[45]Anita Farber-Robertson, *Learning While Leading* (Bethesda, Md.: Alban Institute, 2000) provides a method for doing this kind of self-critical reflection even without the benefit of a supervisor or conversation partner.

[46]Miles, *Pastor as Moral Guide,* 46, suggests similarly that a pastor seek to discern a person's "implicit ethical model," and to ask questions both in keeping with a person's central ethical principles and other principles as well.

[47]Gaylord Noyce, *The Minister as Moral Counselor* (Nashville: Abingdon Press, 1989), 38.

[48]Miles, *Pastor as Moral Guide,* 35; Miles speaks plainly: "In many cases, people have screwed up, are contemplating screwing up, or are seeking help to avoid screwing up." A corollary problem is that they may want to blame others for the screw-up.

[49]Eric Berne, *Games People Play: The Psychology of Human Relationships* (New York: Grove Press, 1964), 116–22.

Conclusion

[1]Saint John of the Cross, "Spiritual Canticle," stanza 24, para. 8, in *The Complete Works of Saint John of the Cross*, vol. 3, trans. E. Allison Peers (Westminster, MD: Newman Press, 1964), 303–4.

[2]Evelyn Underhill, *The Spiritual Life*, 1st ed. (New York: Harper & Brothers 1937), 104–5.

Index